Partisan Approaches to Postwar American Politics

Partisan Approaches
to Postwar American Politics

Byron E. Shafer

with

Harold F. Bass Jr.
John F. Bibby
William G. Mayer
Nicol C. Rae
Randall W. Strahan

CHATHAM HOUSE PUBLISHERS

SEVEN BRIDGES PRESS, LLC

NEW YORK • LONDON

Partisan Approaches to Postwar American Politics

SEVEN BRIDGES PRESS, LLC
P.O. BOX 958, CHAPPAQUA, NEW YORK 10514-0958

PUBLISHER: Patricia Artinian
COVER DESIGN: Antler Designworks
MANAGING EDITOR: Katharine Miller
PRODUCTION SUPERVISOR: Melissa A. Martin
COMPOSITION: Bang, Motley, Olufsen
PRINTING AND BINDING: Versa Press, Inc.

LIBRARY OF CONGRESS CATALOGING-IN-PUBLICATION DATA

Partisan approaches to postwar American politics / Byron E. Shafer,
editor.
    p. cm.
    Includes bibliographical references and index.
    ISBN 1-56643-064-X (pbk.)
    1. Political parties—United States. 2. United States—Politics
and government—1945–1989. 3. United States—Politics and
government—1989– . I. Shafer, Byron E.
    JK2261 .P295   1998
    324.273′009′045—ddc21   98-8999
                                                                CIP

Manufactured in the United States of America
10 9 8 7 6 5 4 3 2 1

Contents

Tables and Figures

Tables

Figures

Acknowledgments

We were fortunate to be able to present what became the chapters of this book as a panel at the annual meetings of the American Political Science Association in August 1996. And we were fortunate to be able to "preview" the final version in a series of public lectures at Oxford University in the fall of 1997. Financial support for these ventures was provided by the Andrew W. Mellon Fund at Oxford University, so thanks are due both to the Andrew W. Mellon Foundation, which created that fund, and to the University Mellon Committee, which authorized this support: Nigel Bowles, Desmond King, Mark Philp, John Rowett, and Alan Ware, along with the administrator, Nancy Cowell.

The book itself was accepted for publication by the late Edward Artinian, in what must have been one of his last publishing decisions. Ed Artinian was a master at locating and supporting work that applied basic political science to contemporary political events; there is no obvious counterpart on the scholarly landscape. "I think they'll be glad to get this one," was his diagnostically brusque review. With his passing, we have one more reason to hope that he was correct.

At Chatham House, in what must have been a very difficult period, Patricia Artinian stepped in quickly to encourage this project. It then fell to Katharine Miller and Melissa Martin to manage the total process of publication, again supportively and without hesitation. At Nuffield College, Maureen Baker managed the total process on the other side of the Atlantic. Steve Moyle contributed his reliably creative efforts to the graphs and tables. And Elaine Herman did the word processing, typing, and retyping what must have seemed an endless stream of minor adjustments on the way to a final manuscript.

Introduction

Political parties and partisanship have long played a central role in our understanding of politics, precisely because they have so often played a central role in practical politicking, as key intermediaries in the political process. This does not require parties to be the main influences on politics, nor even to be reliably independent actors. It does not require partisanship, the divisions and alignments associated with party politics, to reach into all aspects of society. Indeed, whether, to what extent, and in what ways parties and partisanship have contributed to political and social change is one set of questions that the chapters in this book can address.

Nonetheless, parties have often been the main intermediaries of politics. They have gathered and presented the main actors. They have gathered and presented the main programs. They have linked individual citizens with governmental institutions, just as they have linked social forces with public policy. As a result, a focus on partisanship not only assembles many of the larger influences, developments, and trends in the public life of a nation in a fashion that connects one to another. It also brings many of the specific contestants, policies, conflicts, and coalitions—the guts of politics as it is normally understood—back into view.

To that end, the postwar political story of the United States is approached here through six major elements of parties and partisanship: party officeholders, party factions, partisan elites, party organizations, mass partisanship, and partisan rules. These six chapters are then presented in parallel fashion:

- Each begins with a description of the situation for this element of partisanship in the immediate postwar years, roughly 1946 to 1952.
- Each attends to some aspects of the change that followed—and change there has certainly been.

- Each moves on to a description of the same situation in more recent years, roughly 1990 to 1996.
- And each closes with a bit of speculation about how much of postwar American politics is actually picked up by focusing on this particular element.

Parties are certainly there in all their various aspects—they are ubiquitous—throughout American politics in the postwar era. They are there in the foreground, in explicit conflicts among party officeholders over the contents of public policy. But they are there at only one remove, in continuing struggles among party factions to try to move these larger parties in those explicit conflicts. And they are still there in the foreground when the general public adopts, exercises, and alters its principal political—its partisan—identifications.

Yet political parties are also there in the background, when grand social forces—organizational, economic, educational, religious—move society as a whole, in developments that quickly become partisan, just as they are there in the background when parties go about organizing to play their various roles, as intermediaries to coordinate institutions and influence public policy. And they are there—they *are* the background—in the rules of the game, shaping all this subsequent politicking. All these incarnations can be found in the chapters that follow.

Partisanship that is this omnipresent is not, however, stable in its contributions across the postwar years, and the story of change in its major aspects is another central thread in all those chapters. In chapter 1, national party officeholders are showcased as in some sense the ultimate product of any party system. In the beginning, here, they fight the last major rearguard actions of the New Deal, simultaneously establishing the policy boundaries for much of the postwar era. At the end, they turn and fight the last major rearguard actions of that era—intended, by one side only, to be the opening battles of a successor. The tale of these *party officeholders* is the responsibility of Randall W. Strahan.

An enduring factional structure, neither formalized nor informally permanent but recognizable for long periods nonetheless, then helps to link these national officeholders to the main social forces of their time. In the beginning, this factional structure features Democratic complexity and Republican simplicity, making Democratic Congresses and Republican presidencies more easily achieved. By the end, it features Republican complexity and Democratic simplicity instead, thereby conducing in the opposite partisan directions. Analysis of these *party factions,* in chapter 2, is the responsibility of Nicol C. Rae.

The social forces around these officeholders and their factions also shift profoundly during this period. In the process, they generate a circulation of elites: ascendant social groups beget new leadership cadres who translate those original social forces into influences on public policymaking. Four examples, in particular, give concrete life to this abstract dynamic: organized labor and Modern Republicans at the beginning of this period, New Politics Democrats and evangelical Protestants at the end. The resulting *partisan elites* are the responsibility of Byron E. Shafer, in chapter 3.

In most other countries, a focus on "the party" would imply a focus on the party apparatus—its organizational form and character—and would then move "up" to its elites or "down" to its voters. In the American case, parties in this sense begin the immediate postwar years as weak and confederate organizations built on a strong base of citizen attachment. By contrast, they enter the modern era as bureaucratized organizations with a national strategy, pursued uneasily on a base of weakened loyalties in the general public. John F. Bibby handles the analysis of *party organizations* across these changes in chapter 4.

For most of the postwar years, party identifiers in the general public have attracted more attention in scholarly research than the organizations that link them to politics, much less the institutional framework within which that politics occurs. Yet across those same years, public loyalties, too, change in a subtle and complicated fashion. Some aspects shift, others remain remarkably stable, and still others show a surface stability masking thoroughly different behavior underneath. Responsibility for recapping the literature on *mass partisanship,* in chapter 5, falls to William G. Mayer

Finally, all of the above occur within a set of institutional rules that establish ballot form, candidate access, and voter eligibility, as well as the devices for their exercise. These, too, have not been static across the postwar era; they have not lacked partisan impacts; and party operatives have not been innocent of those facts. Even the ability to participate in the most elementary way—to vote—has changed in ways that have partisan implications, while the forums for all such participation (including public primary elections and internal party procedures, with more or less partisan strictures governing each) have changed as well. Harold F. Bass Jr. recounts the difficult story, in chapter 6, of *partisan rules.*

Whether political parties and partisanship are causal engines in these events; whether they are instead simple windows on them; or, more likely, whether parties and partisanship are themselves contingent influences —now merely reflecting other forces, now transforming their impact—is a matter for each author (and then each reader) to judge. At a minimum, the authors believe that a great deal of the *story* of postwar American politics adheres to the major aspects of partisan politics within it, especially when pursued systematically across the postwar years.

1

Partisan Officeholders, 1946–1996

Randall W. Strahan

hough separated by an extraordinary half-century of political change, the elections of 1946 and 1996 produced identical and somewhat odd partisan lineups in Washington: Republican majorities on Capitol Hill facing a Democrat in the White House. Viewed from the perspective of partisan officeholders, much else in American politics has changed from the postwar period to the waning years of the century. The balance between the two major parties in controlling national offices has shifted notably, with Democrats no longer clearly dominant. Parties divide on issues about which they formerly agreed, and elected officeholders act differently in relation to their parties. Yet in one important respect, the initial impression that partisan politics have come full circle from 1946 to 1996 may not be misleading.

As political scientist James W. Ceaser has pointed out, analyzing change in political parties requires attention to their dual character, both as associations of partisans, who seek to advance competing views on how the country should be governed, and as organizations, which are more or less well equipped to maintain themselves coherently over time.[1] Partisan officeholders constitute one very important level of party organization, but they are also the partisans who must put party principles and programs into practice in the face of changing currents in national politics. An analysis of change in American politics from the perspective of partisan officeholders is thus partly a study of organizational or institutional developments affecting these officeholders, but also necessarily a study of the views *of* leading party officeholders on major questions of

national policy—and of their responses to changing problems of governance in the light of those views.

During some periods in American politics, partisan officeholders articulate and actively contest fundamental choices about the direction of
national governance and policy. At those times, leaders of American parties offer sharply contrasting views of governance and policy, views that
would take the country on different paths of development. More commonly, parties contest a narrower ground, in national elections defined by
the greater electoral success of one or the other party in controlling national offices. Party differences are still clearly distinguishable, but the officeholders of one party set the basic terms of the national political debate, while the officeholders *and office seekers* of the other party react,
criticize, and respond. It is here that we find the perspective from which
postwar (1946–52) and late-century (1990–96) partisan politics bear a
genuine resemblance. Both are periods during which national partisan officeholders tested and defined the limits of a major change in national
governance. And both are periods when the leading officeholders of the
party associated with the new governing regime emerged in a position to
articulate the direction and issues on which partisan competition would
center in the future.

From the perspective of parties as associations that advance competing views of governing, the most striking development in partisan politics
from 1946 to 1996 is that the relative positions of the two major parties
are now almost perfectly reversed. During the series of elections from
1946 to 1952, Republican officeholders with ambitions to remain nationally competitive came to accept a Democratically defined agenda focused
on determining the pace at which the federal government role in securing
domestic economic welfare should grow, and how the United States should
act to contain communism abroad. Conversely, the years from 1990 to
1996 found national *Democratic* officeholders testing, then, for a time at
least, coming to terms with a Republican-defined agenda focused on restricting and ultimately reducing the influence of the federal government
in American society.

This chapter addresses the politics of the two six-year periods that
mark the beginning and ending points of the segment of American political history with which this volume is concerned. The major issues and
choices confronting national partisan officeholders during these two periods, their responses, and the political consequences of those choices constitute the principal story to be told. Particularly close attention is paid to
the 80th (1947–48) and 104th (1995–96) Congresses, each of which casts
into relief some important political features of these respective time peri-

ods. If the officeholders of one, the other, or both major political parties can serve to define the terms of partisan politics for a new era, these Congresses demonstrate that they can also serve to confirm the limits of change. Officeholders may contribute to either form of definition, not only by advancing new issues or directions in governance but also by overreaching public support—and thus causing a political response that itself defines the contours of the new politics. In a conclusion, the importance of partisan officeholders in shaping the direction of American politics over this period is reconsidered.

Partisan Politics, 1946–52

By the time of the first national election in postwar America, in 1946, euphoria over the Allied victory in World War II had already given way to frustration over the problems of reconversion to a peacetime economy. Inflation, extensive labor unrest, and shortages of housing, cars, meat, and consumer goods generally were neatly laid at the feet of the incumbent Truman administration and Democratic Congress with a simple but pointed Republican campaign theme: "Had enough?" The competence of President Harry S. Truman, who had managed to alienate major elements of his own party as well as the opposition in the months since Franklin D. Roosevelt's death, had also become an issue, inspiring Republican slogan writers to aver as well that "To err is Truman."

For many Republicans, issues of postwar economic adjustment and of Truman's suitability for the White House were linked to a more fundamental critique of the direction of both domestic and foreign policies during the Roosevelt-Truman years. Opposition to the activist federal government that had been built up during the New Deal and the war years, to its cost, and to its attendant administrative apparatus was the dominant tendency among congressional Republicans, a significant number of whom were skeptical of the internationalist direction of postwar foreign policy as well.

Truman's popularity was at a low ebb by late 1946, so low that he took no public role in the campaign and canceled a planned election-eve address intended to rally Democratic voters. The president had made clear in a message to Congress in September 1945 that he would continue to advance the New Deal agenda in domestic policy, advocating full-employment legislation, an increased minimum wage, expanded public works, housing programs, expansion of social security, and national health insurance. On the other hand, the conservative coalition of southern Democrats and Republicans that had slowed the development of the

New Deal since the late 1930s had *already* checked Truman's domestic legislative program as well, before any input from the first real postwar election, leaving open the question of precisely what the federal role in economic and social welfare matters would be as the postwar era began.

The 80th Congress, 1947–48

When the 80th Congress convened in January 1947, Republicans had gained fifty-six seats in the House and thirteen in the Senate (see figures 1.1 and 1.2), placing them in control of Congress for the first time since 1930. Conditions seemed ripe for a major assault on the New Deal programs that had been a focus of many GOP campaigns. "The main issue of the election," pronounced Robert A. Taft of Ohio, Senate Republican leader, "was the restoration of freedom and the elimination or reduction of constantly increasing interference with family life and with business by autocratic government bureaus and autocratic labor leaders."[2]

Joseph Martin of Massachusetts, the newly elected Speaker, and the rest of the Republican leadership in the House were, if anything, even more hostile to the legacy of the New Deal. Internationalism in foreign

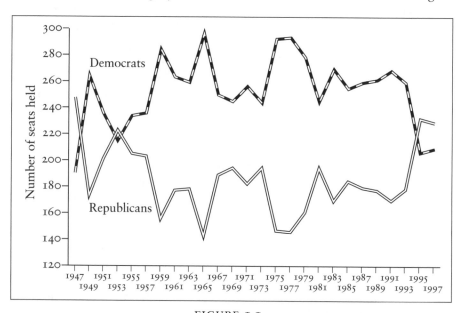

FIGURE 1.1

U.S. HOUSE: PARTY STRENGTH

SOURCE: Norman J. Ornstein, Thomas E. Mann, and Michael J. Malbin, *Vital Statistics on Congress, 1997–1998* (Washington, D.C.: CQ Press, 1997), 42–43.

policy also found less GOP support in the House than in the Senate, where Arthur H. Vandenberg, Republican senator from Michigan, was the leading figure and a key ally of the Truman administration in marshaling congressional support. Speaker Martin later described the 80th Congress as "a continuation of the old battle of the Thirties":

> Many of my differences with President Truman were simply a revival of my fights with Roosevelt. Thus as Speaker of the Eightieth Congress in 1947–48, I led the Republicans in what looks in retrospect like the last stand against heavy federal spending, high taxes, centralization and extravagance.[3]

This "last stand" of congressional Republicans in the 80th Congress consisted primarily of challenges to the legacy of the New Deal in two areas: taxation and labor-management relations. The Republicans had campaigned in 1946 on a promise of tax reduction, and Harold Knutson of Minnesota, incoming chairman of the House Ways and Means Committee, lost no time in proposing a 20 percent across-the-board reduction in

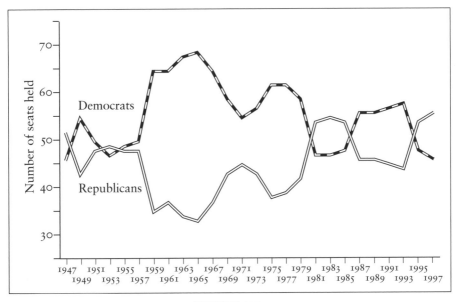

FIGURE I.2

U.S. SENATE: PARTY STRENGTH

SOURCE: Norman J. Ornstein, Thomas E. Mann, and Michael J. Malbin, *Vital Statistics on Congress, 1997–1998* (Washington, D.C.: CQ Press, 1997), 42–43.

income tax rates. Both Knutson and Taft made it clear that tax cuts were intended simultaneously to encourage economic growth and to reduce revenues available for federal domestic programs.

Responding to President Truman's claims that Republican tax legislation was inflationary, would increase the federal debt, and would unfairly benefit the wealthy, Taft declared: "The president's real reason for retaining taxes is obviously to have more money to spend. The best reason to reduce taxes is to reduce our ideas of the number of dollars the government can properly spend in a year, and thereby reduce inflated ideas of the proper scope of bureaucratic authority." In a more colorful comment, Knutson sought to place the tax issue in the context of the long-standing opposition by conservative Republicans to the New Deal and New Dealers. "For years," he pronounced on the House floor, "we Republicans have been warning that the short-haired women and long-haired men of alien minds in the administrative branch of government were trying to wreck the American way of life and install a hybrid oligarchy at Washington through confiscatory taxation."[4]

Tax reduction did become law during the 80th Congress, but only after substantial concessions were made by Republican leaders with regard to its scope and distributional effects. To pass the House, Knutson's original proposal had to be modified to shift more of the tax reduction to lower-income taxpayers. The House-passed version then had to be modified even further in the same direction to win approval in the Senate. After presidential vetoes of this and a second, smaller tax cut were sustained during 1947, Republican leaders finally built a veto-proof coalition in support of a still-broader-based tax reduction package in 1948.[5]

With the demands of a more active international role, as well as those of federal domestic programs, now mitigating against a return to prewar levels, the Republican tax-reduction effort proved modest in the face of the greatly expanded revenue base that had developed during the war years. As a result, the one area in which an argument might be made that the Republican-controlled 80th Congress redirected a major New Deal policy is labor-management relations. New Deal labor legislation, beginning with the National Industrial Recovery Act of 1933 and followed by the National Labor Relations Act of 1935, had created a favorable legal climate for the development of organized labor and had established the National Labor Relations Board (NLRB) to oversee and protect labor interests.

The impressive growth in union membership that followed, together with an extensive wave of postwar strikes and the association in the public mind of strikes and wage demands with postwar shortages and inflation, had by the mid-1940s created a much different political environment for setting federal labor policy. The Democratic-controlled 79th Congress (1945–46) had already responded to a Truman administration request for temporary authority to intervene in some labor disputes by passing permanent legislation deemed too restrictive of unions to receive the president's signature. With Republicans in control of Congress and their business allies mobilized to seek redress for a perceived imbalance in favor of labor, it came as no surprise when the 80th Congress moved almost immediately to enact new labor legislation.

An omnibus bill assembled by Fred A. Hartley Jr. of New Jersey, chairman of the House Education and Labor Committee, quickly cleared the chamber by a large margin. Though widely supported in the House, the effort was not without controversy. Before deliberations began, Hartley's elevation to the chair of the Education and Labor Committee provoked the resignation of former chair and fellow New Jerseyan Mary Norton, who pronounced Hartley unqualified, as evidenced by her claim that he had attended "exactly six meetings" of the panel over the previous ten years she had chaired it.[6] Nevertheless, Hartley was very much in evidence in early 1947, working closely with Charles Halleck, Republican majority leader, and a number of private attorneys to draft legislation to restrict controversial union activities and enhance presidential authority to intervene in strikes.

Some Democrats complained about the direct role business interests played in writing the legislation and about the speed with which it came to a floor vote, but the outcome was never in doubt. As one account had it: "The passage of labor legislation in the House ... was more in the nature of a mass movement than a duel between opposing [party] leaders.... House Republicans felt themselves committed to labor legislation and more than half the Democrats agreed."[7]

When the 80th Congress began, Robert A. Taft had his choice of chairing either the Finance or Labor committees in the Senate. Opting for the latter, he ensured that he, rather than the more moderate George Aiken of Vermont, would oversee the development of the Senate's labor bill. The Ohio Republican's stated objective was to achieve "balance" by producing a bill that would proscribe unfair labor practices in much the same fashion that unfair management practices had been outlawed by New Deal labor legislation. Taft skillfully managed amending activity, fending off amendments from both prounion and antiunion senators that might have hindered his goal of building a coalition broad enough to override an expected Truman veto.[8]

During the House-Senate conference, Taft and his colleagues insisted that a successful veto override would require a final version close to the more moderate Senate version. House conferees generally deferred, and the measure swiftly passed both chambers. When Truman formally submitted his veto message to Congress on 20 June 1947, the House took a total of three minutes to begin the override vote, which succeeded by a 331–83 margin. After a thirty-hour filibuster by Democratic opponents of the bill, the Senate followed suit, voting 68–25 to override.

The resulting Taft-Hartley Act restructured the NLRB and proscribed a wide range of labor practices deemed to give unfair bargaining advantages to unions. To some on the left, who had viewed the growth of union power and governmental planning capabilities during the New Deal and war years as progress toward the development of an American version of social democracy, Taft-Hartley represented a major reversal and a reassertion of the hegemony of business interests.[9] Regardless, the labor legislation of the 80th Congress in fact marks one of the most important instances in which postwar officeholders were engaged in defining the *limits* of changes in American politics wrought by the New Deal and the war years.

The passage of Taft-Hartley thus ended experimentation with new modes of industrial relations that had arisen with the extraordinary crises of the 1930s and 1940s, but it did not return things to the status quo ante or reduce the place of organized labor as a major force in American political and economic life.[10] The Republican-controlled Congress skirmished with the Truman administration over executive appointments, over spending measures, and over the incorporation of additional occupational groups in the social security program. But with the possible exception of labor-management relations, in no other area of domestic policy could it be argued that Republican officeholders delivered—or even came close to delivering—reversals of New Deal policies.[11]

Conservative Republicans who sought to do so in other areas were essentially able to muster only limited support. New federal housing and education programs even made some headway during the 80th Congress, passing the Senate but failing to win passage in the more conservative House. If some congressional Republicans were unrelenting in their attacks on the expanded federal presence ushered in by the New Deal, others, including some not identified with the moderate and liberal wings of the party, had come to accept an expanded federal role in protecting economic security as a desirable, or at least unalterable, feature of the postwar political landscape.

This was evident from interchamber and intraparty divisions among Republican officeholders in Congress, and from public and private comments of party leaders. Senator Robert A. Taft, for example, surely the leading figure among conservative Republicans in the 1940s and early 1950s, consistently maintained a highly critical public posture toward the taxation, bureaucratic regulation, and expanded executive power associated with the New Deal. Yet by the mid-1940s, Taft had also come to acknowledge that some of the central tenets of the New Deal—though taken to unacceptable lengths by the Democrats—were essentially correct.

In typical fashion, Taft delivered his most direct statement of this view before an audience little inclined to agree. Making the case for new federal housing legislation before a group of Cleveland home builders, Taft argued: "While the average is high, the necessary inequality of the [free enterprise] system leaves millions poor. . . . If the free enterprise system does not do its best to prevent hardship and poverty, it will find itself superseded by a less progressive system which does." Hence the federal government should "undertake to put a floor under essential things to give all a minimum standard of living."[12]

In a 1949 letter, Taft also made clear his view that national *electoral success* for Republicans would require acceptance of significant federal involvement in areas such as social relief, housing, and health. Conceding that a "theoretical argument" could be made to eliminate or oppose these kinds of programs, the leading conservative Republican officeholder of his day stated, "I am quite sure that any party that took that position would have only a short tenure of office and the opposition party would soon enact the legislation anyway, in a much more extreme form."[13]

Under the leadership of Taft's Senate colleague, Arthur H. Vandenberg of Michigan, Republicans provided consistent, if not always enthusiastic, support for the basic elements of the Truman foreign policy focused on containment of Soviet communism. As Republican Speaker Joe Martin described the evolution of his party's views:

For Republicans, as for everyone else, the world of 1947–48 was a far different place from what it had been in the days when we were challenging Roosevelt's interventionism. This issue was now dead. Whether one liked it or not, events of the previous decade had made the United States the leader of the non-Communist nations. The country could not, if it wished, isolate itself from a world suddenly drawn close together. We had to carry the burden of leadership, costly as it was. There was no other practical choice.[14]

Aid for communist-threatened regimes in Greece and Turkey, the

Marshall Plan to rebuild Europe, and the Vandenberg Resolution establishing the framework for NATO, all won passage during the 80th Congress, as did an extension of the president's authority to negotiate reciprocal trade agreements. Divisions within GOP ranks between isolationists and internationalists were still visible, however, and Republicans questioned the costs and ideological underpinnings of Truman's policies, as well as the focus of containment policies on Europe to the exclusion of Asia. Hence, Republicans cooperated with the Truman administration on foreign affairs, but with a fair amount of what one party historian described as "peripheral sniping."[15] Yet Republicans during the 80th Congress rightly viewed themselves as having helped lay the groundwork for a postwar regime in foreign policy that would continue to win bipartisan support for almost two decades.

In the minority, and divided between northern and southern wings, congressional Democrats were largely eclipsed in the immediate postwar years by the Democrat in the White House, Harry S. Truman, when it came to drawing distinctions between the parties. Beginning with his "Twenty-One Points" speech in September 1945, Truman advocated not only sustaining and extending New Deal programs but enacting new federal legislation to provide health insurance, protect civil rights, and expand federal aid for education and housing. After the 1946 Republican victory, Truman briefly backed away from an activist agenda. But by the summer of 1947, the president had again "solidly aligned himself with the New Deal and the priorities of the liberals."[16]

Continuing into the 1948 election, Truman took on "the role of an oppositionist" to Congress, in the process transforming his public image from that of a machine politician out of his depth to a plucky underdog battling the odds to defend the common man.[17] Calling the 80th Congress back for a special session in the summer of the (1948) election year, Truman criticized Republican tax and labor legislation for serving special interests and emphasized the need for immediate action on a wide range of proposals including anti-inflation measures, housing legislation, increases to the minimum wage and to social security benefits, federal aid to education, restoration of cuts in federal power projects, and civil rights protection.

Neither as senator nor as vice-president had Truman been part of Franklin D. Roosevelt's inner circle. By all accounts, he was much more comfortable with professional politicians than the intellectuals and reformers who clustered around FDR. As one Washington journalist characterized Truman, "He had an inborn and articulate distrust of and distaste for the Georgetown New Dealer—the pipe-smoking, tweed-jacketed, martini-and-salad man ... while the Truman type of administrator went his unterrified way with his bourbon and cigar."[18] Truman may have had little use for the cultural trappings of some of the New Deal elites—and for that matter, many of the New Dealers themselves[19]—but in response to the Republican capture of Congress in 1947–48, he unequivocally reaffirmed the association of the Democratic Party with the egalitarian liberal activism and class-based politics of the New Deal.

Though the administration's domestic proposals made little headway, the outcome of the 1948 election made clear that Truman's political strategy was more attuned to the national electorate than the anti–New Dealism of the congressional wing of the GOP. Republicans expected to win unified control of both branches for the first time in two decades. Instead, they proved vulnerable to Truman's strident attacks on the "do-nothing Eightieth Congress" and to his claims that Republicans would "do a real hatchet job" on the New Deal if they won control of both branches of government. With some justification, Republicans argued that they might have made a better showing if their presidential candidate, Governor Thomas E. Dewey of New York, had been less complacent and had run a more effective campaign.[20] But the underlying facts were that after taking their first turn at governing since the late 1920s, Republicans had neither reversed the New Deal, nor won the presidency, nor held their majorities in Congress.

Democratic Control, 1949–52

The return of unified Democratic control of Congress and the White House from 1949 to 1952 did not produce any major burst of liberal domestic legislation in Washington. Divisions among Democrats, divisions that had been obscured to some extent by Republican control of Congress, now returned to full view. A Truman pledge to overturn Taft-Hartley went unfulfilled, with Sam Rayburn of Texas, Democratic House Speaker, among those opposed.[21] Indeed, with the exception of new housing legislation (1949) and a major expansion of the social security program (1950), Truman's "Fair Deal" domestic proposals fared little better than when Republicans had controlled Congress.

Two factors were critical in limiting Truman's success in establishing or expanding federal programs: the resistance of southern Democrats in Congress and the eclipse of domestic policy by national security issues with the outbreak of the Korean War in June 1950. National security issues had already become a continuing factor in postwar partisan politics, even before Korea. With both parties committed to a foreign policy of active containment of communism, partisan conflict in this area focused on the conduct of foreign policy and on the adequacy of internal security measures.

By the late 1940s, partly because of questions raised over the fall of China to communism, Republicans had begun to gain partisan advantage by emphasizing the issue of an alleged Democratic failure to protect against security threats posed by domestic communists. The protracted stalemate that followed American intervention in Korea then created a second major opening for Republicans to criticize Democratic management of national security policy. During the 1952 election campaign, General Dwight D. Eisenhower, Republican presidential candidate, emphasized the Truman administration's flawed conduct of the Korean War—issuing a pledge to "go to Korea" to end the war—and focused on the issues of government corruption, high prices, and internal security.

Yet Eisenhower made a concerted effort to keep conservative Republican opposition to the New Deal from becoming a major issue in the election contest with Democrat Adlai Stevenson. "Social security, housing, workman's compensation, unemployment insurance, and the preservation of the value of savings—these are things that must be kept above and beyond politics and campaigns," Eisenhower proclaimed during one campaign address. "These," he added, taking a page directly from FDR, "are rights, not issues."[22] Eisenhower succeeded in making the conduct of the Korean War a central issue of the election instead—and won big (55.1 percent of the popular vote), carrying narrow Republican majorities into both the House and Senate on his coattails.

The 1946–52 period thus ended with Republicans in control of the White House and Congress for the first time in more than two decades. But from the perspective of the issues contested between officeholders of the two parties, even this outcome mostly confirmed the success of *Democrats* in defining the national political agenda.[23] Republicans had regained power by running an extraordinarily popular figure, who explicitly distanced himself from the anti–New Dealism of his party's old guard and focused instead on his ability to resolve the stalemate in Korea and provide better administration of government at home. The Republican loss of Congress in 1954, and the return of Democratic control over both branches for most of the 1960s, demonstrated that the gains of Republican officeholders in the 1940s and 1950s had not fundamentally altered either the governing agenda or the partisan advantage Democratic officeholders had established during the postwar years. The extent to which these features of partisan politics have changed as the twentieth century draws to a close is the subject to which the chapter now turns.

Two Partisan Twists on the Way to the Late Twentieth Century

Some important features of postwar politics are *still* clearly recognizable in the partisan politics of the 1990s. With few changes, the positions of many Democratic and Republican officeholders on economic and social welfare issues such as taxation, health care, and regulation of business remain virtually interchangeable with those of their postwar counterparts. Democrats remain the party of activist government as the means of social and economic progress. Republicans continue to emphasize economic liberty and view government regulation and redistribution as more often a burden than a benefit to society.

Yet the partisan politics of the 1990s bear the imprint as well of two very important intervening twists, which should be considered briefly before taking up the discussion of how partisan officeholders have competed and governed during the late-century years. First is the upheaval of the 1960s, during which national partisan competition began to occur on new political issues. To the economic and social welfare issues that had divided the parties since the 1930s was added a reopening of fundamental questions about American foreign policy, plus a set of cultural issues that pitted moral traditionalists against those preferring greater individual choice in matters of personal behavior and "lifestyle."[24]

As had been the case with economic and social welfare policy, neither party's officeholders were monolithic on these new issues. But the clear tendency of the officeholders of the two parties from the late 1960s through the 1990s was to divide on these issues in a way that Democrats became associated with a less interventionist view of foreign policy and a more permissive stance on the new cultural issues. Republicans, for the most part, remained committed to the older view that national security required the continued projection of American force in the world, and to a more traditionalist orientation on cultural and social issues.

The more complex partisan politics engendered by the alignments of the parties on these issues was not without strains and ironies. Unlike the basic continuity of views among Democratic and Republican officeholders on questions of economic and social welfare, the postwar profiles of the two parties in foreign policy matters became harder and harder to recognize. Reacting against the interventionist policies that were thought to have produced the debacle in Vietnam, many liberal Democratic officeholders repudiated the anticommunist internationalism of earlier Democratic administrations and began voicing concerns about the economic and political costs of international engagement and of a large defense establishment—concerns that were remarkably similar to those expressed by postwar conservative Republicans such as Robert A. Taft.

With the polarization of the parties on cultural issues, each party's prevailing view of the beneficence of government intervention also shifted, depending on the issue in question. Republicans continued to criticize most governmental intrusion into the economic sphere but now argued that government could and should play an important role in fostering traditional moral "values." Most Democrats, conversely, continued to view regulation of economic activity as an essential task of government, but they now questioned governmental regulation of religious practice, abortion, unconventional sexuality, or other aspects of personal behavior that were considered matters better left to individual choice.

The second development that has had a major effect on contemporary partisan politics is the so-called Reagan Revolution of the 1980s. Here, for the first time since the New Deal, a Republican president actually attempted to mount a serious challenge to the premise that the domestic political agenda ought to center on identifying which social or economic problems should be the next target of action by the federal government. As political scientist Charles O. Jones observes:

> In 1980, a president—Ronald Reagan—was elected who judged that government was the problem, not the solution.... So for the first time there was a serious effort to install a contractive agenda. Two approaches were tried. The first was programmatic: seeking to cut back, eliminate or devolve various federal programs. The second was fiscal: seeking to reduce taxes, thereby starving the revenue side so as to prevent enactment of new programs and to force serious evaluation of existing programs.[25]

As Jones and others have pointed out, the first approach fell short because of President Reagan's inability to build support for major cuts in domestic programs beyond an initial round in 1981. Whether by design or not, the second approach had a much greater impact.[26] Against the backdrop of the severe economic problems and foreign policy embarrassments of the Carter years, the Reagan administration succeeded in setting in motion both a massive tax cut, which indexed tax rates for inflation, and a major defense buildup. When combined with an unusually severe recession from 1981 to 1983, the results were spectacularly large federal budget deficits and what some have termed the "fiscalization" of national politics.[27]

With budget procedures that required Congress to enact a comprehensive budget plan each year, and with the adoption of the Gramm-Rudman-Hollings law mandating annual deficit reduction or automatic across-the-board spending cuts, officeholders in both branches by the late 1980s had little choice but to focus on the Sisyphean task of containing budgetary imbalance. Officeholders oriented toward identifying new programs or expanding those already in existence now had to contend with a recurring agenda of determining which taxes could be raised or which programs cut to reduce deficits.

In the final election of the 1980s, both the wider range of issues being contested between the parties and the effects of deficit politics were much in evidence:

- George Bush ran a campaign in 1988 in which social issues —family values, patriotism, school prayer, law enforcement, drugs—figured prominently, and foreign policy matters—arms control, the Grenada invasion, defense spending—were highly visible as well.
- On the other hand, the preferred approach of *neither* party to the deficit problem appeared to be very popular with voters—for Republicans, cutting domestic spending; for Democrats, raising taxes—and neither Bush nor his Democratic opponent, Michael Dukakis, proposed much in the way of specific plans for deficit reduction, excepting, of course, Bush's often-repeated pledge to oppose any new taxes.
- Dukakis called for "good jobs at good wages" and cited problems such as health insurance coverage, but he did not actively propose major new federal programs. Dukakis's initial hesitancy to identify too closely with "liberalism" in the 1988 campaign, and his claim that the election was about "competence rather than ideology," revealed the extent to which the new configuration of issues kept Democrats off-balance in presidential politics—as did their record of losing five of the six elections between 1968 and 1988.

In contrast, Democratic officeholders in Congress continued to flourish in the new political environment. They maintained unbroken majorities in the House of Representatives throughout this period, as they had done for eighteen consecutive elections by 1990, and Senate majorities for all but the years 1981–86 (see figures 1.1 and 1.2, pp. 8 and 9). This basic pattern, of Republican-led divided government, would persist for one more election into the 1990s (see figure 1.3), to be followed by a volatile

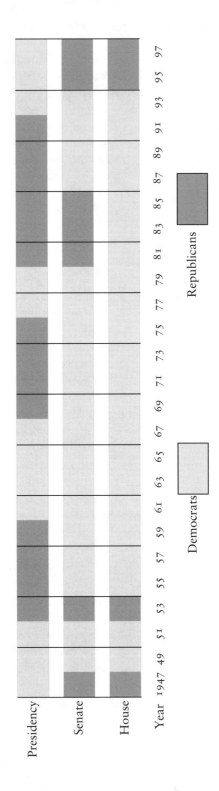

FIGURE 1.3
PARTY CONTROL OF NATIONAL OFFICES, 1947–97

period of partisan politics during which Republicans lost the White House but captured Congress, from which they mounted a renewed effort to advance the project of establishing a more conservative governing agenda.

Late-Century Partisan Politics, 1990–96

By any standard, 1990 was an eventful year in American politics. On 2 August, Iraq invaded and occupied Kuwait, to which the Bush administration responded with a major deployment of American forces in the Persian Gulf plus the assembling of an international coalition to demand Iraqi withdrawal. Both houses of Congress passed resolutions approving the deployment, although Democratic leaders in particular insisted that a separate congressional action would be required before the troops could be used in an offensive action to expel Iraqi forces.

In domestic affairs, the Gramm-Rudman-Hollings legislation finally performed its intended function, as a budgetary "doomsday machine," creating the politically unacceptable prospect of across-the-board spending cuts of $105 billion in fiscal year 1991 if the president and Congress failed to reach agreement on a new budget. In response, neither party's officeholders proved willing to stake their political futures to a clear test of public preferences by unilaterally offering a deficit-reduction package on this scale.[28] They turned instead to what had become the institutional manifestation of this political uncertainty since the 1980s, the repeated use of bipartisan "summits," in which party leaders negotiated while blurring partisan responsibility for the tax increases and program cuts that would ultimately be enacted.

In this case, congressional Democrats declined to produce a budget plan as a starting point for negotiations and succeeded in extracting a retraction of the president's "no new taxes" pledge as a condition for staying involved in negotiations that had been initiated by the White House. The bipartisan summiteers worked from May to October to produce a deficit-reduction plan, only to have the plan rejected in the House by majorities of both parties. Conservative Republicans, including Newt Gingrich, the minority whip, reacted critically to tax increases in the plan. Liberal Democrats reacted critically to savings in the Medicare program, as well as to fuel and other taxes seen as unacceptably regressive.

In a scenario that would be replayed a few years later with partisan roles reversed, President Bush vetoed a temporary measure to keep the government funded, causing a shutdown of nonessential federal offices and services. This impasse was broken after only two days, when Bush agreed to a new budget framework developed by congressional Democrats. With smaller savings from Medicare and tax increases on upper-income households more than three times larger than those in the original bipartisan plan, the resulting package clearly reflected a tilt toward Democrats' budget preferences.

The effective abandonment of the budget process by a majority of House Republicans left Bush with the unpalatable options of either threatening a prolonged government shutdown and Gramm-Rudman-Hollings budgetary implosion, or signing—and providing at least partial bipartisan political cover for—Democratic budget legislation. Not surprisingly, he chose the latter. The fall of 1990 also saw passage of major legislation on air pollution, immigration, and crime. But few would have characterized it as a cooperative session, since completion of work on contentious budget issues kept Congress in session until only nine days before the 1990 election.

Divided to Unified Party Control, 1990–94

The congressional election of 1990 reflected no clear national trend other than the continued success of incumbent candidates—who were mostly Democrats—in winning reelection. Neither the foreign policy crisis in the Middle East nor the fall policy battles in Washington seemed to have had a recognizable effect on the alignment of voter preferences. Consistent with the well-established pattern of the president's party losing strength in Congress at midterm, Republicans did lose one seat in the Senate and nine in the House, leaving Democrats with substantial 56–44 and 268–167 majorities, respectively. The apparent victory of Democrats in moving the budget debate in the direction of higher, more progressive taxation seemed clouded by the politics of some specific election contests, however, particularly the narrow margin (3 percent) by which prominent incumbent Senator Bill Bradley of New Jersey survived a high-profile effort of Republicans to associate him with tax increases initiated by the state's Democratic governor.

The final two years of the Bush administration were marked by extraordinary successes in foreign affairs and by a growing stalemate on domestic policy, with the latter ultimately proving the more important for the president's political standing. Shortly after the 1990 election, the administration had sought and received approval from the UN Security Council for the use of force to expel Iraqi forces from Kuwait. The president then formally requested congressional authorization to implement the Security Council resolution, leading to widely viewed debates in the House and Senate on 12 January 1991.

In keeping with the post-Vietnam divergence of the two parties on the use of force in foreign policy, the debate proceeded mostly along partisan lines.[29] Opposition to the resolution was led by Senator George Mitchell, Democratic majority leader, and by Speaker of the House Thomas Foley. Sam Nunn of Georgia, Democratic senator and Armed Services Committee chairman, also argued against the resolution, helping to produce a relatively close 52–47 Senate vote, in which majorities of both northern and southern Democrats voted no. The resolution passed by a broader 250–183 margin in the House, where a unified Republican conference and a large majority of southern Democrats supported the president over the opposition of other Democrats.[30]

The "Desert Storm" campaign that followed was successfully concluded by March, removing Iraq from Kuwait with minimal American casualties and driving President Bush's public approval to stratospheric levels. Added to the military triumph in the Persian Gulf was the continuing breakup of the Soviet bloc and, by late 1991, of the Soviet Union itself. For the first time since World War II, no direct threat to American national security loomed.

Domestic politics were a different matter entirely. Congress reeled from the perception that the institution was lurching from one scandal to another. House Democrats had ridden out the resignations of their Speaker and whip under accusations of unethical behavior in the previous Congress, only ·to encounter new public embarrassments in 1991 and 1992. The General Accounting Office reported in 1991 that members of both parties had written thousands of overdrafts—some as large as $40,000—on accounts members were allowed to maintain with the office of the House sergeant at arms. Other reports alleged that financial irregularities and even drug dealing had occurred at the post office operated by the House. According to some polls, public approval of Congress reached its lowest point in decades during 1992.[31]

None of the problems of the Democratically controlled Congress redounded to the particular advantage of the White House, however. Indeed, as the economy continued to slow, the president's public approval plummeted. The multiyear budget agreement of 1990 had brought a temporary respite from open conflict in that area, but the Bush administration and Congress now clashed over extending unemployment compensation and over provisions for new civil rights legislation. Both were finally signed into law in late 1991, as was a major transportation measure touted as a stimulus to employment.

The final session of the 102d Congress witnessed sharper partisan conflict and less productivity. Bush proposals for capital gains and other tax reductions to stimulate the economy went unheeded, while measures passed by Congress dealing with taxation, family leave, voter registration, and campaign finance were vetoed. Each side chided the other for the resulting gridlock. "I extended my hand to the congressional leaders, the Democratic leaders, and they bit it," exclaimed the president in his Republican National Convention speech of August 1992. "The president's repeated, gratuitous use of the veto and meaningless deadlines were major sources of deadlock," retorted House Majority Leader Richard Gephardt.[32]

"Change," then, was to be the theme of the 1992 election. Successive scandals, plus frustration over the inability of Washington officeholders to take action in the face of a weak economy, gave new potency to the strategy of seeking office by running against Washington insiders. Some analysts even argued that "outsiderism" merited consideration as an independent dimension of electoral politics in 1992, one that interacted with the issue positions of candidates to provide advantages to those who could plausibly position themselves at a distance from the taint of Washington.[33]

One candidate who clearly benefited from this environment was Texas billionaire H. Ross Perot, who was to win 19 percent of the popular vote despite an on-again/off-again, independent presidential campaign. The Perot campaign focused its own attention on the budget deficit, which would reach a record $290 billion in 1992, but drew support primarily from voters attracted to diffuse appeals to clean up Washington and end politics as usual.[34]

A second distinctive feature of partisan politics in 1992 was the virtual disappearance of foreign policy as an issue area contested between the two parties. The epochal transformation that had occurred in the international sphere was reflected in the ephemeral nature of that extraordinary public approval awarded to President Bush following the successful prosecution of the Gulf War. With the collapse of the Soviet Union, and for the first time since 1940, voters had the luxury of choosing national officeholders without having to consider how their choices might affect the country's chances in the event of war or other international threat.

Presidential voters were thus free to focus on other issues troubling them, and according to polling data, these were primarily economic: jobs, the deficit, health care, and taxes.[35] This devaluation of foreign policy issues also appears to have minimized any political damage suffered by the clear majority of congressional Democrats who voted against the use of force in the Persian Gulf. As Richard F. Fenno Jr. reported on the basis of close observation of the 1992 campaign of one such Democratic senator,

Wyche Fowler of Georgia: "No one I talked to believed that his war vote affected the outcome; and Fowler's own view was, 'I don't think it hurt me much.' "[36]

These proved to be the conditions for a return of unified party control in Washington for the first time since 1980. Positioning himself as a moderate "New Democrat," Bill Clinton, governor of Arkansas, won with a plurality (43 percent) in the three-candidate race. Despite higher-than-average incumbent losses and the largest turnover in membership since 1948, Democrats retained control in Congress, holding their four-teen-seat Senate majority, 57–43, while seeing their House majority reduced by ten, to 258–176. Reflecting voter concerns, the president promised to move immediately on a new economic program and in late January made a commitment to submit a plan for universal health insurance coverage within ninety days. Gridlock seemed finally to have been broken, as "family leave" and "motor voter" bills vetoed by President Bush during the previous session were repassed and signed into law early in 1993.

A more serious test of whether unified Democratic government could deliver the change American voters were seeking came as Congress took up the president's economic and health-care initiatives. A number of post-election analyses held that the election signified a decisive rejection of Republican efforts since 1980 to move national economic and social welfare policy in a more conservative direction. Political scientist Walter Dean Burnham, for example, concluded that the election was "a landslide vote of no confidence in the conservative regime Ronald Reagan and his allies had sought to create on the ruins of interest-group liberalism" and was therefore "of far more than usual significance."[37] "The clearest message of 1992," wrote Wilson Carey McWilliams, "was the majority's demand for active government, engaged to relieve America's discontents and reclaim the future."[38]

While taking care to project a moderate stance on issues such as welfare reform, President Clinton proved more than willing to provide opportunities for congressional Democrats to deliver more active government during the 103d Congress, if they judged that voters were in fact demanding it. The record of 1993 and 1994, however, raises serious questions about whether this was the case. The attempt to revive a more activist agenda initially ran up against the fiscal legacy of Reaganism. Yet it ultimately foundered on the lack of agreement among Democratic office-holders that public support *existed* for a major departure from the status quo. The Clinton economic plan consisted of three major components, the first two of which involved modest steps to advance a more active federal agenda: economic stimulus; new spending ("investments") to increase future productivity; and deficit reduction.

Almost from the beginning, congressional Republicans succeeded in forcing the administration onto the defensive, for planning to enact new spending before acting on deficit reduction and for proposing a budget package weighted toward increased taxes. After congressional leaders altered the planned sequence of votes to have the deficit-reduction measure adopted first, the stimulus component passed the House but fell victim to a Republican filibuster in the Senate. The administration ultimately succeeded in winning passage of a big *deficit-reduction* package, one that restored some of the progressivity of the pre-Reagan tax system, but had to add more spending cuts to the plan, accept reductions of almost half in the proposed new "investment" spending, and weather a divisive intraparty debate over energy tax provisions to do so.[39]

As deliberations on the package continued into the summer of 1993, Democratic congressional leaders found themselves having to shift from appeals based on the political and policy merits of the plan to arguments stressing that the party and the Clinton presidency would be severely harmed by failing to meet the first real test of their ability to govern.[40] On those grounds, the final legislation attracted no Republican votes and passed by the narrowest possible margin in both chambers, 51–50 in the Senate, 218–216 in the House. Nevertheless, by taking up the issue of reforming the health-care system to provide universal insurance coverage, Bill Clinton moved on to a much more ambitious effort to reorient the national agenda, toward a larger and more activist governmental role in providing for economic and social welfare.

Though support for the idea had waxed and waned over the years, health-care reform had long been considered a major programmatic objective of liberal Democrats. The general goals of health-care reform again found broad initial public support in 1993, but it was clear from the outset that finding the revenues to fund a program on this scale would be a major challenge, especially in the face of the resistance of officeholders from both parties to voting increased taxation.

In this respect, the politics of the deficit-reduction plan had set the stage for the health-care debate that followed. Well in advance of the unveiling of the Clinton proposal, for example, Sander M. Levin of Michigan, a House Democratic liberal, observed: "A new general tax increase would have been difficult for us anyway, but the experience of the deficit-reduction bill reinforced what was likely to occur—no general tax increase for health-care reform."[41]

The program introduced by President Clinton in November 1993 attempted to finesse the tax issue by mandating employer contributions to new "health alliances" and by proposing to raise revenues primarily through additional levies on tobacco. This proved insufficient to smooth the way for an immensely complicated proposal, which produced its own immensely complicated politics. Five congressional committees worked independently at the task of writing an acceptable plan, and the affected interest groups mounted high-profile campaigns designed to raise public anxieties about the effects of reform.

In the end, Democratic congressional leaders proved unable to assemble a coalition in support of any plan that would guarantee universal coverage, while liberals who held the balance in their party in both chambers refused to accept compromise proposals that could have attracted support from moderate and conservative Democrats (and some Republicans). Health-care reform never came to a vote in either house of Congress, and George Mitchell, Senate majority leader, announced in September 1994 that the efforts to pass a bill would be dropped.

Postmortems on the demise of health-care reform cited strategic errors committed by the president and Mrs. Clinton and the substantial resources mobilized by economic interests who stood to lose, or, more broadly, alleged systemic incapacities to manage proposals of this complexity or plans involving short-term costs to achieve longer-term benefits. Each of these factors may well have contributed to the outcome. But from the perspective of national partisan politics, the most important fact was that the attempt to reestablish an activist agenda on this scale was widely judged a political disaster. Other legislative accomplishments of the first period of unified Democratic government in more than a decade, including two major trade agreements, seemed greatly overshadowed by the health-care and budget fights. The outcome of the 1994 election would strongly reinforce the view that the attempt to revive an expansive federal agenda had been a costly political error.

The 104th Congress, 1995–96

As James W. Ceaser and Andrew E. Busch have written, "no sane individual in 1992, unless it was Newt Gingrich, foresaw the Republican congressional sweep in 1994." As elaborated in one postelection essay, "The 1994 Midterm: Why the Models Missed It," election analysts had believed they had good reason to consider the Senate as up for grabs, but had little reason to anticipate that House Democrats would fail to extend their forty years in the majority.[42]

While analysts debated the causes of the gains that produced the first GOP majorities in the House and Senate since 1954, House Republicans under the leadership of incoming Speaker Newt Gingrich were organizing a party government regime the likes of which had not been seen since the early years of the century. Though both chambers had experienced increased party unity in voting over the previous two decades (see figures 1.4 and 1.5), and both parties had significantly strengthened their leadership and organization in the House, the new Republican operation, in the words of Roger Davidson, veteran Congress watcher, "was far more than simply a continuation of long-term trends."[43]

Gingrich set the tone for the new partisan regime by naming House committee chairs in mid-November 1994 before the Republican committee assignment body had even met, and by skipping over senior members in naming the leaders of three major panels. Committee chairs were then put on notice that they would be expected to be active in supporting party objectives. Equally important for understanding congressional politics in 1995 was the Republican Contract with America, which had been signed

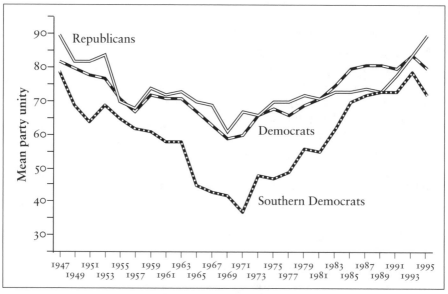

FIGURE 1.4

U.S. HOUSE: PARTY UNITY

SOURCE: *Congressional Quarterly Almanac,* various years.

NOTE: Party unity scores are the mean of party members voting with their own party when party majorities oppose one another. Scores are for the entire Congress beginning in the year indicated.

by the overwhelming majority of GOP candidates during the fall election campaign. The ten groups of legislative proposals in the Contract had been assembled to reflect traditional Republican positions on economic issues (balanced-budget amendment, business tax cuts, legal reform) and cultural concerns (crime provisions, welfare reform, family tax credits), with appeals to the more recent anti-Washington populism incorporated as well (term limits).

Whatever may have been the effects of the Contract on voter choices, the items proposed in the document provided an agenda around which to organize, a set of agreed priorities on legislative goals, and a timetable for voting (100 days) that could be met only by means of centralized direction from the party leadership. This was especially important in establishing a mode of operation for a party whose officeholders had no experience running the House as the majority, and over half of whom had two years' or less experience in the chamber. As a result of the Contract exer-

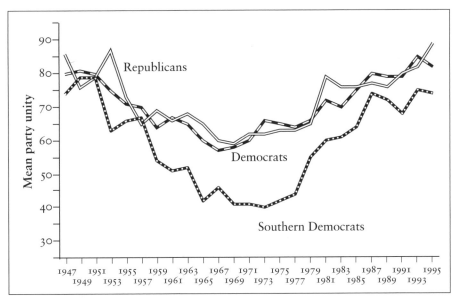

FIGURE 1.5

U.S. SENATE: PARTY UNITY

SOURCE: *Congressional Quarterly Almanac*, various years.

NOTE: Party unity scores are the mean of party members voting with their own party when party majorities oppose one another. Scores are for the entire Congress beginning in the year indicated.

cise, when the 104th Congress convened in January 1995, all but seven members of the Republican majority had committed in writing to spend the next three months addressing a mix of issues carefully preselected to produce party unity.

Even in the flush of an unexpected partisan sweep, the Senate retained its character as the more individualistic and deliberative—or at least, slower moving—institution. Senate Republicans reelected Robert Dole as floor leader, but replaced the party whip, Alan Simpson of Wyoming, with Trent Lott of Mississippi, who was considered more attuned to the activist conservatism that was ascendant in the House. As had been the case when Republicans were in control of both chambers during the 80th Congress, the Senate was to prove a moderating force on both the pace and the substance of legislation emerging from the House during 1995.

Along with changes in the new Republican Congress, the response of the Democrat in the White House was especially instructive for gauging how the surprising Republican victory would affect the terms of national partisan politics. In his first news conference after the election, Bill Clinton offered a ritualistic jab at "those who would use this election to turn us back ... to the policies that failed us before," but devoted much greater emphasis to the theme that he recognized and that the Democratic Party was in step with: voter desires for smaller government.

> [The people are] still not sure that we understand what they expect the role of government to be. I think they want a smaller government that gives them better value for their dollar, that reflects both their interest and their values, that is not a burden to them, but empowers them. That's what I have tried to do, but I don't think we're there yet—by a long shot.
>
> So what I think we have to do is to look at every single government department, every single government program and ask ourselves: Is there a better way to do this? Is this something where the American people will think we're more of a burden than a help? Is there a way to give more flexibility to people at the state and local level and in private life to achieve the same goal?
>
> ... I think we have to analyze the results of the elections, hear what the voters were saying and go back to them and say: We [Democrats] believe that government is not inherently bad. We agree that the government needs to be smaller and more efficient. We believe it needs to reflect our values as well as our interests. And we believe that we have more to offer in that regard.[44]

Before the new Republican Congress convened, President Clinton continued to tack rightward, delivering a televised address on 15 December proposing his own package of tax cuts billed as a Middle-Class Bill of Rights.

As work in the House proceeded at the furious pace required to bring each of the Contract measures to a vote within the promised 100 days, Speaker Gingrich won the assent of Republican House leaders and of Senate Majority Leader Dole to pursue a second ambitious goal: enacting a budget in 1995 that would produce budgetary balance by the year 2002. Both chambers then took up the task of drafting seven-year plans to achieve such a balance, with the White House having little if any role in the process except to offer criticism of Republican priorities, especially the changes being proposed in Medicare and other social programs.

Indeed, White House isolation was such that, in April, an anxious President Clinton reportedly had begun to ask White House advisers, "How do we get into this thing?"[45] By June, the president had decided that endorsing a balanced budget would be the only way to join the debate, and in a televised address on 13 June he announced his support of that goal. Congressional Republicans, meanwhile, proceeded to pass a seven-year package that included $245 billion in tax cuts, $270 billion in savings from Medicare, sharp reductions in other areas of domestic spending, and changes to devolve greater authority to the states in health and welfare programs for the poor.

The president finally became involved directly in budget negotiations with congressional leaders in November 1994, after casting a veto of a temporary spending resolution that resulted in the first governmental shutdown of his administration. While insisting that the budget package provide additional funding for health, education, and environmental programs, the president again moved closer to the Republican position by agreeing to the seven-year time frame for reaching balance. The inability of the president and Republican congressional leaders to agree on the specifics of a seven-year plan nevertheless resulted in a second shutdown in December. Polls showing that Republicans were losing public support as a result of the impasse encouraged GOP leaders to abandon the shutdown strategy, and in January the effort to enact a balanced budget plan during the 104th Congress was itself abandoned.

As the 1996 elections approached, many congressional Republicans became concerned about having overreached what the public would support, in some of the Contract and budget initiatives, and began to focus instead on demonstrating a capacity to pass legislation that could become law. As a result, the second year of the 104th Congress, 1996, witnessed agreements with the White House on major farm, welfare, telecommunications, and health insurance regulation bills, all of which were signed into law. But the fact remained that most of the Republican Contract bills—as well as a balanced-budget package that would have restructured the huge Medicaid and Medicare programs, substantially reduced federal tax revenues, and devolved greater authority to state governments—were not.

Viewed in terms of legislative enactments, there was a certain symmetry between the politics of the 103d (1993–94) and 104th Congresses (1995–96). Democratic officeholders, led by President Bill Clinton, failed in an attempt to enact one of the major programmatic objectives of postwar economic liberalism, the provision of universal health insurance. Only a year later, Republican officeholders, led by Speaker Newt Gingrich, failed in an equally ambitious effort to deliver the programmatic changes needed to complete much of the unfinished conservative agenda from the 1980s.

Yet it would be incorrect to conclude that the Democratic and Republican initiatives were somehow equally inconclusive. Officeholders for both parties lost big battles during the mid-1990s. But Republicans appear to have succeeded in establishing the terms on which future partisan competition and policy debates in the area of social and economic welfare policy will occur. In this respect, the contrast between the political consequences of the 80th and 104th Congresses could not be sharper. In 1947 and 1948, Democrat Harry Truman actively contested the Republicans' agenda and won reelection by reasserting the case for economic liberalism and activist government. In 1996, Bill Clinton also won reelection after jousting with a Republican Congress, but only after working hard to persuade American voters that the Republicans were not the only party committed to smaller government, a balanced budget, and lower taxes.

As a leader, Bill Clinton may "sound a very uncertain saxophone,"[46] but his 1996 State of the Union address could not have been more clear in registering the fact that conservative ideas about social and economic welfare policy now defined the terms of the national partisan debate:

> We know that big government does not have all the answers. We know there's not a program for every problem. We know, and we have worked to give the American people a smaller, less bureaucratic government in Washington. And we have to give the American people one that lives within its means. The era of big government is over.[47]

Confirming that the president's view was shared by some, if not all, Democrats in Congress, Richard A. Gephardt, House minority leader, sounded a similar theme as the 1996 election approached: "They [House Democrats] realize that we did not produce what the American people wanted. You can call it anything you want. I've said many times, we're all 'new Democrats' now.... We have to be. Times change."[48]

The outcome of the 1996 presidential election demonstrated that Republican success in moving the basic terms of national partisan competition to the right does not, by any means, guarantee success in controlling national office. As Republican congressional leaders discovered in the budget confrontation with the White House in 1995, broad public support remains for many existing federal programs and for the idea that government now plays an important role in guaranteeing economic security. If Republicans are perceived to be taking an antigovernment agenda too far, too fast, even voters generally sympathetic to that agenda may find "new Democrats" preferable.

Nor does the reconstruction of the terms of partisan debate along issues previously advanced by the Republicans imply that real differences have ceased to exist among partisan officeholders. In the same 1996 speech in which President Clinton declared the era of big government to be over, he proposed a plethora of smaller steps by which the federal government could act to address social problems—tax credits, vouchers, new regulations, mandated v-chips in televisions—an approach some have termed "lots of little government."[49] As was the case with Republicans in the postwar era, late-century Democrats may concede that changes in the scope of government are inevitable, but most continue to take a different view of the proper role of government in society.

Still, to the extent that the newly established consensus that economic and social welfare policy should be consistent with balancing the federal budget holds into the next century, this new framework of partisan politics can reasonably be expected to produce more strains among Democratic Party officeholders, elites, and supporting coalitions than among their Republican counterparts.[50] National partisan competition organized around an agenda defined by conservative economic policies seems likely to create continual strains between liberal Democratic elites and core constituencies on the one hand, and officeholders on the other.

In particular, it seems unlikely that culturally and economically liberal Democratic elites will continue indefinitely to support the rightward movement of Democratic officeholders on these issues—a conflict that is most likely to manifest itself in presidential politics. Tensions between economic and social conservatives notwithstanding, Republicans would seem to have fewer problems in store for maintaining unity in an environment where partisan competition centers on how to limit the growth of the federal budget and whose taxes to reduce. If, or more realistically, when, foreign policy issues reemerge as matters of concern to voters, the relative advantages of the two parties may well be reshuffled yet again.

Conclusion: Partisan Officeholders and Political Change

One question remains: how much of the change that has occurred in American politics since the postwar years is explained by a focus on national officeholders? Partisan officeholders, of course, act within institutions and in response to political forces over which they have limited control. Governing in the United States is a continuing activity in which multiple institutions, existing commitments, persistent problems, and unanticipated events constrain the options of officeholders. Those who seek to remain in office must also respond to the elites and voters who determine whether they will be successful. For these reasons, the actions and views of partisan officeholders probably register political change more often than they cause it.

Speaking very broadly, changes in partisan institutions since the postwar years have encouraged a less partisan presidency and a more partisan Congress:

• In this, changes in the presidential selection process set in motion in the late 1960s have reduced the influence of party officeholders and elites and have increased the influence of issue activists and mass electorates. Holders of the presidential office have thus become most sensitive to changes in organizational activity surrounding new issues on the one hand, and in mass opinion on the other. The differences in the governing styles of Harry S. Truman and (the Janus-like) Bill Clinton, for example, in part reflect the interplay of changing political conditions with new partisan institutions. Contemporary presidents must run a gauntlet of ideologically polarized issue activists, and simultaneously must appeal to voters for whom partisan attachments have been weakening. Earlier presidents were more closely linked to their partisan colleagues.

• Congressional officeholding, on the other hand, has become more structured by partisan institutions than was the case in the postwar period. Both congressional parties have become more ideologically homogeneous, and both have substantially strengthened their organizational and leadership structures in the House. The Senate remains much more resistant to organization and leadership, but even it has seen voting become more structured along partisan lines. Positions of institutional influence are now granted *on condition that* partisan goals are to be advanced and supported. In turn, the rancorous conflict over budgetary issues in the 1980s and 1990s both reflected and reinforced this more partisan structure of congressional politics. It is almost as hard to imagine a partisan firebrand like Newt Gingrich rising to a position of leadership in the postwar House as it would be to place a factional broker of the Sam Rayburn type in the Speakership at late century.

To note that the actions of partisan officeholders cannot be understood independent of the influence of institutions, of existing governmental commitments, and of larger social forces is not to argue that partisan officeholders do not encounter political situations in which opportunities arise for influencing the course of American politics on a broad scale. The two who loom largest in the politics of the 1946–96 period are Franklin Roosevelt and Ronald Reagan, both of whom left lasting imprints on American *partisan* politics. While it is just too early to tell which, if either, set of party officeholders will gain greater electoral advantage from a new governing agenda of the mid-1990s, Newt Gingrich will also have some claim to an imprint on American politics if this new era of partisan competition, centered on smaller government and balanced budgets, proves at all resilient. If it does not, partisan officeholders should encounter yet another opportunity to redefine the terms of American politics as the next century begins.

Acknowledgment

The author gratefully acknowledges research assistance provided by Matthew Gunning and Vincent G. Moscardelli.

Notes

1. James W. Ceaser, "Political Parties—Declining, Stabilizing, or Resurging?" in *The New American Political System,* 2d ed., ed. Anthony King (Washington, D.C.: American Enterprise Institute, 1990).

2. Quoted in Susan M. Hartmann, *Truman and the 80th Congress* (Columbia: University of Missouri Press, 1971), 10. Wallace H. White of Maine was the formal Republican floor leader during the 80th Congress, but, as Hartmann notes, White was "majority leader in name only." White's frequent practice of turning around on the Senate floor to receive cues from Taft led a group of Capitol Hill reporters to offer him a rearview mirror to assist in the performance of his duties. Taft also chaired the Senate Labor and Public Welfare Committee and the Senate Republican Policy Committee during the 80th Congress.

3. Joseph Martin, *My First Fifty Years in Politics* (New York: McGraw-Hill, 1960), 177.

4. Both quotes are from John F. Witte, *The Politics and Development of the Federal Income Tax* (Madison: University of Wisconsin Press, 1985), 132–33.

5. For the story, see Hartmann, *Truman and the 80th Congress,* 74, 79, 95, 96, 132–36; Donald R. Kennon and Rebecca M. Rogers, *The Committee on Ways and Means: A Bicentennial History, 1789–1989* (Washington, D.C.: Government Printing Office, 1989); James T. Patterson, *Mr. Republican: A Biography of Robert A. Taft* (Boston: Houghton Mifflin, 1972), 373–75.

6. Quoted in R. Alton Lee, *Truman and Taft-Hartley: A Question of Mandate* (Lexington: University of Kentucky Press, 1966), 55.

7. Stephen K. Bailey and Howard D. Samuel, *Congress at Work* (Hamden, Conn.: Archon Books, 1965), 420.

8. Patterson, *Mr. Republican,* 354–60.

9. See Robert Griffith, "Forging America's Postwar Order: Domestic Politics and Political Economy in the Age of Truman," and Nelson Lichtenstein, "Labor in the Truman Era: Origins of the 'Private Welfare State,' " both in *The Truman Presidency,* ed. Michael J. Lacey (Cambridge: Cambridge University Press, 1989); Nelson Lichtenstein, "From Corporatism to Collective Bargaining: Organized Labor and the Eclipse of Social Democracy in the Postwar Era," in *The Rise and Fall of the New Deal Order, 1930–1980,* ed. Steve Fraser and Gary Gerstle (Princeton: Princeton University Press, 1989).

10. As the editors of *Congressional Quarterly* assessed the political situation of labor after Taft-Hartley: "... while postwar legislation narrowed the scope of union rights compared with what it had enjoyed during the New Deal and World War II periods under the Wagner Act, it never went back to the situation which had existed before the 1930s. The rights of workers to organize and to strike relatively free from the previously ubiquitous antilabor injunction ... the requirements that management bargain collectively and refrain from unfair practices—all these rights were preserved throughout the postwar era. And despite the demands of many conservatives and business interests, Congress in the postwar era did not put unions under antitrust laws ... or prohibit the union shop ... or bar strikes in key industries like transportation and public utilities. The limit to how far Congress went in restricting unions and the preservation of the basic rights of unions which had been won in the 1930s reflected in part the strength of organized labor itself, which could oppose changes in federal law too severely unfavorable to it." See Congressional Quarterly, *Congress and the Nation, 1945–1964: A Review of Government and Politics in the Postwar Years* (Washington, D.C.: CQ Press, 1965), 565.

11. Hartmann, *Truman and the 80th Congress,* 35–40, 137–41; and Martha Derthick, *Policymaking for Social Security* (Washington, D.C.: Brookings Institution, 1979), 83, 146.

12. Quoted in Patterson, *Mr. Republican,* 318–19.

13. Quoted in David W. Reinhard, *The Republican Right since 1945* (Lex-

ington: University of Kentucky Press, 1983), 28.

14. Martin, *My First Fifty Years in Politics,* 193.

15. George H. Mayer, *The Republican Party, 1854–1964* (New York: Oxford University Press, 1964), 468.

16. Alonzo L. Hamby, *Beyond the New Deal: Harry S. Truman and American Liberalism* (New York: Columbia University Press, 1973), 185.

17. Alonzo L. Hamby, "The Mind and Character of Harry S. Truman," in Lacey, *The Truman Presidency,* 46. Truman's revived liberal fervor was also consistent with political advice he was receiving at the time on how to win in 1948. At the president's request, Clark Clifford had submitted a document analyzing the upcoming campaign. Clifford counseled that Truman should focus on the western region, alienated by the GOP because of Republican budget cuts in public power and other programs, and on appeals to key voting blocs —farmers, workers, blacks, urban ethnics. Southern Democratic conservatives were to receive little attention in this strategy because the South was safely Democratic in presidential elections and because the presence of the Republican majority in Congress (where southern Democrats held great influence) had relieved the president of the need to build an actual record of legislative achievement. Hamby, *Beyond the New Deal,* 209–12.

18. William S. White, *Citadel: The Story of the U.S. Senate* (New York: Harper and Brothers, 1957), 174.

19. Apparently, the feeling was often mutual. On Truman's strained relationship with many who had been close to Roosevelt, see William E. Leuchtenberg, *In the Shadow of FDR: From Harry Truman to Bill Clinton,* 2d ed. rev. (Ithaca: Cornell University Press, 1993), chap. 1; and Hamby, *Beyond the New Deal,* 41–85, 140–42.

20. Martin, *My First Fifty Years in Politics,* 194, 196; Richard S. Kirkendall, "Election of 1948," in *History of American Presidential Elections, 1789–1968,* ed. Arthur M. Schlesinger Jr., vol. 4 (New York: Chelsea House, 1971).

21. D.B. Hardeman and Donald C. Bacon, *Rayburn: A Biography* (Lanham, Md.: Madison Books, 1987), 349.

22. Quoted in Barton J. Bernstein, "Election of 1952," in Schlesinger, *History of American Presidential Elections,* 3248.

23. The one major exception was the issue of communists in government, but even this was an outgrowth of the goal of active resistance to international communism, which *President Truman* had placed at the center of postwar foreign policy.

24. See Byron E. Shafer, "The Notion of an Electoral Order: The Structure of Electoral Politics at the Accession of George Bush," in *The End of Realignment? Interpreting American Electoral Eras,* ed. Byron E. Shafer (Madison: University of Wisconsin Press, 1991).

25. Charles O. Jones, "Separating to Govern: The American Way," in *Present Discontents: American Politics in the Very Late Twentieth Century,* ed. Byron E. Shafer (Chatham, N.J.: Chatham House, 1997), 62.

26. For the view that creation of large deficits was a brilliant political

strategy "that shifted the entire debate in an economically conservative direction," see Aaron Wildavsky, "President Reagan as a Political Strategist," in *The Reagan Legacy: Promise and Performance*, ed. Charles O. Jones (Chatham, N.J.: Chatham House, 1988).

27. Kenneth A. Shepsle, "The Changing Textbook Congress," in *Can the Government Govern?* ed. John E. Chubb and Paul E. Peterson (Washington, D.C.: Brookings Institution, 1989).

28. Though a final budget resolution was never approved, Democrats on the House Budget Committee initially proposed a revenue amount for 1990 identical to that in the president's budget. The committee's report also stated that no action would be taken on tax increases included in the congressional budget "unless and until such time as there is bipartisan agreement with the President of the United States on specific legislation to meet or exceed such ... requirements." See Barbara Sinclair, "Governing Unheroically (and Sometimes Unappetizingly): Bush and the 101st Congress," in *The Bush Presidency: First Appraisals*, ed. Colin Campbell and Bert A. Rockman (Chatham, N.J.: Chatham House, 1991), 175.

29. See Byron E. Shafer, "We Are All Southern Democrats Now: The Shape of American Politics in the Very Late Twentieth Century," in Shafer, *Present Discontents*, 158–62.

30. It is interesting to note that by the 1990s, the conservative coalition of Republicans and southern Democrats appeared much less frequently than it had in previous decades, but was likely to carry the day on those relatively few votes where it did appear. See table A.1, facing page.

31. Marjorie Randon Hershey, "The Congressional Elections," in *The Election of 1992*, ed. Gerald M. Pomper (Chatham, N.J.: Chatham House, 1993), 162–64.

32. Congressional Quarterly, *Congressional Quarterly Almanac 1992* (Washington, D.C.: CQ Press, 1993), 5.

33. James W. Ceaser and Andrew E. Busch, *Upside Down and Inside Out: The 1992 Elections and American Politics* (Lanham, Md.: Rowman and Littlefield, 1993), 1–10.

34. See William G. Mayer, "Changes in Elections and the Party System: 1992 in Historical Perspective," in *The New American Politics: Reflections on Political Change and the Clinton Administration*, ed. Bryan D. Jones (Boulder, Colo.: Westview Press, 1995), 31–35; Ceaser and Busch, *Upside Down and Inside Out*, chap. 4.

35. Gerald M. Pomper, "The Presidential Election," in Pomper, *The Election of 1992*, 146.

36. Richard F. Fenno Jr., *Senators on the Campaign Trail: The Politics of Representation* (Norman: University of Oklahoma Press, 1996), 195.

37. Walter Dean Burnham, "The Legacy of George Bush: Travails of an Understudy," in Pomper, *The Election of 1992*, 1–2.

38. Wilson Carey McWilliams, *The Politics of Disappointment: American Elections, 1976–1994* (Chatham, N.J.: Chatham House, 1995), 194.

TABLE 1.1

THE CONSERVATIVE COALITION

	Appearances			Victory rate	
Year	House	Senate	Year	House	Senate
1947	21	17	1947	100	97
1949	16	14	1949	84	88
1951	24	16	1951	93	95
1953	17	19	1953	100	98
1955	12	12	1955	85	88
1957	16	15	1957	73	93
1959	17	21	1959	64	67
1961	17	24	1961	59	60
1963	12	18	1963	67	46
1965	22	32	1965	29	45
1967	22	22	1967	67	67
1969	21	27	1969	71	66
1971	28	29	1971	79	75
1973	22	26	1973	70	54
1975	25	27	1975	57	53
1977	21	26	1977	58	61
1979	19	19	1979	70	70
1981	19	22	1981	83	97
1983	16	15	1983	74	92
1985	12	19	1985	81	93
1987	9	9	1987	86	98
1989	12	12	1989	77	95
1991	10	14	1991	87	91
1993	8	10	1993	95	81
1995	12	11	1995	100	96

SOURCE: *Congressional Quarterly Almanacs,* various years.

NOTE: Scores are percentages of votes for the entire Congress beginning in the year indicated.

39. Barbara Sinclair, "Trying to Govern Positively in a Negative Era: Clinton and the 103rd Congress," in *The Clinton Presidency: First Appraisals,* ed. Colin Campbell and Bert A. Rockman (Chatham, N.J.: Chatham House, 1996), 101–9; George Hager, "House Meets Clinton Halfway on 'Investment' Proposals," *Congressional Quarterly Weekly Report,* 3 July 1993, 1717–18. To put the tax changes in perspective, the top statutory rate on personal income was 70 percent when Ronald Reagan entered office and 28 percent when he left. The tax component of the 1993 Clinton deficit package increased the top statutory rate from 31 percent to 36 percent.

40. Sinclair, "Trying to Govern Positively in a Negative Era," 107–9.

41. Alissa J. Rubin, "Budget War Casts Shadow on Overhaul Plans," *Con-*

gressional Quarterly Weekly Report, 14 August 1993, 2225–27.

42. Ceaser and Busch, *Upside Down and Inside Out,* 2; Gary C. Jacobson, "The 1994 Midterm: Why the Models Missed It," *Extension of Remarks,* December 1994, 2–3, 14–15.

43. Roger H. Davidson, "Building a Republican Regime on Capitol Hill," *Extension of Remarks,* December 1995, 1–2, 12. See Ronald M. Peters Jr., *The American Speakership* (Baltimore: Johns Hopkins University Press, 1990); David W. Rohde, *Parties and Leaders in the Postreform House* (Chicago: University of Chicago Press, 1991); Daniel J. Palazzolo, *The Speaker and the Budget: Leadership in the Postreform House of Representatives* (Pittsburgh: University of Pittsburgh Press, 1992); Barbara Sinclair, *Legislators, Leaders, and Lawmaking: The House of Representatives in the Postreform Era* (Baltimore: Johns Hopkins University Press, 1995).

44. Congressional Quarterly, "Presidential News Conference: Clinton Reaches Out to GOP, Assesses Voters' Message," *Congressional Quarterly Weekly Report,* 12 November 1994, 3292–94.

45. Elizabeth Drew, *Showdown: The Struggle between the Gingrich Congress and the Clinton White House* (New York: Simon and Schuster, 1996), 216.

46. McWilliams, *The Politics of Disappointment,* 185.

47. William J. Clinton, "Address before a Joint Session on the State of the Union, 23 January 1996," *Weekly Compilation of Presidential Documents* 32 (29 January 1996): 90–98.

48. Daniel Balz, "The New 'New Democrats,' " *Washington Post Weekly Edition,* 23–29 September 1996, 6.

49. This apt description of Clinton's post-1994 approach is said to have been coined by conservative journalist Kate O'Beirne. See E.J. Dionne Jr., "The GOP's Uncertain Trumpeting," *Washington Post,* 13 December 1996, A23.

50. The most likely scenario in which the agreement on budget balance might fall apart would be a serious economic downturn, which would also likely remind some voters why big government used to be so popular.

2

Party Factionalism, 1946–1996

Nicol C. Rae

Party factions occupy a curious status in the study of American politics. In the traditionally broad-based, catchall, major parties of the United States, various intraparty blocs or wings have usually been easy to discern. Indeed, for most of U.S. history, both observers of and participants in the political process have just assumed that such party factions existed, a perception confirmed by the names, or colorful nicknames—"Mugwump" Republicans, "Cotton" and "Conscience" Whigs, "Radical" Republicans, "Dixiecrats," "Progressive" Republicans, "Liberal" Democrats—that have been habitually awarded to significant party factions.

Nevertheless, by comparison with their counterparts in other advanced industrialized democracies, American party factions have proven to be elusive, and thus resistant to analysis. The analytic problem arises because of the highly fluid and decentralized nature of American parties themselves. Adopting Richard Rose's definition of factions, one drawn from West European models, as "self-consciously organized ... with a measure of discipline and cohesion," it is evident that the loose and porous nature of American parties has prevented party factions from developing the levels of organization, discipline, and durability characteristic of party factions in other Western democracies.[1] As a result, conceptual terms, such as "wings," "tendencies," or "clusters," have been suggested as superior analytic tools for understanding U.S. party factions.[2]

This chapter assumes, however, that while remaining amorphous by comparison with party factions in other advanced democracies, modern U.S. counterparts resemble the general type closely enough to merit the designation "faction." In a previous discussion of party factions in advanced Western democracies, I isolated two main patterns of factionalism: clientelistic and ideological.[3] Clientelistic factions are oriented toward particular constituencies or regional interests and seek to maximize some material gain for their adherents, in terms of money, jobs, or political offices. Because the availability of these resources is contingent on control of the government, clientelistic factionalism has been characteristic of dominant-party systems where one party remains in power over an extended period of time, as occurred in Japan under the Liberal Democrats, Italy under the Christian Democrats, and Mexico under the PRI.

The second type of factionalism has been ideological. Ideological factionalism is more characteristic of a two-party or multiparty system with a strong Social Democratic Party. Typically, the division here is between a faction that emphasizes the ideology of the party and seeks to put it into practice and an opposing faction that is prepared to modify or disregard that ideology for electoral success. To the extent that center-right parties have become ideological mass parties in order to compete with the left, they, too, have displayed this type of factionalism, although it is generally more muted.

Clientelistic factionalism has certainly been an aspect of American party politics for much of U.S. history. The patronage-based "machine" politics so prevalent in American state and local governments between the Civil War and World War II was undoubtedly a variant of clientelistic factionalism, but the absence of a major socialist party has meant that America did not experience ideological party factionalism until relatively recently. Nevertheless, the decline of clientelistic politics in the United States in this century, and its replacement by a party politics based more on ideology since the New Deal era, have encouraged the emergence of ideologically driven factions within U.S. parties. Ironically, then, at the same time as the personal attachments of U.S. voters to political parties have greatly diminished, the parties themselves have become far *more* concerned with ideology, and thus more susceptible to ideological party factionalism.

The first period under discussion in this chapter, 1946–52, was precisely the time when ideological party factionalism began to manifest itself in both major parties.[4] By the time of the second period of analysis, 1990–96, ideology had become the predominant mobilizing agency for citizen participation in party politics, to the extent that loyalty to factions now arguably takes precedence over loyalty to party for most activists.

The years 1946–52 were also a time of transition to what Byron Shafer has described as a new "electoral order," with differing party alignments prevailing at different levels of party competition.[5] During these years, the Democratic Party was translating its New Deal presidential strength to the congressional, state, and local levels, while that very presidential supremacy was itself beginning to come into question.

The outcome of this transition was divided control of the federal government for twenty-six of the thirty-seven years between 1953 and 1990. During the 1990s, in contrast, we have seen the Republican Party gathering strength at the congressional and state levels, while its dominant post-1952 presidential coalition has shown serious signs of erosion. The remainder of this chapter demonstrates how in each time period, the factional balance within both parties played an important role in paving the way to a possible new electoral order. In this, party factions served as a crucial link. On one side were election outcomes, and thus the partisan balance inside governmental institutions; on the other side were elite, and ultimately mass, preferences for public policy. Along the way, these factions tell much of the story of postwar politics.

A Period of Transition I: 1946–52

Within the thirty-year cycle beloved of realignment theorists, the New Deal partisan alignment, based on economic class, is supposed to have lasted until the mid-1960s.[6] But in fact, the top-heavy coalition assembled by FDR during the 1930s was already showing signs of severe erosion in the immediate postwar years. That coalition was formed in response to Roosevelt's program for alleviating mass economic hardship and was forged through anxiety that a restoration of Republican rule would bring a return to the economic policies that were popularly blamed for the Great Depression. The coalition's strength actually peaked in 1936, when FDR was reelected with 61 percent of the popular vote, carrying all but two states, while the Republicans were reduced to eighty-nine representatives and seventeen senators. In demographic terms, all sectors of American society except upper-class northern white Protestants were in the Democratic column.[7]

After the 1938 congressional elections, however, the Republicans began to come back. By 1944, FDR's winning percentage had fallen to 53 percent; by 1946, the Republicans had managed, albeit temporarily, to retake control of both houses of Congress. In the postwar period, the context of political debate moved away from a pure focus on economic issues and on to new terrain, involving civil rights for blacks at home and containment of communism in the world at large. Harry Truman was able to gather enough of the old New Deal coalition for a narrow victory in a four-way race in 1948, but this election also exposed the fault lines that would shatter the Democratic presidential coalition for the better part of half a century. At the same time, the 1946–52 period exposed the shortcomings of the Republicans as a congressional party and ushered in a period when the Democrats would establish an even tighter grip on the U.S. Congress than the Republicans were to attain on the presidency.

In sum, the 1946–52 period was one of intense and close competition between the parties for supremacy, by contrast with the lopsided Democratic alignments of the New Deal period. From 1946 to 1952, control of Congress changed hands three times between the parties, and it would change again in 1954. At the presidential level, 1948 was the closest election since 1916 and the first since then to produce a plurality winner. The year 1952 brought the first Republican presidency in twenty years.

Party Factions at the Opening of the Postwar Years

Intraparty factional alignments within both parties help shed light on the electoral turmoil of the postwar years. In the majority Democratic coalition we can discern four factions in the immediate postwar period: Radicals, Liberals, Regulars, and Southerners (see table 2.1).

The *Radicals* were an amalgam of western—formerly Republican— populists and eastern urban socialists. Their base of support lay mainly in academic and intellectual circles plus some labor unions, and their political agenda was based on a further evolution of the Democratic Party in a Social Democratic direction. Although sparsely represented in Congress, Radicals had served in influential positions in the Roosevelt administration, most prominently Henry Wallace, a former progressive Republican who had served as FDR's agriculture secretary and later as vice-president during Roosevelt's third term. Dropped from the national ticket in 1944 for fear that he might actually succeed the ailing Roosevelt, Wallace served as secretary of commerce in the Truman administration until his resignation in 1946 over what he regarded as Truman's unduly hostile attitude toward the Soviet Union. In fact, this issue came to define the Radical wing of the party, as the Cold War and concerns about domestic communist subversion intensified. Several Radical adherents had been overtly sympathetic to the USSR and, like Wallace, deplored Truman's adoption of a foreign policy based on containing communism. Repudiation of the Truman-Marshall foreign policy from the left was the basis of Wallace's "Progressive" third-party candidacy for the presidency in 1948.

TABLE 2.1

DEMOCRATIC PARTY FACTIONS, 1946–52

	Radicals	Liberals	Regulars	Southerners
Issues	Oppose Cold War Social democracy Support civil rights	Oppose communism Extend government Support civil rights	Oppose communism Extend government Some desegregation	Oppose communism Limit government Support segregation
Electoral support	Urban Northeast, Plains Intellectuals Agrarian populists	Urban Northeast, Midwest, West Intellectuals, professionals Blacks, Jews	Urban Northeast, Midwest Blue-collar whites Catholic ethnics	Southern white Protestants
Interest-group support	Some labor Some media	Lawyers Media	Labor unions	Southern business
Party power base	Urban activists	Presidential party	State and local parties	Southern state parties
Leaders	Henry Wallace	Hubert Humphrey Adlai Stevenson	Harry Truman	Richard Russell Strom Thurmond

The *Liberals* were eventually to emerge as the dominant force in the post–New Deal Democratic Party, and this began to become apparent in the 1946–52 period. While strongly supportive of the New Deal's economic policies and social programs, Liberals abhorred communism in general and Stalin's USSR in particular. They also placed a stronger emphasis on civil liberties than did the other Democratic factions and strove to move the national party behind full support for racial desegregation and civil rights for blacks. Adherents of the Liberal faction generally came from white-collar, professional occupations, with academics, teachers, lawyers, and journalists being heavily featured. The civil liberties focus also made Liberal candidates particularly attractive to Jewish voters and to enfranchised northern blacks. During the 1950s, the Liberals finally became dominant within the presidential party, in part because of their base in the talking professions and their appeal in the national news media, both of which were becoming increasingly important in American electoral politics with the decline of traditional party organizations.[8] In Congress, while a growing force, they had not yet broken the stranglehold of the white South over the (congressional) Democratic Party. Hubert Humphrey and Adlai Stevenson were the leading Liberals of the postwar era, and together with another Liberal, John F. Kennedy, they would win four of the five Democratic presidential nominations between 1952 and 1968.

The *Regular* faction—the clearest example of a clientelistic faction in the party politics of the time—was constituted by the remaining traditional urban party organizations, or "machines," in alliance with organized labor. A dominant force in the presidential party during the New Deal, the Regulars had their base of support in the big cities and major industrial areas of the Northeast and Midwest, among blue-collar workers generally and among Catholic ethnic voters in particular. They stood for class-based economic policies at home and robust anticommunism abroad, reflecting the needs and sympathies of their base constituency. While they were not generally hostile to black civil rights, this issue was less relevant for the Regulars than for the Liberals. In uneasy alliance with the latter, however, the Regulars controlled the presidential Democratic Party during the New Deal, although it became clear by the early 1950s that, due to demographic trends, they were becoming the weaker partner in that alliance. Both factions grudgingly rallied around the apparently unpopular President Harry Truman, whose views were fairly representative of the Regular section of the party, in 1948.

The final party faction in the postwar Democratic coalition was the most apparently incongruous: *Southerners,* which is to say, the *White South.* The overwhelming identification of white southerners with the

Democratic Party was based on the heritage of the Civil War and Reconstruction, reinforced powerfully by the South's position as the poorest and most economically underdeveloped region of the country. While Republican Herbert Hoover had broken the Democrats' grip on the South temporarily in 1928, the onset of the Great Depression reinvigorated Democratic loyalties. FDR also showed masterful political skill in retaining the South's monolithic support for the Democratic Party and simultaneously bringing Liberals and northern blacks into the New Deal coalition. Of course, the only way to perform this balancing act successfully was to avoid the issue of civil rights for disfranchised and segregated southern blacks.[9]

The White South—which, like the Regulars, closely fitted the model of a clientelistic party faction—had two essential sources of institutional power within the Democratic Party: the two-thirds rule at national party conventions and the region's grip on the congressional Democratic Party. The first, quite simply, prevented any candidate unacceptable to the South from being nominated by the Democrats for president. The second arose from the post-1910 committee/seniority system in Congress, which allowed long-serving southerners to ascend to powerful committee chairmanships as long as the Democrats held control. On the other hand, FDR's abolition of the two-thirds rule in 1936 greatly weakened the South's clout within the presidential Democratic Party, as it strengthened the Liberals and Regulars. While the principal southern Democratic leaders in Congress, Democratic House Speaker (or Minority Leader) Sam Rayburn of Texas and Senator Richard B. Russell of Georgia, supported Truman's containment policies along with much of the New Deal, the increasing pressure on Truman from the Liberal faction of the party for federal action on civil rights placed the southerners in a very difficult position.

Among the Republicans, there were just two main factions in the immediate postwar period: Stalwarts (or Conservative Republicans) and Liberals (Liberal Republicans) (see table 2.2, p. 48).

The *Stalwarts* consisted of the solid northern, WASP, rural and medium- to small-city core of the Republican Party: those who had stayed with the GOP even in its darkest hours of 1932–38.[10] The lawyers, bankers, and small businessmen who sustained this wing of the party held firm to the laissez-faire tenets of McKinley, Harding, and Coolidge; they were infuriated by the big-government activism of FDR. In foreign affairs, Stalwart Republicans were highly distrustful of "Wilsonian" idealistic meddling, which they regarded as almost inherently likely to corrupt the yeoman Republic that they had fought to preserve. Their greatest strength

TABLE 2.2

REPUBLICAN PARTY FACTIONS, 1946–52

	Stalwarts	Liberals
Issues	Limited government	Interventionist government
	Isolationism	Internationalism/nationalism
	States' rights	Federal coordination
Electoral support	Northeast and Midwest	Northeast and Pacific West
	Small city/rural areas	Urban/suburban areas
	Northern white Protestants	Professionals
Interest-group support	Main Street	Wall Street
	Small business	Corporate business
	Farm organizations	National media
Party power base	Congress	National Convention
Leaders	Robert A. Taft	Thomas E. Dewey

lay at the grassroots of the party *and in Congress,* where they dominated the Republican leadership after the electoral rout of the 1930s. The figure who epitomized the Stalwart wing of the Republican Party was Ohio Senator Robert A. Taft, the predominant Republican in Congress, whose political credo was based on minimal government intervention, at home and abroad.[11]

The *Liberals*—the *Liberal Republican* faction—were most directly descended from the turn-of-the-century progressive Republicanism of Theodore Roosevelt. In truth, however, their antecedents could be traced much farther back, to the "Mugwump" reformers of the late nineteenth century or even to the activist government tradition of the Whigs and the Federalists. This strain of Republicanism was particularly associated with the northeastern patrician class, with leading "old money" families such as the Roosevelts of New York and the Lodges of Massachusetts. While retaining a generally pro-big-business attitude, these Republicans accepted the need for governmental regulation in the national interest and emphasized the importance of good, efficient public service. Although it lost influence in the GOP after Theodore Roosevelt bolted the party in his 1912 "Bull Moose" campaign, progressive Republicanism reemerged in the "Liberal Republicanism" of the 1940s.[12]

When it became apparent that the unrelenting opposition of the Stalwarts to FDR had led the GOP to electoral disaster in 1936, the Liberals provided a Republican alternative that took account of the changes in the

American political landscape wrought by the New Deal. At home, the emergence of Liberal Republicanism in the presidential campaigns of Thomas E. Dewey and Wendell Willkie in 1940 also reflected the accommodation that much of the eastern business and financial establishment had made with New Deal–style governmental interventionism by the late 1930s. Abroad, Liberal Republicanism was robustly internationalist, reflecting its East Coast, European-oriented, economic and social base of support.[13]

Liberal Republican strength was concentrated in the presidential Republican Party. The major party organizations of the large eastern states, in particular, were attracted to progressive candidates who could win elections. This, coupled with the influence of Wall Street over the nation's businesses and banks, allowed the Republican "eastern establishment" a disproportionate influence at the party's national conventions. Liberal Republican candidates also benefited from the vestiges of western Radical Republicanism in states like Wisconsin, Minnesota, and California. Finally, at a time when southern Republican convention delegations were literally "for sale" to the highest bidder, the Liberal Republicans often had more chips with which to bid.[14]

The predominant Liberal Republican of the day was New York Governor Thomas E. Dewey.[15] A formidable administrator, Dewey had been a major presence in national politics since his time as New York City district attorney in the mid-1930s. Even before getting elected governor of New York, Dewey almost won the GOP presidential nomination in 1940, until the convention was swept by a Wall Street–generated tide of support for an even more liberal, internationalist, Republican business executive: Wendell Willkie. In 1944 Dewey had the Liberal faction of the party all to himself, won the nomination, and ran a creditable wartime race against FDR, securing 47 percent of the national vote. Despite opposition from Taft and the Stalwart forces, he was once again the clear favorite for the party's nomination in 1948, and he appeared a very likely winner against an unpopular Truman and a badly fractured Democratic Party.

Factional Dynamics and Party Transition, 1946–52

The two presidential elections of the 1946–52 period demonstrated the changing factional balance within both parties, as well as the incipient evolution of the New Deal party system toward the divided government of the Cold War era. The defining characteristics of this latter era were to be Democratic majorities in Congress and Republican domination of the presidency. Factional dynamics within both parties in the late 1940s already helped to understand why this would occur.

With Henry Wallace having led the Radical faction out of the Democratic coalition, Truman faced a splintering on his right flank too, as the issue of black civil rights appeared on the national political agenda. The insertion of a civil rights plank in the 1948 Democratic Party platform produced a bolt of several southern delegations from the convention and the subsequent nomination of Governor Strom Thurmond for president on a States' Rights or "Dixiecrat" ticket. In fact, the defections of both factions from the Democratic Party were only partial. Wallace's campaign adopted too much of a pro-Soviet taint even for many Democratic Radicals, and Thurmond was able to carry only the Deep South states of Alabama, Mississippi, Louisiana, and South Carolina. The remainder of the region, and most of the southern faction's most prominent political leaders, including Senator Richard Russell, remained loyal to Truman.[16]

Indeed, the New Deal party system, although beginning to weaken and subject to all this factional stress, was still strong enough to reelect Truman in 1948, as the Regulars, the Liberals, and most of the White South remained loyal. The main theme of the Democratic campaign in 1948 was to castigate the Republican 80th Congress, under the leadership of Taft and House Speaker Joseph Martin, as harsh and uncaring toward average citizens, thereby arousing memories of Herbert Hoover and the Great Depression. Despite the onset of the Cold War, the economic issue still weighed sufficiently with most voters to assist the Democrats, and Truman played on it cleverly and relentlessly. In the Plains and western states that provided his eventual margin of victory, for example, Truman accused the GOP Congress of having "stuck a pitchfork in the farmers' back." The Democrats also profited from organized labor's resentment at the restrictions on their privileges and practices contained in the 1947 Taft-Hartley Act.

For the Republicans, who had expected to retain Congress and easily defeat Truman, the effect of the 1948 election was devastating. Dewey had secured the nomination again, on the second ballot over Taft and Minnesota Governor Harold Stassen (see table 2.3). The key to Dewey's success, again, was the "two coasts against the middle" geographic alignment that had emerged in 1940, and Dewey confirmed the bicoastal alliance by choosing California Governor Earl Warren as his running mate. The party platform also reflected Liberal Republican policies, rather than the preferences of the more Conservative Republican leadership in Congress. In turn, one of Truman's most effective tactical ploys in the 1948 election was to call the Republican Congress back into session and challenge the Republican leaders on Capitol Hill to implement parts of their own party platform.[17]

TABLE 2.3

REPUBLICAN PARTY FACTIONS

AT THE 1948 NATIONAL CONVENTION:

PRESIDENTIAL NOMINATION, SECOND BALLOT

Candidates	Liberal	Stalwart	Percent[a]
Taft		274	25
Stassen	149		14
Dewey	515		47
Vandenberg		62	6
Warren	57		5
Other Liberal	19		2
Other Stalwart		18	2
Total Liberal	740		68
Total Stalwart		354	32

SOURCE: Richard C. Bain and Judith H. Parris, *Convention Decisions and Voting Records,* 2d ed. (Washington, D.C.: Brookings Institution, 1973).

a. Total delegates = 1,094.

The two factions then drew opposite lessons from Dewey's defeat. For Taft and the Stalwarts, Dewey's "me-tooism" and failure to stand for true Republican principles were responsible for the outcome. For the Liberals, it was the intransigence of the Stalwarts in Congress that was primarily responsible because it identified the GOP once again with the hard-faced economic conservatism of the 1930s.

Between 1948 and 1952, the global situation also affected Republican Party factionalism in one significant respect. During the 80th Congress, the Stalwart chairman of the Senate Foreign Relations Committee, Senator Arthur Vandenberg of Michigan, had begun to demonstrate significant Republican support for Truman's foreign policy of Soviet containment, by helping to maneuver aid for Greece and Turkey and the Marshall Plan through a skeptical Congress. Senator Taft, in contrast, retained his distaste for U.S. military interventions abroad, as evidenced by his vote against the 1949 NATO treaty. The wave of the future, however, was the emergence of a new generation of Republican Conservatives, perhaps best represented by Richard Nixon, who combined Stalwart positions in domestic affairs with a militant anticommunist posture in foreign policy.[18]

This new militancy in foreign affairs first manifested itself in 1949–50, after the "fall" of China and the onset of the Korean War, when Conservative Republicans mounted a ferocious rhetorical assault on the

Truman-Acheson foreign policy. This was coupled with allegations from Senator Joseph McCarthy and others that the Democrats had at best been duped by, and at worst connived at, domestic communist subversion. Such a change in the Conservatives' approach to foreign policy actually helped to bridge the gulf between the party factions, while it broadened the GOP's potential appeal to hitherto Democratic, Catholic, ethnic voters.[19] Truman's commitment of American forces to the Korean conflict, and the subsequent loss of more than 50,000 American lives, focused the national political debate on national security issues to an even greater extent.

Once this had occurred, the Democrats were in serious trouble, not because Republican allegations of "softness on communism" were evidently true, but because a Republican Party with both major factions converted by anticommunism to internationalism was no longer vulnerable on the security issues that were becoming increasingly important in presidential politics. The focus on national security and domestic subversion hurt the Democrats among some key constituencies and moved political debate away from the economic issues that had sustained their grip on the White House for twenty years.

As the postwar economic boom began to accelerate, the Democrats' presidential coalition also fell victim to demographic change. It was already apparent from the two Dewey elections that the Republicans were benefiting from the economic development and urbanization of the South and West, plus the migration of business-oriented northerners to those regions.[20] Suburbanization and the expansion of educational opportunity were also weakening the solidary ties that had bound northern, urban, white, working-class Democrats to their ethnic communities, again to the long-term detriment of the Democratic Party.[21] The Democrats' sole consolation was the increasing Democratic allegiance of the growing urban black vote in the North.

The Democrats had to face all these problems in the 1952 election, coupled with the perhaps inevitable corruption and exhaustion of a party that had been in power for two decades. To complete the sale for the Republicans, however, factional conflict between Liberal Republicans and Stalwart Conservatives over the presidential nomination still had to be resolved in a manner that united the factions in a new internationalist consensus. This meant that Robert Taft, whose views on foreign policy certainly did not reflect that consensus, would have to be denied the presidential nomination once again. For the Liberal Republicans, badly bruised from having led the GOP to three consecutive presidential election defeats, this was no easy task.

Nevertheless, facing the prospect of a Taft nomination, Dewey was able to rally the troops one last time, in support of the candidacy of General Dwight D. Eisenhower, who held fairly routine Stalwart views on domestic issues but was also strongly committed to NATO and to containing the Soviets abroad. Eisenhower's narrow triumph at the 1952 GOP convention was taken as another disappointment by the existing Stalwart faction of the party, but younger Conservatives who supported Eisenhower, such as Nixon, had already adapted to the changed international environment. Indeed, Eisenhower's nomination of Nixon as his vice-presidential running mate unified the Republican factions around the issue of anticommunism and served as a strong symbolic statement of the new order in the GOP.

With the unpopular Truman driven out of the race early, there was no clear favorite for the Democratic nomination. The ultimate compromise choice promoted by Truman and the Regulars, Illinois Governor Adlai Stevenson (see table 2.4) was a patrician moderate, ideologically closest to the Liberal faction but somewhat tepid on civil rights and therefore

TABLE 2.4

DEMOCRATIC PARTY FACTIONS

AT THE 1952 NATIONAL CONVENTION:

PRESIDENTIAL NOMINATION, FIRST BALLOT

Candidate	Liberal	Regular	White South[a]	Percent[b]
Harriman		123		10
Kefauver	340			28
Russell			268	22
Stevenson		273[c]		22
Other Liberal	29			2
Other Regular		101		8
Other White South			87	7
Total Liberal	369			30
Total Regular		497		40
Total White South			355	29

SOURCE: See table 2.3.

a. The impact of the Cold War and McCarthyism ruled out any possibility of a serious presidential candidacy from the Radical wing of the party between 1948 and 1968.

b. Total delegates = 1,230. Nine delegates (0.5 percent) could not reasonably be classified.

c. Although stylistically and ideologically Liberal, Stevenson was very much the favorite of President Truman and the Regular wing of the party in 1952.

acceptable to the White South—particularly after he chose Alabama Senator John Sparkman as his vice-presidential running mate. Vilified and harassed by anticommunist hysteria, the Radical faction retreated for what would become another decade or so to its intellectual and academic redoubts, from which it would later reemerge as a much stronger force within the Democratic Party.

The presidential majority assembled by Eisenhower and the Republicans, largely on the basis of national security issues, would give the GOP a lock on the White House for much of the next quarter-century. As long as the Cold War persisted and the profile of the presidency in foreign and security policy remained high, the Republicans held a crucial advantage in presidential politics over a Democratic Party that was never quite able to overcome the suspicion of naïveté in foreign affairs. Ironically, the perception of the Republicans as hardliners on foreign policy allowed Republican presidents to be far more flexible and innovative in international affairs than their Democratic counterparts during the Cold War. By contrast, fears of a resurgence of Republican McCarthyism contributed to the decisions of the Democratic Kennedy and Johnson administrations to escalate American involvement in Vietnam.

During the 1960s and 1970s, Republican presidential supremacy was reinforced by the action of the federal courts in opening up sensitive social and cultural questions such as racial desegregation, abortion, busing, school prayer, and the rights of criminal suspects, questions that divided the Democrats as a national party far more than they did the more homogeneous Republicans. White southern realignment also continued to favor the Republicans in presidential politics. In 1952 Eisenhower repeated Hoover's presidential breakthrough in the Outer South. Over the next two decades, as the White South was gradually eased out of the Democratic presidential coalition, there was no other place for it to go but the GOP.

Yet in a development unique in American electoral history, at the same time that the GOP was establishing its presidential dominance during the 1950s, it began to lose ground in congressional elections. While Eisenhower won by a landslide at the presidential level in 1952, the Republicans barely gained control of Congress. In 1954 they lost control of the U.S. Senate for what was to become twenty-six years—and of the House of Representatives for forty.

The Democrats initially gained a grip on Congress during the Eisenhower era because the American public apparently remained distrustful of the traditional economic conservatism advocated by the Conservatives who predominated among Republicans in Congress. Since the New Deal, the legislative branch had become increasingly oriented toward the provision of governmental services and programs to multifarious constituencies.[22] The decentralized committee system—decentralized even further to a subcommittee system in the 1970s—was structured to maximize the electoral benefit for individual Democratic members. The price that was paid for this was, of course, a fundamental incoherence in the overall direction of Congress and the national party.

To accomplish this strategy of distributive benefits, the Democrats perforce became the "everyone" party, eventually embracing social categories as disparate as urban minority activists and rural white southerners. But this very incoherence became the Democrats' greatest *asset* in congressional elections, as long as federal government programs offering benefits to each group could be maintained. Even the White South, which was finally to leave the presidential party in the 1960s, remained a vital part of the Democratic congressional coalition, thanks to the seniority system and to the fact that as long as Democratic control of Congress persisted, conservative southerners saw more advantage for themselves as part of a congressional majority than of an (ineffectual) Republican alternative.[23]

The events of the 1960s institutionalized the new electoral order of 1946–52. Vietnam opened up new Democratic divisions on foreign policy, while the White South essentially left the presidential party as a result of the civil rights revolution. When Democrats did win the presidency, as in 1960 and 1976, it was by narrow margins that were pale reflections of their broad congressional coalition. Republicans, in contrast, remained a narrow, white Protestant, upper-middle-class party. Although they did succeed in breaking into the White South, they did so at the expense of alienating themselves completely from the black vote nationwide.

Latent factional tensions remained within the GOP, but the substantial weakening of the Liberal Republicans after Dewey's retirement led to a more ideologically homogeneous Republican coalition. This coalition was ideally equipped for fighting presidential elections, but too ideologically shrill and socially narrow to threaten the Democratic hold on Congress. Conversely, in the electoral order of 1952–90, multifactionalism in the Democratic Party cost it the presidency most of the time but became a simultaneous asset in maintaining Democratic control of Congress. The pattern of factionalism within each party thus operated to maintain divided control of the U.S. federal government for the better part of forty years.

A Period of Transition II: 1990–96

Seen one way, the Cold War years were characterized by the persistence of a factional alignment that came into focus from 1946 to 1952. From this standpoint, what results is a vision of flux: of candidates, issues, and social groups coming and going within established factional contours. Seen the other way, however—from the vantage point of the 1990s, after the apparent end of the Cold War—these years also contained the forces and trends that would ultimately produce a new factional alignment, one first explicitly recognized from 1990 to 1996. From this perspective, these years are of course the making of the modern world.

Factional Evolution during the Cold War Years:
The Democrats

The societal upheavals of the 1960s had found a focus in—indeed, they were perhaps best distinguished by—intense factional strife within the Democratic Party. The dominant alliance of the Regular and the Liberal factions, built around governmental economic intervention at home and containment of communism overseas, could not withstand the twin challenges of black civil rights and the Vietnam War. While the White South more or less exited from the presidential Democratic Party after the 1964 Civil Rights Act, much of the base constituency for the Regulars—northern, white, ethnic, blue-collar voters—also became disenchanted with the Democratic Johnson administration after outbreaks of racial rioting in several major northern cities in the mid-1960s. George Wallace's third-party candidacy in 1968 appealed to both these groups, picking up their pro-Vietnam constituents in particular, and acted as a catalyst for their growing alignment with the Republican Party in presidential politics during the 1970s and 1980s.[24]

While the Democrats' two clientelistic factions were in decline, the anti–Vietnam War movement revived the old Radical faction of the Democratic Party, the faction that had been read out of the party by McCarthyism in the 1950s but had reemerged as a component of the New Left in the 1960s. This group also allied itself with a new and more militant black and Hispanic leadership, plus a significant contingent of Liberals who could no longer stomach the war, to form a *New Left/Minorities* faction. That faction then effectively drove President Lyndon Johnson from the White House. After Hubert Humphrey's defeat in 1968, the same alliance implemented a drastic reform of the presidential nominating process, which led to the nomination of Senator George McGovern in 1972.[25]

Ironically, while this group had ostensibly been formed as an alliance against the old clientelistic or "pluralist" politics, adherents of the New Left/Minorities faction began to evince their own variant of clientelism, directed toward the "empowerment" of previously excluded or disadvantaged constituencies, such as blacks, Hispanics, women, native Americans, and gays. Instead of relying on old-fashioned graft, patronage, and log-rolling, however, this version of empowerment was to be achieved by means of "affirmative action" and "diversity" policies, in government and in the private sector, along with an emphasis on cultural symbolism and language—methods that were more likely to polarize other social and ethnic groups than encourage them to aggregate their interests behind a revised party platform.

The trauma of McGovern's landslide defeat, in turn, resulted in a schism within the emergent McGovern constituency. As a result, no single, gradually dominant faction was established by the turmoil of the late 1960s and early 1970s. Instead, this incipient schism was eventually to work its way into a new, bifactional structure for the national Democratic Party, though only after the key section of this schism had itself become a continuing faction and only after each of the old, prior factions had met its particular and peculiar fate.

In any event, the key section in this post-McGovern schism, led by McGovern's campaign chairman (later a U.S. senator) Gary Hart, established a *Neoliberal* faction within the Democratic Party. The Neoliberals were distinguished from traditional Liberals and from Regulars by their heavy emphasis on social and cultural liberalism, plus the dovish foreign policy that they still shared with the New Left/Minorities faction. They departed most dramatically from the Regulars *and* the New Left in their efforts to move the Democrats away from the governmental interventionism of the New Deal and toward an emphasis on free markets and fiscal conservatism. On these issues, the Neoliberals stood closer to the remnants of the old White South faction in Congress. Because of their strength among suburban, upper-middle-class voters, their roots in the baby-boom generation, and the favorable response their views evoked from media elites, the Neoliberals had become dominant within the presidential party by the late 1980s.

The old (New Deal) Liberals and the remnants of the Regulars had their last hurrah with Walter Mondale's nomination (and landslide defeat) in 1984. With the decline both of traditional party machines and of organized labor—the linchpins of Regular power within the party—they were becoming a decreasingly relevant intraparty influence, although the old Regular constituency of northern, blue-collar, lower-middle-class, ethnic, and Catholic voters remained crucial to Democratic prospects in presidential elections.[26]

The White South had made a superficial comeback with the nomination of Jimmy Carter in 1976, but appearances were to prove misleading. Carter, and later Bill Clinton, may have won the presidential nomination from a southern base. Yet they did so by sounding Neoliberal themes while actually downplaying traditional white southern conservatism, and neither proved able to win back a majority of the southern white vote for the Democratic Party.[27] This failing only reflected the larger fate of their faction, in rapid decline in Congress as well, where a key event had been the breach of the seniority system in 1975, when the House Democratic caucus stripped three elderly southern Democrats of their chairmanships.[28] Amendments to the Voting Rights Act of 1965, amendments that concentrated the Democratic base constituency of southern black voters in overwhelmingly black districts, had left most remaining white southern Democrats to run in lilywhite districts where they were now much more vulnerable to defeat by Republicans. By the time of the Republican revolution of 1994, Democratic white southerners had been reduced to a marginal and diminishing force in both chambers.

By the late 1980s, the Democratic Party's long-term problem of internal coherence—so often at least a mixed blessing in the past—had intensified. Of its four contending factions, the new ideological ones, the Neoliberals and the New Left, were clearly in the ascendant; the old clientelistic factions, the Regulars and the White South, were just as clearly a diminishing force. In 1984 and 1988, the Reverend Jesse Jackson assumed the leadership of the New Left/Minorities faction and mobilized unprecedented numbers of black voters on behalf of his presidential candidacy. Jackson, however, had no substantial appeal outside his own faction. Walter Mondale exploited the vice-presidency plus heavy support from organized labor to defeat Neoliberal Gary Hart (and Jackson) for the presidential nomination in 1984. But this was a kind of last hurrah.

After Mondale's overwhelming defeat at the hands of President Ronald Reagan in the fall, the position of the Regulars within the party began to look hopeless. Even the unions, their last remaining intraparty power base, moved increasingly into alignment with the New Left/Minorities section of the party, as the unions' public-sector and minority membership increased. And while Neoliberal candidates (and themes) had emerged as the dominant force within the presidential party by the late 1980s, they were still too liberal culturally and too dovish in foreign policy for the general electorate, as the abject failure of Michael Dukakis, the 1988 presidential nominee, demonstrated.[29]

Democratic multifactionalism might thus have been a drag as far as forging a winning coalition in presidential elections was concerned, but in elections to Congress and in the states it remained the party's greatest strength. The Democrats had created a system of distributive politics at the congressional and state levels, and they continued to exploit it to their advantage. Indeed, their control at these levels was even further consolidated by the Watergate scandal, which led not only to severe Republican losses in the 1974 midterm elections but also to the passage of a series of reforms in the congressional elections process that worked to the advantage of (mainly Democratic) incumbents. The latter proved additionally adept at exploiting their visibility and name identification (through, for example, the congressional franking privilege), which had become decisive assets in congressional campaigns with the drastic decline of party identification among the electorate.[30] Of course, the Democratic grip on the House was also aided by the fact that Republican control of the White House subjected the GOP to a series of typical anti–White House swings in midterm congressional elections.

Factional Evolution during the Cold War Years: The Republicans

The Democrats did lose control of the U.S. Senate in 1980, largely because the Republicans were able to "nationalize" the Senate elections in that year and ride on Ronald Reagan's coattails as he swept to victory in the presidential race. The Senate's higher profile on foreign affairs, and the cultural conflict associated with judicial nominations in particular, continued to make the Republicans more competitive in Senate elections during the 1980s, although they were unable to institutionalize their grip on the chamber. Indeed, having failed to increase their margin of control in 1982 and 1984, they lost most of their 1980s gains in 1986, as the Democrats regained control after a midterm election campaign focused on domestic issues and agricultural discontent.

The broader point is that Democratic Party multifactionalism continued to enable the Democrats to cater to a wide spectrum of American society in congressional elections. Apart from the White South, the GOP had made no substantial advances beyond its white, suburban, upper-middle-class base in Congress. In fact, the Republicans in Congress actually lost ground in some of their traditional strongholds in the Northeast and Midwest as a result of Watergate, and northern upper-middle-class distaste for the cultural conservatism that was gradually coming to influence the national GOP did not help them in regaining these areas.[31]

As long as the Cold War persisted, however, the Republicans retained their advantage in presidential politics. Kennedy and Johnson appeared to threaten that advantage in the early 1960s, but their efforts foundered on the rocks of Vietnam. After 1968, the Republicans won over the Wallace voters and reassembled Eisenhower's electoral college coalition in even stronger form, taking the Deep South and not just the Upper South. Apart from a few isolated liberal bastions—Massachusetts, Minnesota, Maryland, West Virginia—the Republicans won a *series* of presidential landslides between 1968 and 1992, broken only by the narrow, post-Watergate victory of Jimmy Carter in 1976. And the victories of 1980 and 1984 could still be argued to represent only the "maturing" of the victories of 1952 and 1956.

Moreover, within the GOP there was a long, slow evolution toward a very different factional world. For a time, the story of this evolution appeared to be one of increasing dominance for one of the two main factions from an earlier era. Then the old factions appeared to be reborn, in a continuing bifactional division with somewhat different ideological programs and social coalitions. At the end, however, by the 1990s, there was a new, and now multifactional, array to characterize life inside the national Republican Party.

The earliest changes in this factional array, destined to underpin the eventual new order of the 1990s, arrived in the American South. During the Eisenhower era, the Republicans had established themselves as a serious political party in the southern states. The new southern Republicans, in turn, could no longer be bought off by patronage from the eastern Liberals, but instead—in a clear instance of clientelistic factionalism being supplanted by ideological intraparty alignments—allied themselves with their ideological brethren in the Conservative faction.

The new nationalistic Republican Conservatism pioneered by Eisenhower and Nixon also succeeded in winning over much of the economically booming Southwest to the GOP, particularly southern California with its heavy concentration of defense industries. The shift in population, wealth, and power toward the Sunbelt also weakened the party's traditional financial power base in Wall Street—a change that became brutally apparent in 1964 when Arizona Senator Barry Goldwater, who had been perceived as being on the far-right fringe of the Conservative faction, easily won the Republican presidential nomination.[32]

Goldwater consolidated the alliance of traditional (Taft) Stalwarts and nationalist conservatives from the South and West into a powerful Conservative faction that took the presidential Republican Party away from the Liberal Republicans. They never got it back. Those who provided the money, resources, and manpower for the Republican Party at the presidential level were now indubitably Conservative. Moreover, as the New Deal coalition finally collapsed, Republican "me-tooism" on economic issues no longer made such good electoral sense in presidential politics. Since Nelson Rockefeller's third, and final, failed attempt at the GOP presidential nomination in 1968, there has not even been a serious presidential candidacy of the Liberal Republican stripe. The only section of the national party where the Liberals were able to hang on was Congress, particularly the U.S. Senate, where they were still the only Republicans who stood a chance of electoral success in the states of New England, the Middle Atlantic region, and the Pacific Northwest.

The whole basis of Republican Party factionalism thus moved sharply to the right. For a time, this could still be seen as a simple recasting of the old bifactional structure. On one side were the Traditional Republicans, economic conservatives from the Northeast and Midwest who were logical heirs to the old Stalwarts. On the other side, they faced off against the New Right Republicans, those from the South and the West who placed a greater emphasis on cultural issues. The old Liberals were absorbed by the first of these factions. The growth areas for the party as a whole were found in the second.

Moreover, this further twist on an old (bifactional) alignment continued to be moderated in the same manner as previously. Both factions were still united in staunch opposition to the Soviet Union, so the level of factional animosity between them did not normally approach the scale of the Democrats' internal conflict. New Right social conservatives were particularly influential in the presidential party, where, like their New Left counterparts among the Democrats, they had resources such as direct-mail fund raising and a mass manpower base from a series of right-wing single-issue groups, including gun owners, tax reformers, and anti-abortionists.

Richard Nixon as president had continued to bridge the gap between these factions, with New Right rhetoric but moderate policy outputs. His Stalwart successor, Gerald Ford, however, almost lost the 1976 GOP presidential nomination to the New Right champion, Ronald Reagan. Four years later, Reagan easily won the nomination but quickly mollified Traditionalists by putting their leading standard-bearer in the 1980 campaign—George Bush—on the GOP ticket. Reagan's espousal of radical, free-market, supply-side economics was also at odds with the Traditional Republican emphasis on fiscal rectitude, but it provided a basis for Republican factional unity on a popular policy, diverting attention from the more divisive social issues of the New Right.

Factional tensions persisted during the Reagan and Bush administrations but were generally muted. Traditional Republicans, while wary of social conservatism, recognized the strength of the New Right at the party's base. New Right activists chafed at the country-club orientation of many state and local Republican officials, especially their lack of enthusiasm for the New Right's social agenda. But during the final tense phase of the Cold War in the 1980s, the two factions suppressed their divisions for the higher goal of keeping the presidency in Republican hands.

At the congressional level, however, the shrill ideological tone of many Republican candidates, and continuing wariness by the voters of Republican rhetoric about scaling-back federal government programs, kept the GOP in a minority position—normally in the Senate, reliably in the House. The intraparty divisions among Republicans in the 1980s were divisions of degree and tone, as opposed to the fundamental cleavages among Democrats. Yet this very fact undermined the Republicans' chances in congressional races, where they failed to be as responsive to individual states and districts as their rivals.

Party Factions, 1990–96

Events in the first half of the 1990s have suggested an unraveling of the postwar, split-level, electoral alignment. From one side, a Democrat won the presidency in 1992, after twelve years of Republican rule. From the other side, and even more surprisingly, the Republicans then won control of Congress in 1994—and of the U.S. House for the first time since 1954. Externally, the end of the Cold War and the final collapse of Soviet communism have had a significant effect on the party system and on the nature and balance of factional alignments within both parties. Internally, a renewed focus on domestic politics has created opportunities for the Democrats in presidential elections.

Accordingly, within two years of a Democrat's reentering the White House, voters had expressed their concern over economic and moral issues by returning the first *Republican* Congress in forty years. Lacking the degree of hindsight available to us for the 1946–52 era, we cannot yet say with confidence what kind of electoral order is emerging from this confusion, and presumably this transition. What is apparent is that this period of flux in the party system has already had an impact on factional struggles in both parties. At a minimum, with some limited but crucial perspective, this period has contributed the *raw materials* for a sharply different factional landscape.

Such a landscape is too new to be delineated with certainty. But it did exist by 1990, so its general outlines can be rendered. Moreover, the factors driving it, and thus interacting to shape those contours, can also be seen. If they have not yet achieved forty years of resolution, they do make some options available while eliminating others. So, we can attempt a broad outline of the factional landscape as it exists today. And a survey of key elements producing this landscape must have further implications for how it evolves.

The emerging pattern of factionalism within the Republican Party is depicted in table 2.5 (p. 64), which, if it is not yet institutionalized, certainly demonstrates the way in which the Republicans are becoming multifactional. Interfactional conflict in such an array is likely to be bitter, with the Religious Conservatives perhaps achieving a disproportionate influence over the presidential party because current presidential nominating politics is structured to favor candidates who can arouse zealous and committed grassroots activists.[33] Even apart from this, however, the advent of the economic insecurity/trade issue has made factional conflict within the GOP more complex and more difficult to resolve. None of this augurs well for the Republicans in presidential politics. Nevertheless, as we have seen, simultaneously appealing to such a diverse group of constituencies can be turned into a positive asset in *congressional* politics. Moreover, like the congressional Democrats of the 1950s, a national consensus on economic issues—this time on balanced budgets, downsizing government, and tax reform—may well favor the GOP.

In contrast, Democratic factionalism will most likely fall along free trade/protectionist lines, with the degree of emphasis on cultural liberalism as a secondary area of potential dispute between the Neoliberal and Radical-Minority factions (see table 2.6, p. 65). The White South and the Regulars have disappeared as significant forces *within* the party, though to win presidential elections, Democrats still need to secure the votes of the constituencies that formerly supported these factions. In congressional politics, that will probably be a much more difficult proposition because the Democratic congressional party has become so much more ideologically narrow. The party's shrunken base—minorities, socially liberal activists, labor, and the teachers—is now smaller than that potentially available to the Republicans, although in the face of the threat of unhindered rule by Republican Congresses, that base will unite behind Democratic presidential candidates who vow to protect programs vital to these constituencies. Democratic presidential candidates should thus be given a free hand to exploit Republican divisions on culture, trade, and foreign policy. Along the way, Democratic factionalism has become less complex and more muted, reflecting the minority and defensive status of the party.

A factional "snapshot" for the 1990s is clear enough. How it will be expressed in a more lasting, institutionalized picture is less clear. In 1988

TABLE 2.5

REPUBLICAN PARTY FACTIONS, 1990–96

	Traditional Republicans	Supply-side Libertarians	Religious Right	Populist Conservatives
Issues	Balanced budget Free trade Cultural conservatism Unilateralism Downsizing government Empowering states Restricting immigration	Tax cuts and flat tax Free trade Cultural moderation Multilateralism Downsizing government Empowering individuals Encouraging immigration	Family tax cut Values-based trade policy Cultural conservatism Values-based diplomacy Ending government secularism Empowering families/communities Generally pro-immigration	Tax breaks for workers Protectionism Cultural conservatism Nationalism Reducing federal intrusion Empowering workers Anti-immigration
Electoral support	Small city/suburbs Mainline Protestants Midwest	Wealthy suburbs Mainline Protestants Northeast/Southwest	Middle-class whites Fundamentalists/evangelicals South/Midwest/West	Blue-collar workers Fundamentalists/Catholics Industrial Midwest/Northeast
Interest-group support	Chambers of Commerce Small business	Wall Street Banking and finance	Christian Coalition Antiabortion movement	Term-limits movement Militias
Party power base	Congress State and local parties	Northeastern governors National media	State and local parties Party caucus participants	Presidential primary voters "Flash" movements
Leaders	Bob Dole Bob Michel	Jack Kemp Steve Forbes	Pat Robertson Dan Quayle	Pat Buchanan Jesse Helms

TABLE 2.6

DEMOCRATIC PARTY FACTIONS, 1990–96

	Neoliberals	Radical Minorities
Issues	Free trade	"Fair trade"/protection
	Downsizing government	Extending government
	Cultural liberalism	Cultural radicalism
	Environmentalism	Environmentalism
	Multilateral foreign policy	Multilateral foreign policy
	Balanced budget	Help for disadvantaged
	Pro-immigration	Pro-immigration
Electoral support	Suburban voters	Urban voters
	Upper-middle-class whites	Blacks and Hispanics
	Women	Gays and lesbians
Interest-group support	National media	Labor
	Trial lawyers	National minority organizations
	Banking/finance	Feminist organizations
	Entertainment industry	National gay organizations
	Teachers' unions	Public interest groups
Party power base	Presidential primary voters	Caucus participants
	Governors	Congress
		State/local parties
Leaders	Bill Clinton	Jesse Jackson
	Al Gore	Jerry Brown
	Tom Daschle	Dick Gephardt

Republican George Bush defeated Michael Dukakis for president while failing to capture either house of Congress, an outcome that would have been recognizable at any point back to 1956. Yet Bush's victory over Dukakis probably marked the *end* of an earlier factional era, and events since then have served to unravel and/or recombine factional alignments in both parties, while changing each party's competitive position in congressional and presidential elections. American electoral outcomes in the 1990s have been influenced, more specifically, by four interrelated developments that have undermined the electoral order of the Cold War era.

The first and most important of these is the end of the Cold War itself, an event that erased the Republican trump card in presidential elections. The second factor for change is a widespread sense of economic insecurity on the part of major sectors of the American workforce—from traditional blue-collar through middle-management occupations—associated with the communications revolution and the advent of an integrated global economy. The third factor is a perception at both the elite and popular levels that the overall federal policy process had broken down or become "gridlocked" as a result of the failure of the national government, and particularly the U.S. Congress, to cope with critical issues facing the country. Finally, there appears to be a widespread public belief that even more fundamental American values, essential to society as a whole, are under threat from a variety of economic and social forces.

The Cold War was the defining issue of the electoral order established in the 1946–52 period. As we have seen, resistance to the Soviets and popular suspicion of the Democrats on national security issues were decisive in establishing the Republican grip on the federal executive branch. When the Berlin Wall fell in 1989, the whole basis of U.S. foreign policy changed. Moreover, the changed nature of the foreign policy *debate* began to favor the Democrats because post–Cold War policy became more concerned with international economic integration, with human rights, and with encouraging and protecting democracy abroad—themes that accorded better with the Democrats' Wilsonian heritage of multilateralism in foreign policy than with the nationalistic tradition of the GOP.

The end of the Cold War also solidified the control of one of the two main Democratic factions of the 1990s, the Neoliberals, over the Democratic Party. Ardent free trading, liberal internationalism—the credo of Democratic Neoliberals led by President Bill Clinton—seemed more attuned to the times than the Third Worldism of the New Left, much less the anticommunism of the Regulars. In this, the end of the Cold War effectively removed the major source of division between Democratic Party factions, as was demonstrated when the entire congressional Democratic Party, from the Black Caucus to the remnants of the White South, proved able to unite in support of President Clinton's military interventions in Haiti and Bosnia.

Democrats also appeared ideally placed to exploit the issues of middle- and working-class economic insecurity because of their long-standing identification with the economically disadvantaged. The sources of this insecurity could be traced to a variety of factors: a sense of anomie flowing from globalization of the economy, the effects of corporate downsizing on older white-collar workers, and the economic recession of the early 1990s. As the economic issue came back to the forefront, the Democratic Party's factions reunited on a traditional New Deal–style assault against a "gridlocked" federal government led by the allegedly "uncaring" patrician Republican president, George Bush. Clinton's 1992 election slogan—"It's the economy, stupid"—perfectly encapsulated the new Democratic intraparty consensus on the priority of economic issues.

Beyond 1992, however, the emergence of the issue of economic insecurity had the potential to change the pattern of factionalism in *both* parties. This was particularly true on the issue of free trade. Free-trade enthusiasts, who predominated in both parties during most of the postwar years, argued that America could compete effectively in the new global economic order only by continuing to pursue global and regional free-trade agreements, even at the short-term cost of American manufacturing jobs. With support from Republican leaders in Congress, Clinton thus completed and passed two major free-trade agreements, the North American Free Trade Agreement (NAFTA) and the General Agreement on Tariffs and Trade (GATT), during his presidency. Yet a majority of the Democrats in Congress voted against NAFTA, and Democratic congressional *leaders* such as Dick Gephardt and David Bonior actually went against it as well. Moreover, labor leaders had become the most prominent Democratic opponents of the expansion of free trade, believing, probably correctly, that their members would pay the short-term price in terms of U.S. jobs exported.

The potential for a bitter new intraparty cleavage on trade issues was not confined to the Democrats. In both 1992 and 1996, conservative commentator Patrick J. Buchanan ran for the Republican nomination on a platform highly critical of the unlimited free-trade position of his party. Buchanan won about a quarter of the total Republican primary vote in each year, suggesting significant grassroots support for a more interventionist, or nationalist, economic policy, particularly among less economically advantaged Republican social conservatives. Tangential issues, such as restricting immigration and dismantling affirmative action programs for women and minorities, have also emerged from the broader focusing of economic insecurity. Buchanan unhesitatingly incorporated these issues into his platform in 1996. And while Democrats at the elite level were inclined to preserve affirmative action in response to their continuing strong support from minority activists, elements of the party, ranging from blacks to Neoliberals, had concerns about the economic impact of immigration on Democratic constituencies.

The changing basis of foreign policy and the emergence of the issue of economic security thus had the potential to create a new basis for factionalism in both parties, and the outlines of this new factional pattern could in fact be perceived by the mid-1990s. The entrance of governmental reform and values issues nevertheless complicated the picture. A series of scandals affecting the U.S. Congress, beginning with the removal from office of Speaker Jim Wright and Democratic Whip Tony Coelho in 1989 and culminating in the House Post Office and Bank scandals in 1992, succeeded in doing what the Republicans had singularly failed to do in forty years, namely, focusing national attention on Congress and its problems. Partly because the Democrats had become so adept at focusing congressional activity on district and state services, the chronic inability of the Democratic majority to discipline itself and pass measures to deal with the budget deficit or health-care reform also appeared all the more glaring.[34]

As the notion of gridlock in Congress gained ground among the electorate, movements to limit congressional terms gained strength at the state level. Ross Perot strongly emphasized reform of congressional procedure and campaign finance in an independent presidential candidacy that secured 19 percent of the popular vote in 1992. The Republican minority in Congress, led by Minority Whip Newt Gingrich, jumped on the congressional reform bandwagon as well and rode it to victory in the 1994 elections.[35] Moreover, the first Republican House majority in forty years did implement some major reforms in House procedure, centralizing power in the party leadership as opposed to the dispersed committee and subcommittee system of the Democrats.[36] It appears likely that the reform agenda will continue to work for the GOP, as long as they do not cede the issue to Perot's Reform Party, and to damage the Democrats, whose core electoral constituencies—labor, minorities, and the economically disadvantaged—have little to gain from congressional reform.

Finally, there are the values issues, which are akin to the cultural issues that generally worked for the Republicans and damaged Democrats in presidential politics during the 1980s. Such issues probably help the Republicans less in the 1990s because, as the Religious Right has become more visible and more active within the party, there has been a significant electoral backlash from northern, suburban, upper-middle-class, business-oriented, and professional Republicans—particularly women—who feel threatened by the Religious Right's vehement opposition to, for example, abortion and homosexuality. Moreover, the values issue has broadened beyond sexual morality in the 1990s to encompass a questioning of *business* values, values that have been equally as subversive as the "counterculture" of the 1960s and 1970s to traditional morality and community in the United States.

Values issues remain problematic for Democrats, however. The ascendant Neoliberal faction in the Democratic Party and the New Left/Minorities faction both espouse generally liberal positions on values issues. If the much-weakened Regular and White South factions remain more circumspect, they lack the grassroots strength to have much impact within the party. To win elections, however, Democrats must avoid alienating the old electoral constituencies of the Regulars and the White South too much, as President Clinton discovered when the issue of "gays in the military" dominated the first weeks of his presidency. In his successful 1996 reelection campaign, in contrast, Clinton effectively nullified potential damage on values issues not just by utilizing "profamily" imagery and rhetoric, but by emphasizing issues such as gun control and restrictions on tobacco sales to teenagers, where the Democrats could get on the "correct" side of the values question. He also signed the Defense of Marriage Act, passed overwhelmingly by Congress in the summer of 1996, to preclude the possibility that states or the federal government would be legally compelled to recognize gay marriages sanctioned by other states.[37]

The ultimate electoral impact of the four factors discussed above is not yet clear. A new electoral order that emerges from this confusion might always yield unlimited control of the federal government to either major party, if that party is able to define the policy debate around their preferred issues. But a new split-level outcome appears more likely. It is quite possible, for example, that in reaction to the Democrats' perceived abuses of congressional power, the GOP will succeed in controlling Congress for an extended period of time. Just as the Democrats were able to unite an extraordinarily diverse congressional majority for forty years around the principles of distributive politics and constituent service, so the new Republican congressional coalition, ranging from southern evangelical Christians to northern suburban professionals, is disunited on many issues but united on the fundamental principle of reforming the federal government and simultaneously reducing the impact of that government on citizens' daily lives.

Yet, by the same token, a Republican return to the presidency might be rendered problematic simply by the nature of the politics required to keep Congress under GOP control. The presidency might even carve out a new role in the system, as the branch that pursues free trade and multilateralism in foreign affairs while protecting various important constituencies at home—minorities, gays, women, immigrants, the poor— against the excesses of a rambunctious, populist, Republican majority in Congress. An electoral order along these lines would in fact reflect the preferences of the likely swing constituency in the new millennium's electoral alignment: upscale, business-oriented, and professional voters, who are globally internationalist, noninterventionist in economics, and culturally liberal.

With so many crosscutting issues and an electorate that lost its partisan moorings long ago, even an attempt to refine the contours of a future electoral order is foolish. Perhaps the economic/trade issue will become of such overwhelming importance that one or the other party will realign the party system totally in its favor. Or perhaps the reform agenda will become so powerful that one or the other major party is *replaced* by some new reform alignment: Perot still secured 8 percent of the popular presidential vote in 1996, despite being an evidently damaged candidate. Given what we do know about the emerging electoral alignment in the United States and its nascent party factions, something along the lines suggested here appears to be the more likely outcome.

Conclusion: Party Factions in a New Millennium

In both periods under discussion in this volume, party factions played an important role in the transition from one type of electoral alignment or electoral order to another. In both the 1946–52 and the 1990–96 periods, we can see clear and consistent lines of intraparty division. Although U.S. party factions may not have approached the degree of organization and discipline we might associate with party factions in pre-1992 Italy or Japan, they nevertheless have been important actors in the American political process. Moreover, as overall levels of identification and support for parties have declined, ideological party factions have become *increasingly* powerful agents of political mobilization in American politics.

As American politics has become more driven both by national electronic media and by ideologically motivated activists, so traditional clientelistic party factions grounded in regionalism or patronage, such as the Regulars and the White South in the Democratic Party, have become increasingly marginal. In the electoral universe of late-twentieth-century American politics, the counterpart rise of ideological factions has also made intraparty factional divisions more difficult to accommodate. Even if one accepts the proposition that some contemporary party factions retain a clientelistic dimension in their political operations—most notably the Radical-Minorities faction in the Democratic Party but even the Religious Right in the GOP—these factions have focused on issues of moral or cultural symbolism and language, issues that tend to foster intraparty divisiveness and polarization, rather than the coalition-building characteristic of the old clientelistic party politics.

Given these circumstances, the party with the greater number of intraparty factions is likely to have more difficulty in presidential elections, which demand that the national party unite behind a single candidate and platform. From 1952 until the early 1990s, this problem consistently bedeviled the Democratic Party, which had four clear and contending intraparty factions for most of this period. By contrast, the Republican Party, with only two significant factions, one of which was clearly in the descendant from 1952 onward, was much better equipped for presidential politics. Nonetheless, the relative ideological narrowness of the Republicans prevented them from seriously challenging Democratic control of the U.S. House for forty years.

This pattern of intraparty factional division contributed strongly to the creative Madisonianism or "divided government"—take your pick—that has characterized American electoral politics for most of the post-1952 period. At a time when both parties had become "ideologized" on the major issue of the day, it made perfect sense for a broad national consensus within the general public—that America should have limited governmental intervention in economic and social policy at home, combined with vigilant containment of communism abroad—to be reflected in divided control of the national institutions of government. With the end of the Cold War, and the growing sense that the United States has been living beyond its means, this electoral order has been unraveling in the 1990s.

As the Republicans have expanded beyond their narrow, white Protestant, business base to incorporate southern evangelical and northern Catholic voters, their pattern of intraparty factionalism has become more complex, principally because much of the old base is uncomfortable with the social agenda that appeals to the newer groups that the GOP is also trying to embrace. The emergence of such issues as trade, immigration, and global integration, which fall along the party's factional cleavages, have put strains on the GOP that now make it much harder for the *Republicans* to unite behind a common candidate and platform in presidential politics. The end of the Soviet threat has removed the most adhesive element in the glue that held together the expanding but increasingly fractious Republican coalition during the 1980s.

Among Democrats, the marginalization of the old Regulars and of the White South has left a much more ideologically coherent Democratic coalition, united around issues of civil liberties, environmentalism, feminism, and minority rights. The major division among Democrats in the 1990s has been over the degree to which, in an era of large budget deficits and widespread popular disillusion with governmental economic intervention, the party should embrace a free-trade, free-market agenda or return to the labor-oriented economic and welfare polices that defined the Democratic Party during the New Deal era. As the Democratic Party has become narrower ideologically, it has impeded its chances of regaining control of both houses of Congress on a long-term basis. Much of the institutional structure that underlay that control in terms of the committee/seniority system has also been discredited and swept away in this decade.

In sum, the GOP has the advantage on values issues and on the question of restraining government spending. Yet a distinct unease with the Republican agenda on civil liberties and the environment, plus continuing wariness of the GOP's unlimited support for free markets and free trade, is likely to help Democratic candidates in presidential contests. Of course, major world events could overturn this nascent alignment quickly. A major international crisis might restore the Republicans to presidential supremacy, as the idealistic hopes of the post–Cold War era are shattered and the international situation requires a more unilateralist or nationalist approach in foreign affairs. Similarly, a major economic downturn could tear the new GOP apart on free trade and allow Democrats to reassemble a New Deal–like, interventionist coalition, dominating all branches of the government.

In the absence of these developments, however, the American electoral order for the first decade or so of the new millennium is more likely than not to produce a divided federal government. And under this new electoral order, observers of American party politics will continue to witness the interplay of highly visible and durable party factions—reflections of, as well as engines for, this change.

Notes

1. Richard Rose, *The Problem of Party Government* (London: Macmillan, 1974), 320–21.

2. Ibid.; Howard L. Reiter, "Intra-Party Cleavages in the United States Today," *Western Political Quarterly* 34 (1981), 287–300; Thomas H. Roback and Judson L. James, "Party Factions in the United States," in *Faction Politics: Political Parties and Factionalism in Comparative Perspective,* ed. Dennis C. Beller and Frank C. Belloni (Santa Barbara: ABC-Clio, 1978), 329–55.

3. Nicol C. Rae, *Southern Democrats* (New York: Oxford University Press, 1994), 6–26.

4. According to historian Joel H. Silbey, the advent of television and the continued expansion of the national government during the postwar years confirmed the irrelevance of traditional American political parties, which had been in decline since the 1890s. Since 1948, Silbey argues, America has experienced a "nonpartisan-personalist" political era that he characterizes as "postalignment" in terms of voter ties to political parties. See Joel H. Silbey, *The American Political Nation, 1838–1893* (Stanford, Calif.: Stanford University Press, 1991), 1–10 and 237–51.

5. Byron E. Shafer, "The Notion of an Electoral Order: The Structure of Electoral Politics at the Accession of George Bush," in *The End of Realignment? Interpreting American Electoral Eras,* ed. Byron E. Shafer (Madison: University of Wisconsin Press, 1991), 37–84.

6. James L. Sundquist, *Dynamics of the Party System: Alignment and Realignment of Political Parties in the United States,* rev. ed. (Washington, D.C.: Brookings Institution, 1981).

7. Ibid.

8. See James Q. Wilson, *The Amateur Democrat: Club Politics in Three Cities* (Chicago: University of Chicago Press, 1962).

9. See Nancy Weiss, *Farewell to the Party of Lincoln: Black Politics in the Age of FDR* (Princeton: Princeton University Press, 1983).

10. On the Stalwarts, see James T. Patterson, *Congressional Conservatism and the New Deal* (Lexington: University of Kentucky Press, 1967).

11. On Taft, see James T. Patterson, *Mr. Republican: A Biography of Robert A. Taft* (Boston: Houghton Mifflin, 1972).

12. The progressive Republicans under discussion here should be distinguished from the genuinely radical Western Republicans of the early twentieth century, such as Robert LaFollette of Wisconsin, George Norris of Nebraska, and Henry Wallace, who also claimed the "progressive" label but were generally absorbed into the Democratic New Deal coalition during the 1930s. See Ronald A. Feinman, *The Twilight of Progressivism: The Western Republican Senators and the New Deal* (Baltimore: Johns Hopkins University Press, 1981).

13. See Nicol C. Rae, *The Decline and Fall of the Liberal Republicans: From 1952 to the Present* (New York: Oxford University Press, 1989).

14. Ibid., 25–45.

15. On Dewey and his impact, see Richard Norton Smith, *Thomas E. Dewey and His Times* (New York: Simon and Schuster, 1982).

16. On the Dixiecratic impact in the South, see V.O. Key Jr., *Southern Politics: In State and Nation* (New York: Knopf, 1949), 329–44.

17. See the comments of Dewey's 1948 campaign manager, Herbert Brownell, in Rae, *The Decline and Fall of the Liberal Republicans,* 34–35.

18. On the rise of the "new nationalism" in the Republican party, see Michael W. Miles, *The Odyssey of the American Right* (New York: Oxford University Press, 1980).

19. On McCarthy and the Catholics, see Seymour Martin Lipset, "Three Decades of the Radical Right: Coughlinites, McCarthyites, and Birchers," in *The Radical Right,* ed. Daniel Bell (Garden City, N.Y.: Doubleday, 1962), 391–421.

20. On the rise of the GOP in the South, see Earl Black and Merle Black, *Politics and Society in the South* (Cambridge, Mass.: Harvard University Press, 1987).

21. See Everett Carll Ladd with Charles D. Hadley, *Transformations of the American Party System: Political Coalitions from the New Deal to the 1970s,* 2d ed. (New York: Norton, 1978).

22. See Theodore J. Lowi, *The End of Liberalism: The Second Republic of the United States,* 2d ed. (New York: Norton, 1979); and Morris K. Fiorina, *Congress: Keystone of the Washington Establishment* (New Haven, Conn.: Yale University Press, 1977).

23. Rae, *Southern Democrats,* 65–110.

24. See Kevin P. Phillips, *The Emerging Republican Majority* (New York: Anchor Books, 1970).

25. Interestingly, Senator McGovern had been a youthful supporter of Henry Wallace in 1948.

26. See Steven M. Gillon, *The Democrats' Dilemma: Walter F. Mondale and the Liberal Legacy* (New York: Columbia University Press, 1982).

27. See Rae, *Southern Democrats,* 55–58 and 128–42.

28. Ibid., 65–110.

29. On Dukakis, see William Galston and Elaine Ciulla Kamarck, *The Politics of Evasion: Democrats and the Presidency* (Washington, D.C.: Progressive Policy Institute, 1989).

30. See Gary C. Jacobson, *The Politics of Congressional Elections,* 2d ed. (Boston: Little, Brown, 1987).

31. See Rae, *The Decline and Fall of the Liberal Republicans,* 157–95.

32. Ibid., 46–77.

33. This advantage was largely canceled out in 1996 by the dramatic frontloading of the primary schedule, which favored well-known Traditionalist frontrunner Bob Dole. See Harold W. Stanley, "The Nominations: Republican Doldrums, Democratic Revival," in *The Elections of 1996,* ed. Michael Nelson (Washington, D.C.: CQ Press, 1997), 14–43; William G. Mayer, "The Presidential Nominations," in *The Election of 1996: Reports and Interpretations,* ed. Gerald M. Pomper (Chatham, N.J.: Chatham House, 1997), 21–76; and Barbara Herrera and Nicol C. Rae, "The Insider Advantage: The Impact of 'Frontloading' on the 1996 Republican Presidential Primaries," paper presented at the annual meeting of the Midwest Political Science Association, 1997.

34. On the collapse in confidence of the congressional Democrats, see Dan Balz and Ronald Brownstein, *Storming the Gates: Protest Politics and the Republican Revival* (Boston: Little, Brown, 1996).

35. Ibid.

36. Ibid., and James G. Gimpel, *Legislating the Revolution: The Contract with America in Its First 100 Days* (Boston: Allyn and Bacon, 1996).

37. The Defense of Marriage Act (DOMA) was prompted by the likelihood that state courts in Hawaii would strike down the legal prohibition on same-sex marriages in that state.

3

Partisan Elites,
1946–1996

Byron E. Shafer

The governing elite is always in a state of slow and continuous transformation. It flows on like a river, never being today what it was yesterday. From time to time, sudden and violent disturbances occur. There is a flood—the river overflows its banks. Afterwards, the new governing elite again resumes its slow transformation. The flood has subsided; the river is again flowing normally in its wonted bed.
— Pareto, *Compendium of General Sociology*, 279 [809]

The coming to partisan politics of new social groups, flagged by the arrival of new group leaders, is not a phenomenon easily missed by even the casual observer. And indeed, a steady stream of such leaders and their groups has characterized American politics across the postwar period. From organized labor and "Modern Republicans" to "New Politics Democrats" and evangelical Protestants—to take only leading examples from opposite ends of the postwar era—each has nevertheless met certain common criteria. Thus each began with the emergence of an arguably new social base. Each generated the critical further element, an aspiring institutional leadership. That leadership then managed the transition to an explicitly partisan home. And in the process, invariably, it bid to shape the policy agenda of its time.[1]

So, partisan elites seem an obvious element among partisan approaches to American (or perhaps any) politics. Even if they were no more than the partisan product of social forces in the background, they would bring those forces, concretely, into the analysis of a changing politics. But, in fact, in the United States as presumably elsewhere, such elites also play a partially transformative role. That is, in linking ascendant social groups to organized political parties, these elites never precisely translate group wishes into institutionalized demands for public policy. Instead, they make choices about the coalitional prospects associated with various preferences, and they sometimes add preferences of their own.

Yet social scientists have found the study of this phenomenon to be a treacherous realm. What distinguishes an elite? What makes it new? What makes such elites, if they can be demarcated, effectively partisan? How do they become so? To what extent does this matter to the conduct of politics? To the resulting public policy? In a socially egalitarian and politically democratic society, the term itself carries excess baggage, an unattractive, even mocking, overlay: is not the very presence of "political elites" evidence of incomplete democratic development? In application, most neutral definitions manage to shuck this baggage only by converting the notion into a category so formalistic as to empty it of most behavioral implications: what is the social background of those who occupy, say, the presidency, or the Senate, or the U.S. Supreme Court?

The Circulation of Elites

These problems did not always seem inherent. When the self-conscious social sciences were themselves arriving, in the late nineteenth and early twentieth centuries, elite analysis appeared to hold the prospect of being both analytically detached and substantively rich. Few social analysts of the time would instinctively have shied away from the concept. Nevertheless, its most central application surely came in the work of the Italian sociologist Vilfredo Pareto, especially in his framework for studying the *circulation* of elites—the "heterogeneousness of society and circulation among its various elements," to use his language.[2]

One secondary advantage of using partisan elites as a route into American politics, then, is to reclaim some of the argument offered by Pareto, now nearly a century ago. Yet there are two more immediate and practical advantages from beginning with Pareto. One is the opportunity to excise, from the start, any normative overlay in the basic concept. Social groups will require group elites as part of their definition, as a condition of their movement from category to group. In turn, this fundamental connection should invigorate the resulting analysis, making it descriptively richer *and* analytically more dynamic, by imposing a search for the link between emerging social groups and emergent leadership behavior, as well as for the factors that produce it and the outcomes that follow from its production.

In the beginning, in any case, five decades before there was a postwar world, the notion of an elite was essentially structural in character:

> So let us make a class of the people who have the highest indices of their branch of activity, and to that class give the name of *elite.* It is obvious that the line that separates the elite from the rest of the population is not, and cannot be, precise, no more than is the line that separates youth from maturity. This, however, does not detract from the usefulness of considering this division of things.
>
> For the particular investigation with which we are engaged, a study of the social equilibrium, it will help if we further divide that class into two classes: a *governing elite,* comprising individuals who directly or indirectly play some considerable part in government, and a nongoverning elite, comprising the rest.... In moving from one group to another, an individual brings with him certain inclinations, sentiments, attitudes that he has acquired in the group from which he comes, and that circumstance cannot be ignored. To this mixing, in the particular case in which only two groups, the elite and the non-elite, are envisaged, the term "circulation of elites" has been applied.
>
> — Pareto, *Compendium of General Sociology,* 273–75 [792–96]

Such circulations, evidently, were to contain three integral elements. There was a social group, with rising consciousness of itself, increasing consequence to society, and *potentially* increasing consequence to politics. There was a leadership component, not necessarily arising in its entirety from within the broader social group but effectively able to speak in its name. Needless to say, this component would play the crucial role in operationalizing the arrival of the larger group in politics. And there were values (and hence preferences) distinctive to this group, values that were at least passed along by, and often initially embodied within, its emergent elite. These became the policy wishes that would characterize the contribution to political debate of the new elite.

Pareto was confident that this process was reliably central to politics, regardless of institutional arrangements, regardless of societal composition. The specifics would vary—that was part of the power of the framework—but the generic process would inevitably recur. A further consequence of this formulation, apart from its analytic neutrality and structural differentiation, was that it did not insist that the relevant elite be located in any one specific place. Hence an emergent *partisan* elite could be located within an organized group, putting pressure on a political party. It could surface instead within the aggregate of those who did the actual work of the party, even coming to constitute "the party" itself. Or it could be found increasingly among the incumbents of public offices secured by that party.

A newly relevant social category; newly influential spokesmen for it; distinguishing values and preferences as a result: those remained the essence of the quest. And beyond that, Pareto would have been the first to argue that the utility of this framework had to reside in the specifics of its application, to a particular nation in a particular historical period:

> Such considerations serve to explain, along with the theoretical difficulties, how the solutions that are usually found for the general problem have so little, and sometimes no, bearing on realities. Solutions of particular problems come closer to the mark because, situated as they are in specific times and places, they present fewer theoretical difficulties; and because practical empiricism implicitly takes account of many circumstances that theory, until it has been carried to a high state of perfection, cannot explicitly appraise.
>
> — Pareto, *Compendium of General Sociology,* 309 [902]

The Immediate Postwar Years
Organized Labor

> When, in a country, classes that for any reason have long remained separate mingle or, in more general terms, when a class-circulation that has been sluggish suddenly acquires an intensity at all considerable, almost always observable is an appreciable increase in intellectual, economic, and political prosperity in the country in question. And that is why periods of transition from oligarchic to more or less democratic regimes are often periods of prosperity.
>
> If the prosperity in question were due to different systems of government, the prosperity should continue as long as the new regime endured. But that is not the case. The fluorescence lasts for a certain length of time and then comes a decline.
>
> — Pareto, *Compendium of General Sociology,* 372 [1057–58]

Few observers, no matter how casual, could have failed to notice the emergence—really the explosion to prominence—of the first great partisan elite in postwar American politics. Its social group was *organized* labor. The elite was its recognized formal leadership. And the policies thereby championed included not just worker organization and collective bargaining but also, in a secondary but major way, the general social welfare programs that would support and supplement the gains of organized workers in their life outside the workplace. Moreover, in all of this, the new labor elite was itself inescapably central. In one sense, it was of course produced by the conversion of an industrial working class into an organized labor movement. Yet it was also the group that *managed* that conversion.

And here, as in all the major postwar cases, the details of this management mattered. For this new labor elite was also the body of specialized actors who determined, this time, to have not just an active role in both electoral and institutional politicking but a specific partisan linkage as well, in opposition to the dominant theory guiding the labor movement in the United States to that time. Having effectuated this partisan link, the new labor elite went on to establish the machinery to make it concrete and ongoing, and to pursue labor interests through that machinery. By extension, this new labor leadership, most centrally, translated those interests—which determined that the agenda for this machinery would be sharply expanded, beyond bread-and-butter "union issues."

Nevertheless, in a more pronounced fashion than with any of the other main elite infusions of the postwar period, the emergence of both this social group and its organizational leadership were rooted in formal, national legislation; they could in fact be traced directly to changes in the law. The existence of an industrial working class certainly predated legal reform. It was a national presence by the late nineteenth century; it was arguably present in specific sectors and locales before the Civil War. Likewise, there had been previous upticks in the translation from industrial working class to organized labor movement, gathered most centrally in the American Federation of Labor (AFL). Union membership had surged at the turn of the twentieth century; organized industrial conflict—strike activity—had surged at the end of World War I.

Yet the scale of growth in the immediate postwar years was sufficient to suggest a qualitative change. Again, there was a chain of important events helping to convert a social class into a labor movement in the years immediately following World War II. The onset of the Great Depression; the coming of the New Deal; widespread, genuine, and explicit class conflict; reconstitution of the national Democratic coalition; bifurcation in the labor movement itself, producing the Congress of Industrial Organizations (CIO) but ultimately reinvigorating the AFL: all these contributed to the rise of this first and most inescapable of postwar partisan elites. In none of the counterpart cases, however—Modern Republicans, New Politics Democrats, or evangelical Protestants—was the simple role of law so central, both in creating the group basis for a new elite and in institutionalizing that elite.[3]

The key precursor to this was the National Industrial Recovery Act of 1933, whose section 7(a) attempted to create an employee right to organize and bargain collectively, and did create a National Labor Relations Board (NLRB) to oversee implementation of that right. When the full act was struck down by the Supreme Court, in *Schecter Poultry Corporation v. United States* (295 U.S. 495, 1935), supporters responded with the National Labor Relations Act (NLRA) of 1935. The NLRA attempted not just to reestablish the right to organize and bargain collectively but to guarantee the integrity of union selection, and it established a second NLRB with substantially expanded powers, charged explicitly with preventing unfair management behavior. By the narrowest of margins, 5–4, the Supreme Court, in *National Labor Relations Board* v. *Jones & Laughlin Steel* (301 U.S. 1, 1937), sustained this NLRA.

There were to be other pieces of New Deal legislation with direct relevance to organized labor, including the Fair Labor Standards Act of 1938. There were to be other *purposes* even to the NLRA of 1935: directly partisan goals like embedding American working people in the Democratic coalition; more systemic goals like regularizing labor-management relations; even broader aspirations like underpinning an economy built on mass consumerism and consumption. And there were to be partially autonomous contributions to the growth and institutionalization of American labor from, most notably, the new CIO. But it was the NLRA that institutionalized all of these, along with the recordkeeping that would chart their progress. Michael Barone captures the mix of social forces and legal buttresses that were to produce a major player in partisan politics:

> They knew they faced steep odds. The Wagner Act [the NLRA] might be ruled unconstitutional, as NRA had been; the companies might prevail, as they had in the 1920s. But at least some of these unionists must have been encouraged by the hope, which turned out to be fulfilled, that they were creating a new institution which would become a part of the fabric of American life and would play a major role in the economy and politics of their country.[4]

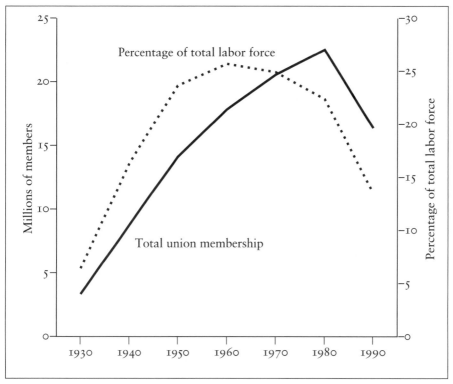

FIGURE 3.1
UNION MEMBERSHIP ACROSS THE POSTWAR YEARS

SOURCES: *Historical Statistics of the United States, Colonial Times to 1970* (Washington, D.C.: Department of Commerce, 1975); *Statistical Abstract of the United States* (Washington, D.C.: Department of Commerce, various years).

And for the next thirty years, that progress was to be as prominent as it was remarkable. Figure 3.1 shows the growth of union membership, both in raw numbers and as a share of the total labor force. Membership growth on this scale could hardly fail to produce the sense of an explosive new social presence, especially since it was concentrated in those economic sectors, most notably manufacturing, that came to embody the great postwar economic boom—and because it represented an immediate (and again inescapable) change in power relations within those sectors. Yet, at this point, the leadership of organized labor, as militant and as newly numerous as it obviously was, was still not evidently a "political elite," much less a partisan one. A social base had become an organized group, and this group was generating a professionalized leadership rapidly. But the latter had not yet moved decisively into politics, partisan or not.

Ironically, it was to be another national law—deleterious, not beneficial—that led directly to this second conversion. The Labor-Management Relations Act of 1947, known more generally as the Taft-Hartley Act after its (Republican) sponsors, represented the first serious counterattack by those unhappy with the growing role of organized labor. To that end, it added a (longer) list of unfair labor practices to the roster of unfair management practices that the NLRA had created, while complicating the process of union certification and slowing the use of the ultimate weapon of a certified union, the strike. But what it produced, in Paretian terms, was the final link in this causal chain: the conversion of an organized group into a political elite, while reminding this elite that the exercise of its power had an almost inevitably partisan dimension.

The seeds of Taft-Hartley had been sown during the rise to social power by organized labor. The continuing militancy of some labor leaders during the Second World War—John L. Lewis of the United Mine Workers, a founding figure in the CIO, stood out—had already produced some restraining legislation. But the overall growth of labor unions in American society had been an increasing worry not just to corporate business, its "natural" opponent, but also to the mainstream Republicans who represented the areas where small (not corporate) business was still dominant. It was actually the latter who would remain most impressed by the "threat" from organized labor, as the section on Modern Republicans suggests.

In any event, these seeds then flowered in the early postwar years, years characterized, as figure 3.2 indicates, by unprecedented strike activity. There were other great bulges to such activity in American society during the twentieth century—immediately after World War I, for example. But 1946 was to set the historical record—most strikes, most days lost to strikes—a record that remains unchallenged a half-century later. And on this, figure 3.2 still sharply understates the situation. For the record set in 1946 is all the more remarkable in that the workforce generating it was less than half the size of its modern counterpart. Said differently, in 1994 there was a man-day lost to strikes for every twenty-six American workers; in 1946 there was a man-day lost for every *half* worker! That was labor strife on an imposing level. It led directly to the Labor-Management Relations Act of 1947. It led indirectly but ineluctably to a newly partisan strategy for the new labor elite.

Previous upticks in labor organization had been characterized by a doctrine of explicit nonpartisanship, growing partly out of a tradition of

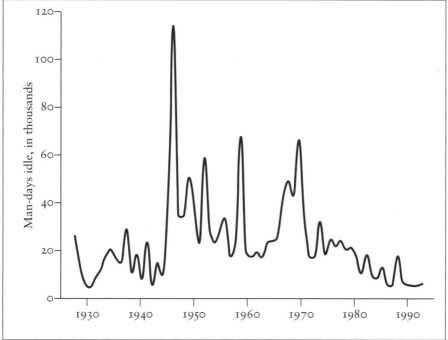

FIGURE 3.2
WORK STOPPAGES

SOURCE: *Statistical Abstract of the United States* (Washington, D.C.: Department of Commerce, various years).

syndicalism in the American labor movement, partly out of a sense that labor interests were best served by possessing partisan alternatives, and partly just from the apparent unattractiveness of both major political parties. Samuel Gompers, the dominant figure in AFL history to that point, had argued forcefully that "labor must learn to use parties to advance our principles, and not allow political parties to manipulate us for their own achievement." The constitution of the AFL thus averred that "party politics, whether they be Democratic, Republican, Socialistic, Populistic, Prohibitionist, or any other, shall have no place in the conventions of the American Federation of Labor."[5]

In response to restrictive governmental legislation during World War II, the CIO had formed a political action committee (CIO-PAC). One other immediate response to the passage of Taft-Hartley, then, was the creation by the AFL of the Labor League for Political Education (LLPE), a deliberate counterpart to CIO-PAC. Moreover, the national AFL convention that created the LLPE called on *each* of its constituent units to create further counterpart organizations for attending to matters political, and urged them to replicate these at every level of the organization, in time for the 1948 election.

From there, the partisan die was probably cast. For however much the LLPE leadership might flirt with the old AFL maxims, the implicitly partisan facts about the distribution of labor strength argued otherwise, and these had just been powerfully (and painfully) emphasized by the election of 1946. As figure 3.3 demonstrates, the geographic distribution of labor gains during the preceding decade was hardly uniform. If nearly a quarter of all working-age Americans was now unionized, there were also areas, like the Middle Atlantic states, the industrial Midwest, and the far Northwest, where this figure was more than a third; there were like-

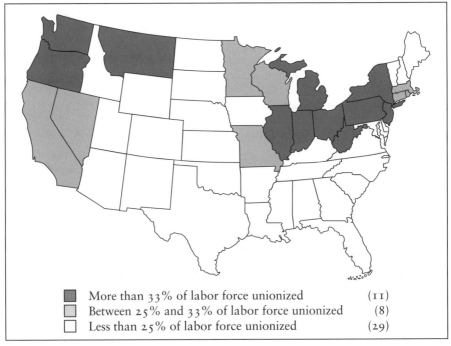

	More than 33% of labor force unionized	(11)
	Between 25% and 33% of labor force unionized	(8)
	Less than 25% of labor force unionized	(29)

FIGURE 3.3

GEOGRAPHIC DISTRIBUTION OF UNION MEMBERSHIP, 1953

SOURCES: Leo Troy, *Distribution of Union Membership among the States, 1939 and 1953*, Occasional Paper no. 56 (New York: National Bureau of Economic Research, 1975), 18–19; *Statistical Abstract of the United States* (Washington, D.C.: Department of Commerce, 1954).

wise regions, especially the American South but also the agricultural Midwest, where the figure for unionization was derisory. Yet if these were "merely" facts of institutional economic life, they were also key facts of political life, and implicitly partisan facts at that.

The election of 1946 was to make them explicit. For what happened in 1946, at one level, was a huge resurgence—observers at the time could not know how temporary it was—of the national Republican Party. But what this implied was not just that the putative party of owners, rather than workers, came to control both houses of Congress. It also meant that the largest surviving contingent of the national *Democratic* Party was in the South, where Republican competition was nugatory and where labor was scantily organized. Table 3.1 shows the fate of those northern and western Democrats whose constituents were the bulk of organized labor for the elections of 1944, 1946, and 1948, of which the 1946 election was crucial to the fortunes of the Taft-Hartley Act.

The path from there to the status of major *partisan* elite—indisputably the major Democratic elite of the ensuing generation—was short and direct. That path ran through the merger in 1955 of the two great federations, the AFL and the CIO. But by then all the major means of operating in politics, along with the fact that these would be exercised reliably in conjunction with the Democratic Party, were effectively established. What

TABLE 3.1

PARTISAN IMPACTS OF THE 1946 ELECTION

| | A. The House | | | |
	Democrat	Southern Democrat	Republican	Nonsouthern
1948	160	103	171	1
1946	85	103	246	1
1944	140	103	190	2

| | B. The Senate | | | |
	Democrat	Southern Democrat	Republican	Nonsouthern
1948	32	22	42	0
1946	23	22	51	0
1944	35	22	38	1

SOURCE: *Guide to U.S. Elections* (Washington, D.C.: CQ Press, 1975), 447–880.

the creation of the AFL-CIO did was only to institutionalize them, in the formal framework for the dominant voice of the dominant partisan Democratic elite.[6]

The original schism that produced two labor federations during the 1930s had been rooted in different approaches to organizing the industrial workforce. The AFL had long proceeded by organizing workers within trades and across industries. The unions that became the CIO argued that faster progress would come from organizing workers within industries and across trades. By 1955 the CIO unions, the apparent winners of the early argument on the numbers, had been established and stabilized but had reached an apparent plateau in their growth. By 1955 the AFL unions had in turn resumed growing, so they were by far the larger of the two great families of organized labor. The generation of leaders responsible for the initial split had likewise passed from the scene.

If future Taft-Hartleys were to be avoided, then, in an environment where the easier economic sectors had already been unionized, labor had to marshall every resource. In such an environment, unification made sense to most major players. By the time of unification with the CIO, the AFL had also delivered its first-ever presidential endorsement, of Democrat Adlai Stevenson against Republican Dwight Eisenhower in 1952, thereby crossing yet another historical barrier. It had also had its first experience—though 1956 was to be much worse in this regard—of having to carry the Democratic campaign in areas where the official party was either enfeebled or sat on its hands in the face of the personal popularity of Eisenhower.

A partisan political orientation thus became the "logical" approach for the new Committee on Political Education (COPE) of the newly merged AFL-CIO, even though it represented a double change: not just away from determined nonpartisanship but away from a concentration on legislative politics, on lobbying, and toward serious and sustained emphasis on electoral politics, on electioneering at every stage of the process. Lobbying activity hardly retreated, and organized labor had powerful resources to commit to it. Indeed, these resources were effectively augmented once it had established major *electoral* connections to many congressmen and senators, while those connections were simultaneously given definition by the content of the lobbying campaign.

COPE thus developed and constantly revised a labor program of public policy and made sure that amenable legislators knew its contents, through direct national communication in Washington, through communication from the state and local chapters of these legislators, and, occasionally, through communication efforts from the mass membership. The result was the single most important lobbying operation within the majority party in American politics. With it came a consistent and ongoing, parallel electoral effort, which always involved voter registration drives, targeted initially at union members but expanded subsequently to general geographic areas where members were concentrated. When there was a nominee who was programmatically attractive to organized labor—a Democratic nominee, with the rarest of exceptions—this electoral effort could involve major get-out-the-vote drives as well, complete with all the modern technology for such drives as it evolved. As all of *this* became institutionalized, in turn, labor became more comfortable intervening in the primary elections that nominated such candidates, so as to have someone attractive to support in the general election.

As it happened, these developments also transpired at a point in which the electoral machinery of the official Democratic Party, which would historically have assumed priority for all these activities, was becoming increasingly enfeebled in large areas of the country. As a result, organized labor would often substitute, in effect, for the official party. To that end, it could even dispatch experienced operatives to help in the practical management of a campaign. And the fact that its funding capacities were never, in the aggregate, equal to those of corporate business did not mean that its funds were not crucial to mounting and sustaining such campaigns. A generation later, this trend would come full circle, when governmental workers, once the patronage base for an organized Democratic Party, themselves became unionized, in the main recruiting success for the labor leadership of that generation. But already by the late 1950s, organized labor *was* the Democratic campaign in major geographic areas.

The ascendant labor elite that undertook these newly partisan activities was additionally distinctive in important ways, in its collective structure as well as its policy program, by comparison to labor elites in other countries as well as by comparison to other elites in American politics. Seen one way, these distinctions were important to the manner in which an emergent partisan elite could organize itself. Seen another, they were central to the values—to the transformation of values—that this elite brought forcefully into American politics.

One aspect of this distinctive character was the fact that American union officials—full-time, fully paid, union bureaucrats—were considerably more *numerous* than those in other nations. A variety of characteristics of the American context underpinned this difference, including the decentralization of bargaining, the individualized character of politics, and the expected autonomy of workers in pursuing their own interests. In any case, table 3.2 suggests how substantial it was. Needless to say, a numer-

TABLE 3.2
UNION OFFICIALS AND UNION MEMBERS

Country	Number of full-time officials	Ratio of officials to members
United States	60,000	1: 300
Denmark	1,000	1: 775
Australia	2,750	1: 900
Sweden	900	1: 1,700
Great Britain	4,000	1: 2,000
Norway	240	1: 2,200

SOURCE: Adapted from Seymour Martin Lipset, "Trade Unions and Social Structure: II," *Industrial Relations* 1 (February 1962): 93. Data are from various years in the late 1950s.

ous body of specialized actors, fully supported by extended formal organizations, was thereby advantaged in pursuing its policy goals.

All this leads directly to the other distinctive characteristic of this cadre in the period of labor ascendancy, one that Pareto himself might have expected. For this vastly expanded cadre of labor operatives had grown so fast that it had to emerge, by and large, directly out of the organized occupations themselves, again at least in this initial generation. Certainly more than at any subsequent point in the evolution of American labor, this meant that new labor bureaucrats brought the general social views of their members directly into politics. Earlier labor activists had been nurtured by union ideology; later counterparts would be trained in labor relations courses. This crucial ascendant generation was neither.

In terms of the values guiding conflict over public policy, this combination of bureaucratic muscle and social background had three main implications. First, these new political operatives—this new partisan elite—still gave its highest priority to issues of worker organizing and collective bargaining. Such an emphasis, backed by all the resources of a newly partisan federation, was to prove sufficient to find ways of living with the provisions of the Taft-Hartley Act, as well as to defuse subsequent legislative attacks. On the other hand, this emphasis, even when backed by all these resources, was never to prove sufficient to repeal Taft-Hartley as a framework.

Second, the entire operation was also turned to supporting (and potentially expanding) the welfare state, those social welfare programs that benefited working people when they were not at work and were intended to benefit others of similar circumstance. Union membership stalled by the late 1950s. Nevertheless, this orientation made organized labor central to another great increment to the welfare state, courtesy of the New Frontier and the Great Society in the early 1960s. And it remained central to the rearguard defense of these programs, when its own membership was in decline and when they were under counterattack. Two great elite initiatives were thus represented by, and came together in, this second policy concentration: the decision to make organized labor a central element of the Democratic coalition, and the decision to use a place in that coalition to widen the focus of labor in politics generally.

As a result, third and finally, the fact that labor would thereafter be crucial in keeping economic and social welfare issues at the center of Democratic *Party* affairs implied an essential moderation on those alternative social and cultural issues that did nevertheless also make their way intermittently into politics. On these, labor was to be, for example, anti-communist in foreign affairs and traditionalist in social values. As important, however, a focus on social welfare from a central place in the Democratic coalition implied a conscious decision to try to sustain the general societal consensus on social and cultural issues and thereby keep such issues *out* of politics.

Modern Republicans

> One might suppose that since the interests of employees and strike-breakers are directly contrary to the interest of the strikers, they would use the opposite derivations. But that is not the case, or if they do, they do it in a very mild, apologetic way.... As regards employers of labor, the reason is that many of them are "speculators" who hope to make up for their losses in a strike through government aid and at the expense of consumer or taxpayer. Their quarrels with strikers are quarrels between accomplices over the division of the loot.
>
> — Pareto, *Compendium of General Sociology,* 315 [913]

The other newly ascendant partisan elite of the immediate postwar years was utterly different in structure from organized labor, though it was also—as Pareto might have hypothesized—curiously symbiotic in its political behavior. It was different in the superficial sense of being based in the institutional nemesis of labor, namely, corporate business. But this group was also structurally different, in a whole host of ways. Most fundamentally, it lacked the membership base that characterized labor. In that sense, it was very close to being an elite without a mass. Likewise, it lacked a defining moment, one crystallizing its move into politics, being instead the product of a historical period and a strategic context. Nevertheless, it was to shape the opening years of postwar politics in important ways *in conjunction with* organized labor. Indeed, to add to the curiosity of the relationship, it was to share certain major policy preferences with its hypothetical adversary—an internationalism in foreign affairs, for example, and support for civil rights.

The elite in question is perhaps best denominated as the "Modern Republicans," in deference to the first self-conscious attempt by practitioners to classify it. In truth, many others acknowledged its distinctiveness in its own time, attaching their hopes or (more often) fears to its prospective rise. Yet their designations normally derived, in effect, from their private political preferences. Democratic opponents referred to this group merely as "corporate Republicans." Intraparty rivals dubbed them "me-too Republicans" instead. The term "Modern Republicans" at least leaves their designation to the group itself, while remaining sufficiently vague as to leave its substantive content to the analyst. Despite all that, this second distinctive postwar elite did offer all the classic hallmarks demanded by Pareto.

At bottom, there was a newly ascendant, or at least freshly ascendant, social stratum. Beyond it, there was a body of specialized actors emerging directly from this stratum. This elite, for so it certainly was, held clearly distinguishing values and preferences. As a result, its fortunes had potential policy consequences. And their pursuit was destined to influence American politics well into the 1970s. More than with any other postwar elite, this group would have a differential success with different public offices. More than with any other, the *process* by which the Modern Republicans acquired both a political role and partisan attachments was to remain decentralized and amorphous. Yet, allowing those facts to obscure its rise would obscure the second main manifestation of the circulation of elites in postwar American politics.

The roots of this new, incipient, partisan elite were actually in an organizational form, rather than in a specific organization, much less an overhead agency. That form was the modern business corporation, and if it was not strictly new to American life, it was about to acquire a dominance it had never previously possessed, along with further associated characteristics that were arguably new. The form itself had been born a generation before the American Civil War. It had come to dominate specific sectors of the economy (transportation, communication) in the late nineteenth century. And it had shown every sign of becoming broadly dominant in the first quarter of the twentieth century, before the Great Depression brought corporate growth to a halt and tarnished the public standing of corporate elites.[7]

Yet the newly invigorated American economy of the postwar years was destined to return to a focus on the business corporation. Wartime production had actually conferred particular benefits on corporate, rather than small or family, business. The consumer boom of the postwar years was a further contribution to the apparently dominating destiny of the form. So was the coming of a huge standing defense establishment, courtesy of new international defense commitments. And so, especially, was the spread of U.S. corporations into foreign markets, at a time when the other major developed economies were in spectacular disarray and when the modern corporation had not so clearly displaced either small business or the family firm elsewhere. A new corporate leadership, a truly "managerial" leadership in every sense of the word, then completed the picture.

None of this was hidden from public view at the time, and much was made of the social phenomena associated with the resurgence of corporate America. Nevertheless, contemporary social analysts could not know how temporally distinctive this evolution was. From one side, the evidently increasing concentration of employment inside the manufacturing sector was real enough, as figure 3.4A (p. 92) indicates. Yet even there, the great firms, those with more than 1,000 employees, were to peak early as a share of all American workers, then begin to recede; their share of value added would follow. Moreover, from the other side, not only would all such concentration reach a ceiling by the 1960s, but the place of manufacturing within the American economy had itself already crested, as in figure 3.4B (p. 93), so that corporate gigantism was not effectively the wave of the future.

In its time, nevertheless, that gigantism was impressive. Big government had obviously come with the New Deal and World War II. It did not go away. Big labor had arrived with the Great Depression and the NLRA. It remained an obvious mountain on the postwar landscape. Business, *big* business, was a central part of the postwar recovery, and this fact was widely noted within its society.[8]

The rise of an economic form, of course, was not itself a social base, a political elite, a partisan link, or a programmatic orientation—although growth on this scale of what was also a form of *social* organization did bring incipient possibilities for all of the above. Corporate growth did automatically imply an increase in "corporate numbers." That category, however, was still too abstract to have much meaning, and indeed the largest share of corporate employees were actually the people who made up the social base for organized labor! As a result, the social base for what was to become Modern Republicanism was really a burgeoning "middle management" instead.

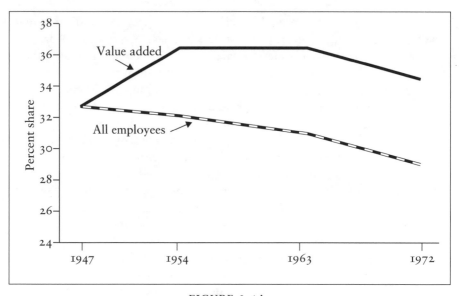

FIGURE 3.4A
GROWTH OF THE POSTWAR CORPORATE WORLD —
EMPLOYMENT AND VALUE ADDED IN FIRMS OF 1,000 AND OVER

SOURCE: *Statistical Abstract of the United States* (Washington, D.C.: Department of Commerce, various years).

Yet here, for a time, this growing social base did actually possess a new and growing residential location: the burgeoning suburbs, which were also a critical part of the immediate postwar scene. Suburbanization would ultimately become a defining characteristic of American society, and this period would see the greatest raw explosion of housing construction in American history, almost all of which, as in table 3.3 (p. 94), was intentionally suburban. As a result, it would see the transition of the United States to an archetypically suburban society. Eventually, the status of dominant residential form would lessen the distinctiveness of the suburbs as a political base, as they came to encompass most of the conflicts characterizing American society. But in the immediate postwar years, the suburbs were still disproportionately home to lesser managerial employees of the burgeoning corporations.

To the extent that Modern Republicanism had a mass constituency, then, it was increasingly suburban. William Chafe puts the social context around this:

If the "organization man" came to symbolize the new corporate personal-

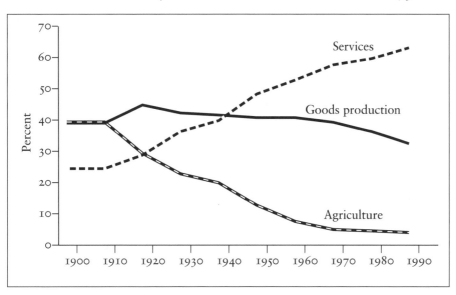

FIGURE 3.4B

GROWTH OF THE POSTWAR CORPORATE WORLD —
EMPLOYMENT DISTRIBUTION BY MAJOR SECTOR

SOURCES: *Historical Statistics of the United States, Colonial Times to 1970* (Washington, D.C.: Department of Commerce, 1975); *Statistical Abstract of the United States* (Washington, D.C.: Department of Commerce, various years).

ity, the suburban housing development came to symbolize the middle-class lifestyle he went home to. . . . In one of the most astounding migrations in history, suburbanites flocked to the new communities that blossomed in ever-widening circles around the nation's metropolitan areas. At the height of the great European migration in the early twentieth century, 1.2 million new citizens came to America in a single year. During the 1950s, the same number moved to the suburbs every year. . . . During the 1950s, suburbs grew six times faster than cities. Between 1950 and 1960 alone, 18 million people moved to the suburbs.

The move to suburbia represented a miraculous fusion of need and desire. After the war, the number of marriages doubled, and most of the new households had nowhere to go. Over 2 million couples in 1948 were living with relatives. It was against such a backdrop that easy housing loans through VA and FHA combined with a booming economy to make possible a massive program of housing construction. Between 1950 and 1960 more than 13 million homes were built in America—11 million of them in the suburbs. Building contractors wanted cheap land; county gov-

TABLE 3.3

HOUSING CONSTRUCTION
IN THE TWENTIETH CENTURY

	Total units started (in thousands)	As a percentage of total stock
1990	1,193	1.2
1985	1,742	—
1980	1,292	1.5
1975	1,160	—
1970	1,469	2.2
1965	1,510	—
1960	1,275	2.2
1955	1,646	—
1950	1,952	4.2
1945	326	—
1940	603	1.6
1935	221	—
1930	330	1.0
1925	937	—
1920	247	1.0
1915	433	—
1910	387	1.9
1905	507	—

SOURCES: *Historical Statistics of the United States, Colonial Times to 1970* (Washington, D.C.: Department of Commerce, 1975); *Statistical Abstract of the United States* (Washington, D.C.: Department of Commerce, various years).

ernments were happy to welcome them to empty space crying for development.[9]

The new corporations, with which this suburban constituency was at first so closely associated, also possessed a higher leadership—a growing corporate elite—by definition. More to the practical point for an inquiry into the rise and fall of partisan elites, the leadership of this newly triumphant corporate form had distinctive values and preferences, for incipient transfer into politics. These values differed not just from those of other social groups in contemporary society but, in important ways, from those of counterpart individuals in an earlier period. Accordingly, these values, along with the geographic distribution of their holders, were to be more crucial to their place in postwar politics than any institutional device that their holders controlled.

To begin with, because these were the key operational elites from corporate management, they were the individuals most likely to encounter the leadership of organized labor across the bargaining table. Not surprisingly, they focused on labor-management relations, as a central concern of their economic life and of any related politics. Where they differed from other regular opponents of organized labor—and from their own predecessors in an earlier incarnation—was in an acceptance of labor as part of the normal landscape. There was just no point in denying its existence, its power, or the recurrent need to reach some accommodation with it. Instead, the point was to be sure that any resulting agreement was mutually beneficial and that the rules governing labor-management negotiations were not additionally tilted in favor of the former.

More abstract thinkers within this newly ascendant managerial stratum actually accepted the virtues of governmental action to maintain consumer demand and full employment. Others, while hardly saluting these values, did their business with government, and in a major way now that big government was a feature of the economic marketplace. If they did not want that government to ingest (or even regulate) further sectors of the economy, or to tax away the rewards of business and enterprise, neither did they want it to stop doing business with *them*. Geography then added a key twist to these values, converting them into a much more general political program while providing the incentive structure to pull their holders into partisan politics.

For, in fact, the new managerial elite was also geographically concentrated, as figure 3.5 (p. 96) demonstrates, in the Northeast, then the industrial Midwest, and then the West Coast. As a subset of American regions, however, these areas shared a number of other characteristics: (1) they were the places where the general societal consensus on the welfare state was at its most supportive; (2) they were the places where union membership was at its highest—major corporate states were also major labor states; and (3) they were the places where liberal Democrats had *their* best prospects of becoming the dominant partisan group. Accordingly, if this new managerial elite was not necessarily keen on extending social welfare programs, its members were encouraged to accept an overall social welfare consensus as contributing the boundaries of public life, within which all subsequent politicking had necessarily to occur.

Those were the contours of a distinctive political outlook. They gained some further practical prospect—this particular elite gained some further prospect in practical politics—from the increased legitimacy of the giant corporations generally in the immediate postwar world. This was never sufficient to carry the Modern Republicans to political dominance.

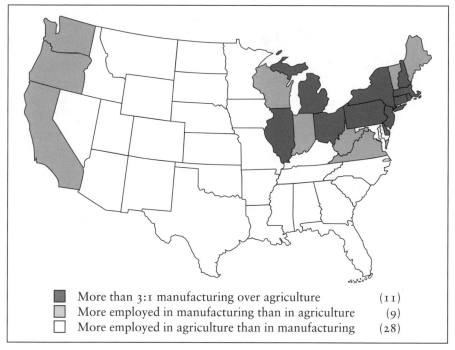

More than 3:1 manufacturing over agriculture   (11)
More employed in manufacturing than in agriculture   (9)
More employed in agriculture than in manufacturing   (28)

FIGURE 3.5
CORPORATE EMPLOYMENT IN THE STATES, 1950

SOURCE: *Statistical Abstract of the United States* (Washington, D.C.: Department of Commerce, 1952), various tables combined.

Corporate failings remained linked with perceptions of the Great Depression; the public was not even vaguely interested in rolling back the main programs of the New Deal. But the phenomenal growth of the American economy in the immediate postwar years, along with the growth of corporate enterprise in an inextricably entangled fashion, did provide substantial background legitimacy.

And that growth and its products were truly phenomenal. Table 3.4 shows an array of indicators, including that central summary number on well-being, namely, per capita income, and the main capital asset following from it for most people, namely, homeownership. The same point could be made with an aggregate: gross national product, up 250 percent between 1945 and 1960. It could be shown through productivity: 310 hours to make a car in 1945, 150 hours in 1960. It could be demonstrated

TABLE 3.4

THE "CORPORATE BOOM" AT THE PERSONAL LEVEL

	Disposable income ($1,987 per capita)	Home-ownership (%)	Possession of a television set (%)
1990	13,824	64.2	98
1980	11,221	65.5	98
1970	9,875	62.9	95
1960	7,264	61.9	87
1950	6,214	55.0	9
1940	4,787	43.6	0

SOURCE: *Statistical Abstract of the United States* (Washington, D.C.: Department of Commerce, various years).

with consumer goods generally: clothes dryers, air conditioners, *second* cars. It could be shown even in the means for expanding the ability to purchase such goods: short-term consumer credit, up 500 percent from only 1946 to 1958. It could be shown, as in table 3.4 again, in the spread of the device most commonly used by cultural critics to talk about the period, namely the near-blanketing of the nation by television.

What was still missing in this equation was the "draw," some pull from the other side that would bring emergent elites with this distinctive outlook into partisan politics. Yet the background forces for such a draw were already present in other associated aspects of politics in those same states where a corporate Republicanism was resurgent. Or at least, if there was to be a Republican alternative in those states, its contours were clear enough. In coalitional terms, it needed to constrain labor but accept its legitimacy and not threaten its members. In programmatic terms, it needed to control the costs of social welfare programs while accepting *their* legitimacy and not threatening beneficiaries, at least of the major social insurance programs. It needed, in short, to wear the Republican label but be attractive to moderate Democrats.[10]

In the abstract, the new corporate elite could offer these assets. As it developed, again at least in these particular states, there was usually an existing elite—outside of Modern Republicanism, at first—ready to benefit from this apparent fit between strategic needs and elite assets by introducing its newer counterpart to partisan politics. Or at least there was normally an existing party leadership ready to do the essential operational tasks to convert this new elite, first into partisan candidates, then into partisan officeholders. By definition, these states already possessed some established partisan leadership, within the regular Republican Party. Given their inherent competitive difficulties, members were often prepared to support a new corporate elite in Republican politics—what would come to be called the Modern Republicans—if its members could in fact bring returns.

Accordingly, the fortunes of these implicit Modern Republicans were critically shaped by a combination of geographic location and inherent assets from one side, and of the needs and norms of the regular Republican Party from the other. For, in truth, the natural field of this elite, within partisan politics, remained the Republican Party. This was so by way of ongoing programmatic attachments: the Republicans remained the party of lower spending, lower taxes, and less intervention in private business. It was so by way of contemporary social alignments as well: the Democratic Party, besides being the home of more of those with contrary preferences, was most centrally the home of organized labor, the opposition to corporate management in purely economic terms.

This never led to any overarching political action committee, the counterpart to the AFL-CIO's COPE, which would then register middle-management voters in the suburbs, recruit sympathetic candidates from corporate leadership, and contribute the techniques of campaign organization and campaign finance. Indeed, what was in formal terms the opposite number to the AFL-CIO, namely the National Association of Manufacturers, never undertook systematic electioneering and focused its lobbying activity—which it took very seriously—much more on scaling back labor gains in labor-management relations and on restraining the welfare state generally. As a result, the new managerial elite, the seedbed of Modern Republicanism, percolated into politics more individually and very much on a person-by-person basis.

Yet in practice, while the "blue ribbon" assets of this new managerial elite might be welcomed by the existing Republican Party—especially, as it turned out, its fund-raising capabilities—the *values* associated with those assets just as often were not. This was a further reason why members tended to enter practical politics as individuals, one by one. It was a further reason why they were never to possess even associated interest groups, much less an overhead agency. But more to the practical point, this conflict over public values and policy preferences, plus the need to be actively slated by the regular party, explained the peculiar pattern of success (and failure) of the Modern Republicans, once they had entered postwar partisan politics.

The Republican Party overall was based in small (not corporate) business, and it was local (not national) business leaders who played an active role in organized party politics across the country. These individuals were most decidedly *not* happy with the prospect of "living with" organized labor; they became the force behind the Taft-Hartley counterattack of 1947. They were not really happy with the prospect of accommodating the welfare state; they regarded themselves as paying its bills, while its beneficiaries were inherently unsympathetic to their needs or values. They were happy, even delighted, to win elections and run government, but if that implied endorsing the products of the New Deal, then the point of it was likely to escape them.

Given this division between an established old and a potential new Republican elite, a clear pattern of success for the Modern Republicans —a clear pattern of conversion from social base to partisan officeholding—followed ineluctably. They were to be reliably successful at the presidential level, fluctuatingly successful at the senatorial level, and only marginally successful at the congressional level. In this, it was not surprising that the new elite showed its greatest gains at the presidential level. Wendell Willkie in 1940, Thomas Dewey in 1944 and 1948, and then Dwight Eisenhower, explicitly and operationally, in 1952 and 1956: these were the presidential candidates of the new managerial elite, and they contributed a generation of presidential dominance within the Republican Party.

These candidates were accepted by the old elite—not necessarily embraced, just accepted—because, as with Dewey most diagnostically, they had shown that they could win in a Democratic area, which the entire country in some sense was! In that sense, they were easily preferable to rallying the established base, and losing. On the other hand, in those areas where the old Republican elite continued to be successful on its own, there was no evident need to search out these new corporate Republicans. And there was good reason, given the difference in values and preferences, not to defer to them if they edged forward.

The home of this attitude, in contraposition to the presidency, was the House of Representatives, where a sizable minority of seats were normally Republican and where a substantial majority of these were aligned with an established Republican elite. The new managerial elite was welcome—if it really wished, which it usually did not—to undertake those remaining contests with normal Democratic majorities. But this would not add many Modern Republicans to the Republican Party nationwide in the average year, and these offices were, in any event, least attractive to a numerically limited elite whose principal focus was not politics.

In between the presidency and the House, in every sense, was the

Senate, so the Republican Party in the Senate acquired the clearest *divisions* along old elite/new elite lines. There were states with reliable Republican majorities here, and they tended to be in the hands of the old (small business) elite. But there were others with substantial Republican minorities and a chance—but only that—of winning statewide, behind a candidate who at least did not alienate Democrats. In these, even old-line Republicans were willing to try the new managerial alternative. These were the states, unsurprisingly, which did produce a leaven of Modern Republicans across the 1950s: Prescott Bush in Connecticut, 1952; Clifford Case in New Jersey, 1954; Jacob Javits in New York, 1956; Kenneth Keating in New York and Hugh Scott—the true archetype—in Pennsylvania, 1958.

The collective term for this group, "Modern Republicans," owed its currency to the great partisan success of this period, Dwight Eisenhower and the Eisenhower presidency. The crucial moving figures in getting Eisenhower to run were in fact from the key "managerial" states: the Northeast, the industrial Midwest, and the West Coast. Likewise, the crucial figures in guaranteeing the *funds* that would encourage this effort were top managerial leaders from this incipient party elite. Eisenhower was then nominated with the support of those states that most clearly fit this mold, and opposed by those where the older Republican elite was still dominant. When Eisenhower won by drawing *Democrats* across the partisan line, he became entitled to contribute the summary term for a new and partisan elite. Figure 3.6 tells this story, a story that would be repeated, if less dramatically, at the state and not just the national level for the next fifteen years.

The Eisenhower archetype also commented powerfully on the limitations of this emergent Republican elite. Eisenhower did explicitly harry corporate business figures about their need to "get involved," especially in electoral politics. Yet this was not their natural theater. What they wanted overall was a public policy that did not interfere excessively in business management. Moreover, the limits on the political reach of their underlying social stratum—their mass base—were always a problem. Explicitly corporate suburbs plus a few "silk stocking districts" in central cities were never going to be numerically dominant, even within the Republican Party.

Nevertheless, the extent to which they did come to constitute a critical element of the national Republican Party during the 1950s and 1960s was impressive. In battles over international involvement, for example, they provided a Republican presence behind both pursuing the Cold War *and* maintaining an active presence in international agencies of coopera-

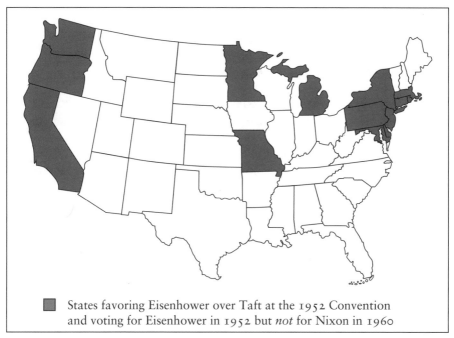

States favoring Eisenhower over Taft at the 1952 Convention and voting for Eisenhower in 1952 but *not* for Nixon in 1960

FIGURE 3.6

HOME BASES FOR MODERN REPUBLICANS

SOURCES: Paul T. David, Malcolm Moos, and Ralph M. Goldman, *Presidential Nominating Politics in 1952* (Baltimore: Johns Hopkins University Press, 1954), vol. 1, *The National Story*, 95–97; and *Presidential Elections since 1789*, 5th ed. (Washington, D.C.: CQ Press, 1991), 205 and 207.

tion. In the fight over civil rights, perhaps *the* great issue of the late 1950s and early 1960s, they provided most of the Republicans who joined with northern and western Democrats to support civil rights legislation. Even in the more tangential elements of social welfare, such as disability insurance or health-care regulation, they provided the crucial middle ground that made legislation possible and shaped its specifics critically at times.

The Modern Period
New Politics Democrats

Observable, on occasion, is the parallel development of another literature chiefly designed to affect changes in the apportionment of profits between the governing class and its adjutants.... The larger the total to be appor-

tioned, the hotter the battle and the more copious the literature it in-
spires.... Not a few "intellectuals" and humanitarians, sincere of faith
and poor of spirit, gape in open-mouthed astonishment at such portentous
demonstrations, and dream of a world that will some day be ruled by
them....

Early in the nineteenth century, either because it was richer in Class
II residues than now or because it had not yet been taught of experience,
the governing class by no means considered such derivations innocuous,
and much less to its advantage. It persecuted them, therefore, and tried to
control them by law. Gradually in course of time it discovered that they in
no way constituted obstacles to ruling-class profits, that sometimes, indeed oftentimes, they were a help. In those days, rich bankers were almost
all conservatives. Nowadays, they hobnob with revolutionaries, intellectuals, Socialists, even Anarchists.

— Pareto, *Compendium of General Sociology*, 351–52 [1011–12]

The third great elite infusion to postwar American politics, despite
being Democratic, actually shared more structural characteristics with the
Modern Republicans than with organized labor. Like the Modern Republicans, this third great infusion was to grow out of a distinctive social base
rather than an organized constituency. Like the Modern Republicans, it
would always lack a single overhead agency to coordinate its activities,
though here, a variety of issue and cause groups, drawing on the same social base and very much aware of each other, would coordinate common
values and positions. Like organized labor, however, its strength as a self-
conscious elite would be powerfully augmented by changes in the rules of
the game, albeit the formal rules of politics rather than of economics in
this case. And to complete the circle, those revised rules would then has-
ten both the demise of the Modern Republicans and the rise of the final
elite group in postwar politics to date, the evangelical Protestants.

This third group, in any case, was the New Politics Democrats. As
with any serious candidate for a Paretian circulation, there was a newly
ascendant social stratum; there were newly emergent specialized spokesmen; there were distinctive values, to give these phenomena policy implications; and there was an ultimate and explicit partisan connection.
Moreover, as with all the other serious candidates, this newly emergent
elite was not just structurally essential for connecting an ascendant social
base with the institutions of government. It was also extremely important
in defining, and partially transforming, the policy desires that this elite
then pursued through partisan politics. It was arguably ironic that this

new, insurgent elite was Democratic, rather than Republican, given its greater structural affinities with Modern Republicans than with organized labor. It was inescapably ironic that its major direct opponents, at the time it was coming to power, were *not* Modern Republicans, but organized labor.

Harbingers of a "new politics" was what elite spokesmen for this group considered themselves, and the Democratic Party became their institutional—partisan—home, so New Politics Democrats became a logical moniker. Once more, there are good reasons for allowing this self-description to stand, in that it avoids alternatives adapted for explicitly tactical purposes, while it leaves the analyst free to put further defining characteristics into the general label. Within the Democratic Party, Al Barkan, director of the AFL-CIO's COPE, was frequently unprintable in his description of New Politics Democrats: *his* definition would certainly not serve. Within the partisan competition, Spiro Agnew, vice-president on the Republican ticket at the critical moment, fired off some pithy and memorable summary epithets. The phrase "New Politics Democrats" at least avoids these.

It was a particular slice of the New Politics Democrats—in effect, their "shock troops"—that first brought them to public attention and probably served as their collective catalyst. These were the university-based political activists of the mid-1960s. Heavily influenced by the civil rights revolution of the preceding decade, they borrowed its protest tactics to deal with the central issue of direct concern to them, the Vietnam War and opposition to it. On the one hand, they would prove to be but a fraction, albeit an active one, of the social group they initially represented. On the other hand, the *substance* of their main issue, involving cultural and national values rather than economics and social welfare, would remain diagnostic. Yet as ever, even here, this "elite within the elite" itself had a growing social base to underpin it. And this base, in turn, had two key aspects.

One was the "baby boom" of the immediate postwar years, and figure 3.7A (p. 104) certainly attests to its reality. But this boom occurred additionally within the general context of postwar prosperity, and it was augmented most particularly by the burgeoning share of Americans actually going to college. Indeed, it was this "college bulge"—a rapid increase in college enrollment—that was truly distinctive, much more than just the raw (baby boom) numbers beneath it, as figure 3.7B (p. 105) affirms. That these individuals had grown up in a world in which neither depression nor war had touched them, before Vietnam, and that they had achieved the historically privileged status of a college education without personal

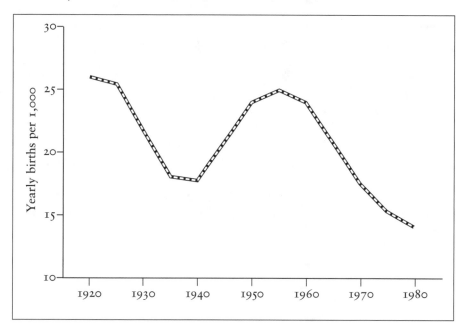

FIGURE 3.7A
A SOCIAL BASE FOR THE VANGUARD
OF THE NEW POLITICS DEMOCRATS —
THE BABY BOOM

SOURCE: Richard A. Easterlin, *Birth and Fortune: The Impact of Numbers on Personal Welfare* (New York: Basic Books, 1980), 8.

sacrifice in so many cases, were often taken to be a further key to their values and behavior: political constraints on lifestyle choices seemed merely the residue of a time lag in social thinking. In any case, the 1960s was the decade of their most rapid growth in the entire twentieth century.

This combination of issue substance and social base would have been easily sufficient to produce extended campus unrest. It was hardly sufficient to produce a major partisan elite, imparting new directions to national political conflict. Instead, the larger social base for that elite lay in a striking increase in the share of the Democratic Party composed of higher-status and higher-education individuals. The college-based shock troops came out of this stratum; in some sense, they were both its symbolic incarnation and its real children. But the stratum was much broader, and therefore much longer lasting.

Figure 3.8 (p. 106) shows the increase in the share of the Democratic Party contributed by those completing a college education across the post-

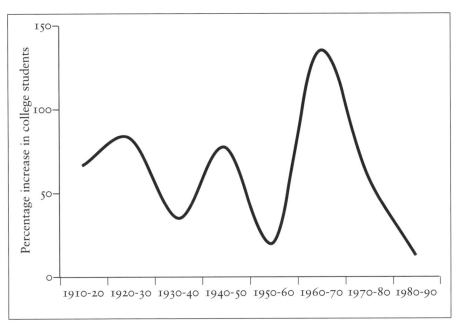

FIGURE 3.7B

A SOCIAL BASE FOR THE VANGUARD
OF THE NEW POLITICS DEMOCRATS —
THE COLLEGE BULGE

SOURCES: *Historical Statistics of the United States, Colonial Times to 1970* (Washington, D.C.: Department of Commerce, 1975); *Statistical Abstract of the United States* (Washington, D.C.: Department of Commerce, various years).

war years, and the change inherent in it was remarkable: there were two, quite different, partisan social worlds at the beginning and end of this period. In 1950, college-graduate Democrats were evident rarities and anomalies to their class. By 1980, they were an obvious and distinctive part of the coalition. Along the way, the share of Democrats with a college education actually rose faster than the share of all Americans with same. For reasons addressed below, the late 1960s became the historic breakpoint.[11]

Opposition to the Vietnam War did unite this larger population, albeit more moderately, with the university-based activists. While Vietnam as an issue would ultimately dissipate, this preference for international accommodation would remain characteristic. A general cultural liberalism united both parts of the group as well, though again more moderately for the mass base than for those activists who styled themselves as a de-

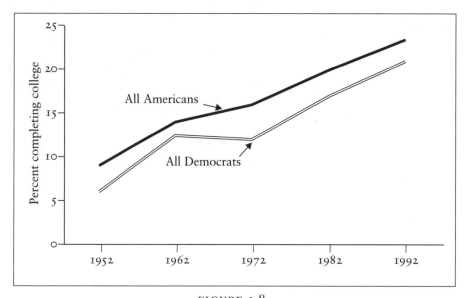

FIGURE 3.8

THE RISE OF THE COLLEGE-GRADUATE DEMOCRATS

SOURCE: *National Election Study* (Ann Arbor: Interuniversity Consortium for Political and Social Research, various years).

liberate "counterculture." The enduring position here was progressive rather than traditional, emphasizing choice rather than constraint, and hence rights rather than responsibilities.

But the true unifying theme, and the one destined to carry by far the most political weight, concerned the character of politics itself, its proper institutions and the proper behavior within them. The progressive position on this would prove to be what propelled the New Politics Democrats over time. It would allow their elite to add more international accommodationism and cultural liberalism than the mass base would have demanded. It would simultaneously unite them with an earlier incarnation of the same social tendency and political preference.

In their own view, spokesmen dubbed this phenomenon *new* precisely because it would center on a putative "new politics," one focused on solving problems rather than dispensing patronage; one addressing issues rather than just rallying loyalties; one dealing with the quality rather than just the quantity of life. Emphasizing opposition to "machine politics," as this view certainly did, its constituents were destined for conflict with the regular party, which in this case came to mean the regular Democratic Party. Emphasizing opposition to "organized interests," as it also did, its constituents were destined for conflict with the main organized interest inside the regular Democratic coalition, which by this time was, of course, organized labor. Emphasizing those views, its constituents were destined to be in favor of the reform of political (and especially partisan) institutions, and they reliably were.

As ever with such elite eruptions, these views appeared to follow "naturally" from—they were entirely consistent with, though they did not necessarily exhaust—the social experience of the group from whence they came. Thus members of this group were suburban rather than urban; cosmopolitan rather than local; and white-collar rather than blue-collar. In turn, they were inclined to get their political information more from the formal media than from social intermediaries, were motivated more by substantive content than by partisan loyalty, and deferred more to voluntary organizations that they chose to join, rather than to community organizations provided for them, including the political party.

Such preferences in political style were joined by distinctive substantive values and policy preferences. This stratum, while more economically liberal than social counterparts in the Republican Party, was both less liberal and less concerned with economic and social welfare issues than were most other Democrats. Conversely, concerned about the environment, tolerant of social deviance, in favor of personal choice in such matters as divorce and abortion, focused on the social roots of problems like crime, and hostile to most forms of social control, they were even more liberal on cultural and social issues than the Modern Republicans, whom they otherwise resembled. Needless to say, they were wildly more liberal on these matters than other Democrats, whom they did not resemble.

The preconditions for what was to become this new partisan elite had begun with the postwar economic boom, most especially with a few key social changes intimately connected to it. There would be a full generation before these preconditions led to the indisputable arrival of the New Politics Democrats; nevertheless, the preconditions for their emergence did trace directly to the postwar boom. The general characteristics of that boom, of course—rising family income, rising homeownership, the spread of new consumer goods of all sorts—had been crucial both to the appearance and to the improved legitimacy of the Modern Republicans as well. But two further elements of this change were to be crucial to the emergence of the New Politics Democrats as a full-blown partisan elite.

The more general of these was a rapid transformation of the occupational structure of a booming postwar American economy, from a blue-collar base with a substantial component of unskilled labor to a white-collar base with a growing sector of professional occupations instead.

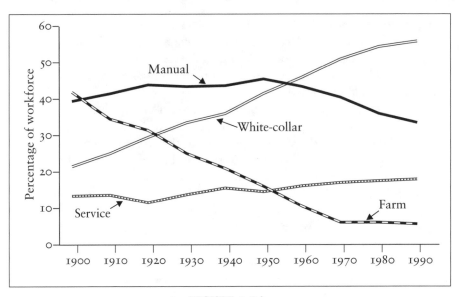

FIGURE 3.9A

THE COMING OF THE WHITE-COLLAR WORLD —
OCCUPATIONAL CHANGE ACROSS THE TWENTIETH CENTURY

SOURCE: *Statistical Abstract of the United States* (Washington, D.C.: Department of Commerce, various years).

Decennial census figures, as in figure 3.9A, confirm that the crucial division between a blue-collar and a white-collar majority was reached by 1960, but interim samples suggest, remarkably, that the divide was actually crossed by 1956. Part and parcel of this occupational (and class) shift were sharply rising educational levels, as shown in figure 3.9B. This was largely a further by-product of the postwar boom, though it also owed a huge amount to direct governmental intervention in the form of the postwar "GI Bill," which allowed many returning servicemen to resume an education interrupted by war but many more to gain an education they would never otherwise have secured.

Had this occupational and educational evolution gone hand in hand with the occupational and educational distribution of partisan attachments from the immediate postwar years, its eventual resolution in politics would have been clear. Blue-collar workers were more Democratic, white-collar workers were more Republican; less-educated Americans were more Democratic, more-educated Americans were more Republican. Ergo, as the share of society that was white-collar and more educated increased, so would the share of Republicans in society as a whole. In fact,

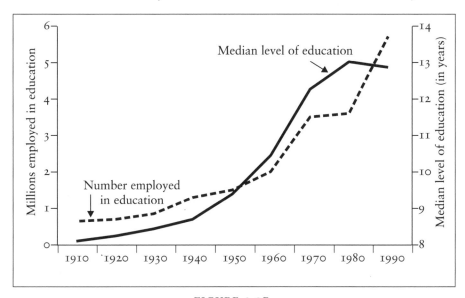

FIGURE 3.9B

THE COMING OF THE WHITE-COLLAR WORLD—

EDUCATIONAL CHANGE ACROSS THE TWENTIETH CENTURY

SOURCES: *Historical Statistics of the United States, Colonial Times to 1970* (Washington, D.C.: Department of Commerce, 1975); *Statistical Abstract of the United States* (Washington, D.C.: Department of Commerce, various years).

however—and this was the crucial intermediary fact about the emergence of the New Politics Democrats—this did not occur. The Democratic share of the total population fluctuated randomly for another generation but left no doubt that the Democrats remained the majority party. The Republican share, despite all those favorable social preconditions, *did not rise*. Table 3.5 (p. 110) shows the actual trend, measured two ways.

Many explanations suggested themselves for why initial postwar projections about partisanship would not prove accurate. Most of these, however, were ultimately some mix of programmatic appeal and generational effect. To wit: the programs of the New Deal, its social insurance programs in particular—social security, unemployment compensation —proved immensely popular. So did immediate postwar extensions, such as the GI Bill and the governmental commitment to full employment. The changing internal composition of society, even to this remarkable degree, just did not dent that essential popularity.

As long as the Democrats were centrally connected with supporting and the Republicans with *opposing* these programs, then, no shift in par-

TABLE 3.5
TREND OF PARTY IDENTIFICATION
ACROSS THE POSTWAR YEARS
(IN PERCENTAGES)

A. For all those leaning Democratic or Republican

	1952	1962	1972	1982	1992
Democrats	57	53	52	55	50
Republicans	35	34	33	32	37
All others	9	12	14	13	13

Democrats = Strong Democrats + Weak Democrats + Independent Democrats; Republicans = Strong Republicans + Weak Republicans + Independent Republicans; All others = Pure Independents.

B. For all those identifying clearly

	1952	1962	1972	1982	1992
Democrats	47	46	41	44	36
Republicans	28	28	23	23	25
All others	26	25	35	32	39

Democrats = Strong Democrats + Weak Democrats; Republicans = Strong Republicans + Weak Republicans; All others = Independent Democrats + Independent Republicans + Pure Independents.

SOURCE: *National Election Study* (Ann Arbor: Interuniversity Consortium for Political and Social Research, various years).

tisan attachments of any seriousness was in evidence. And indeed, for more than a generation after the Second World War, as table 3.6 suggests, most of society still remembered—had personally experienced—the Great Depression to which these programs responded. To expect these survivors to shift their partisanship, especially when the Modern Republicans failed to gain overall control of their party, was almost to expect them to disavow that experience.

So, what was happening in partisan terms was different. Again, if the occupational and educational nature of society was changing but the partisan balance in society as a whole was not, then the occupational and educational composition of identifiers with the two major political parties had to be changing substantially. As it developed, these changes were to be especially critical for the Democratic Party, the majority party *and* the party whose previous composition had been most unlike the growth areas of the evolving society. As a result, if an ideological assertion of a new po-

TABLE 3.6

VOTING-AGE AMERICANS WITH CONSCIOUS
ADULT EXPERIENCE OF THE GREAT DEPRESSION
AND WORLD WAR II
(IN PERCENTAGES)

	1952	1962	1972	1982	1992
Cohorts born 1927 or later	8	28	55	68	82
Cohorts born 1926 or earlier	92	72	45	32	18

SOURCE: *National Election Study* (Ann Arbor: Interuniversity Consortium for Political and Social Research, various years).

litical style (reformed, "clean," open, participatory) was one side of the equation creating New Politics Democrats, a social base—the more highly educated middle and upper-middle classes among Democratic identifiers —was the other side of that equation.

Once again, as with the Modern Republicans, there had arguably been an earlier incarnation of the same tendency in American politics. Or, at least, the Progressive movement at the turn of the twentieth century had been nothing if not focused ideologically on reforming political institutions, while being based socially in a newly assertive, educated middle class, with a serious leaven of the independent professions.[12] At that time, however, the dominant party, the party of government, had been the Republican Party; the Democratic Party was little more, in national terms, than an amalgam of disparate interests seeking policy gains. In such an environment, the progressive tendency was perhaps inevitably the reform faction within Republicanism.

Seventy years later, the same contextual things had changed. The dominant party was now the Democratic Party. It had acquired both a national policy program and a national coalition, courtesy of the New Deal. As a result, this time, the successor tendency to progressivism, again perhaps inevitably, surfaced as the reform faction of the *Democratic* Party instead.

There was, nevertheless, a specific politics to bring this development into being, one catalyzing the "New Politics" tendency, and catalyzing it as a Democratic elite. This politics gained consequence from the fact that the partisan outcome of this process was incipiently predisposed, but hardly preordained. Indeed, organized labor, the dominant interest group in the Democratic coalition, did not share at least the priorities of what became the New Politics Democrats, while the Modern Republicans arguably did. Moreover, many of the most active members of what was to become the New Politics elite were consciously *anti*partisan, opposed on the record as much to the existing Democratic as to the existing Republican Party.

Events underlined a partisan necessity, however, and made clear to the activists that this partisanship was Democratic. The flashpoint for anti-Vietnam activity proved to be the Eugene McCarthy nominating campaign of 1968, an insurgent campaign within the Democratic Party; the Republican alternative was effectively foreclosed by the return of Richard Nixon as its nominee. The frustration of the McCarthy campaign—its active defeat by the regular party coupled with organized labor—only widened the potential "new politics" base for what became the McGovern nominating campaign of 1972. Its success was then half the story of the institutionalization of the New Politics elite inside the Democratic Party.

Again, the activist fringe of this elite was often explicitly hostile to both parties, even coming out of families whose parents were Modern Republicans. But the realization of its antiwar wishes was fought out within the Democratic Party, and that proved crucial. Perhaps even more crucial was the fact that when Jimmy Carter captured both the Democratic nomination and the presidency in 1976, initially raising high anxieties for Democrats of all stripes, Carter then ran a classic administration of New Politics elites: accommodationist in foreign affairs, tolerant of lifestyle choices in cultural matters, unconcerned with social welfare policy. By that point, a very significant share of those active in Democratic Party politics had come to be New Politics Democrats.[13]

They were helped immeasurably in their rise to prominence by a continuing reform movement, emphasizing precisely the assets—education, disposable income, control of working schedules—that New Politics Democrats possessed. But in truth, while reform continued to be central to the New Politics ideology, and while New Politics Democrats would drive it farther in institutional terms, they were not directly responsible for the reforms that initially benefited them. A conscious reform drive around the turn of the century whose implications had been working their way gradually through society as time passed—the Progressive movement, once again—had both opened the internal processes of party politics to those participants who might turn out in any given forum *and*, most especially, weakened the ongoing organization of the regular party in opposition to them.

The point, then, is merely that by the 1960s, the organized Democratic Party had become an increasingly feeble shell, capable of being captured by a newly energized elite that was more effectively adapted to an increasingly participatory politics. In this, the New Politics Democrats did little more than finish off a century-long evolution. Alan Ware summarizes the situation accurately:

> There can be little doubt that what happened to the Democratic parties in America between the early 1960s and the late 1970s was truly extraordinary.... Why did this transformation occur? In doing this, it is perhaps most useful if we attempt to classify the numerous factors which seem to have contributed to party collapse....
>
> The first category is the most obvious; it includes the development of new technologies which could be employed in political campaigning, and the resources which helped incumbents, especially legislators, to divorce themselves from the nominating and electoral activists of their party's organization. The second category includes several different factors which would have affected the parties, irrespective of the state of campaign technology or of political controversies in the 1960s. There were demographic changes in the cities ... there were declining resources available for attracting professional activists into the parties ... there was the declining strength and commitment of the Democrats' labor union allies. The third category includes a number of forces which seem to have been the direct product of the convulsions of the 1960s—intra-party divisions and increased party disloyalty; issue extremism; the opportunity for "exit" to non-party political activity; and the institutional reforms which emanated from the conflicts.[14]

By the early 1970s, the New Politics Democrats had driven their preferred formal arrangements to the presidential level as well. When these institutional reforms were combined with the natural growth of their social base, an augmented role in the national Democratic Party followed more or less automatically. In a primary electorate, where turnout might be 30 percent or less and where it was highly tied to educational background, they could bulk very large indeed. In lesser forums, such as party caucuses, where turnout could easily be 2 or 3 percent, they were often a genuine majority. In internal party affairs, then, there were increasing areas where this emergent elite could expect to overwhelm the "old" party—and become the new.

This process still required new and congruent issues to sustain the involvement of the New Politics Democrats. These were, however, to be present in abundance. The Vietnam War might inevitably fade, but the women's movement and feminism would fit comfortably into the same co-alition. Environmentalism might lose some of its energizing role, but ho-mosexual rights would arrive to provide another stimulus. In parallel fashion, a succession of interest groups, of issue and cause organizations, would succeed each other in tandem with these issues and would provide a diagnostic operational element for the New Politics Democratic elite. In-deed, these groups were to be singularly successful in defining what it meant to be a "progressive Democrat," in a fashion that the Modern Re-publicans, for example, had never even approximated. In so doing, they contributed a distinctive, but highly effective, dynamic to the operation of the third great postwar partisan elite.

Evangelical Protestants

> It has often been noted that there were times when religious sentiments seemed to lose ground, others when they seemed to gain strength, and that such undulations corresponded to social movements of very consider-able scope. The uniformity might be more exactly described by saying that in the higher stratum of society, Class II residues gradually lose strength, until now and again they are reinforced by ties upswelling from the lower stratum. . . .
>
> An instance in our day would be the United States of America, where this upward thrust of members of the lower classes strong in Class II resi-dues is very intense; and in that country one witnesses the rise of no end of strange and wholly unscientific religions . . . that are utterly at war with any sort of scientific thinking, and a mass of hypocritical laws for the en-forcement of morality that are replicas of laws of the European Middle Ages.
>
> — Pareto, *Compendium of General Sociology,* 277 [801-803]

The fourth and last great elite infusion to postwar American politics shared some characteristics with each of its three major predecessors. It was probably closest in structure to organized labor in that it possessed not just a fully crystallized organizational framework to complement its underlying social base but a single overhead agency to (attempt to) coor-dinate its many other explicit organizations. Yet it was also distinguished in substance by its conscious opposition to *all* these other elites. This fourth great elite was born, most directly, in a hostility to the values of New Politics Democrats. Indeed, it was mobilized around many of the same values, but from the opposite direction. Yet the greatest direct op-probrium from its leaders was still reserved, albeit intermittently, for the handful of descendants of the Modern Republicans. They were the partisan apostates who muddied the message and thwarted its transmission. If organized labor did not receive the same pyrotechnic treatment, finally, that was because labor remained, forever and in principle, beyond the pale.[15]

The group in question, seedbed of this fourth and last great elite infusion, was, of course, evangelical Protestants. And it was to contribute, from the late 1970s onward, what became known as the New Christian Right. Yet this particular incarnation was only the latest resurgence of what had been a major contributor to the circulation of elites across all of American history. From the beginning of American politics—from before the beginning, really—there had been surges of evangelical Protestants into "secular" politics, as table 3.7 suggests. And in every case, there had been a clear change in the agenda of political conflict as a result.

TABLE 3.7

PROTESTANT SURGES ACROSS AMERICAN HISTORY

	Designation	Substantive thrust	Dominant issues
1730–1760	First Great Awakening	Religious autonomy	Christianizing and independence
1800–1830	Second Great Awakening	Social leveling	Evangelism and abolition
1890–1920	The Great Divide	Political populism	Temperance and creationism
1970–	New Christian Right	Moral rejuvenation	Family values and abortion

The First Great Awakening, and the first great evangelical Protestant surge, had come in the 1730s to 1760s and had contributed, powerfully if indirectly, to the Revolutionary War. There could hardly be a more critical contribution to the "agenda for political conflict." The Second Great Awakening, roughly 1800 to 1830, had represented a second major Protestant upsurge in church membership and involvement with politics, and this had contributed, again indirectly but powerfully, to the Civil War. Both of these awakenings, however, occurred in a world where "evangelical Protestantism" began as the reform movement within Protestantism generally and ended by being effectively synonymous with it, renewing the elite structure of mainstream Protestantism as it progressed.

The next subsequent evangelical surge, the one preceding the modern incarnation, was different. Evangelicals did continue to see themselves as fighting morally degenerative forces, which in the 1890s meant fighting the big interests and the socially privileged. On just those grounds, evangelicals threw in their lot with the Populists. William Jennings Bryan became their symbolic champion; but this time, they were defeated. They managed a dramatic afterword in the first decades of the twentieth century, when they were the crucial further influence in securing Prohibition, via the Eighteenth Amendment to the Constitution. But policy success again crashed in ignominious defeat in the 1920s, when they fought an unsuccessful rearguard campaign—Bryan was once more the symbolic champion—against the teaching of (Darwinian) evolution.[16]

The Protestant evangelical movement appeared politically spent at that point, and subsequent events were to sweep politics in very different directions for several generations. Yet it is important to understand the divisions that occurred within Protestantism at the turn of the century because it was to be one side of these divisions, this time, that would generate the New Christian Right. Most of the underlying forces contributing to a split were consequences of the massive industrialization of the late nineteenth and early twentieth centuries. Nevertheless, part of the resulting split was explicitly ecclesiastical, and part was social. Together, the two parts contributed a new and different Protestant stream, submerged for nearly fifty years and then bursting forth in a major elite effervescence in the late twentieth century.

In doctrinal terms, the difference could be summarized as one of modernists versus fundamentalists. What would become the modernist strand of contemporary Protestantism came to emphasize the adaptation of Scripture to a newly scientific world, the place of formal liturgy in religious practice, and the application of sacred organization to secular betterment. In social terms, this proved a much more congenial approach to the more urban and then suburban, more middle-class and then upper-middle-class, and more and more highly educated sectors of Protestantism. In contrast, what would become the fundamentalist strand of contemporary Protestantism continued to emphasize the inerrancy of the Bible, the role of Christ in direct personal salvation, and the necessity of applying moral (Christian) principles to individual life. In social terms, this remained a more congenial approach for the more rural, the more lower-middle and working classes, and the less educated among Protestant identifiers.

Fundamentalism was probably also an approach inherently more suited, in its theology, in its organizational form, and in its social base, to maintaining distance between religion and politics. But dramatic defeats over the teaching of evolution in the 1920s certainly gave it a push in that direction, and depression, war, and the postwar economic boom then intervened for all Protestants—the mainline and the evangelical, the liturgical and the pietistic, the modern and the fundamental—providing quite other focuses for their energies and their politics. This half-century of apparent quiescence, on top of a general sense of the fundamentalists as a disadvantaged minority in intellectual and social decline, surely exaggerated the impact of evangelical Protestant elites when they returned to American politics in the late 1970s, and clearly it inflated the press response to their return.

Three main factors were ultimately to reverse the evangelical withdrawal from politics. One was an underlying pattern of religious growth, accompanied by a set of social changes that were very unlike those suggested by historical caricatures. A second, and the key for a Paretian analysis, was the generation of a new elite with additionally different social advantages, an elite consciously intending to capitalize on growth and change. And the third was a set of particular events to serve as the catalyst, interacting with broader changes to elicit and encourage a strong and active *partisan* connection between evangelical Protestants and modern American politics, in the guise of the modern Republican Party.

At the social base for American politics, the long period of political quiescence among the evangelical Protestants was actually characterized by a number of undercurrents important to their eventual reemergence. The prewar years were in truth a period of *Catholic* growth in the United States, as a massive immigrant influx from southern and eastern Europe fed through society. The immediate postwar years were then a period of growth for the modernist Protestant denominations—often known as "mainline Protestantism"—with new suburbs generating new churches, and new churches generating new members as well (table 3.8, part A, p. 118). By the early 1960s, however, this trend, too, had stalled. The major current in denominational affiliations was still one within Protestantism, but away from the mainline and toward the evangelical (table 3.8, part B, p. 118). The fact that the share of the population who acknowledged no religious tradition was also growing surely magnified the consequence of this particular current.

In any event, a number of factors appeared to be involved in the huge shift within Protestantism, the one among the three such trends destined to underpin a new partisan elite. Evangelical Protestant supporters argued, and mainline Protestant opponents feared, that the apparent change in vitality that this shift suggested was in fact a reflection of changing theological attractiveness, between denominations with moral certainties,

TABLE 3.8

DENOMINATIONAL TRENDS IN POSTWAR AMERICA
(IN PERCENTAGES)

A. Membership trends across the great "families"
of American religion

	1952	1962	1972	1982	1992
Protestant	72	74	69	65	58
Catholic	22	20	24	22	24
Jewish	3	3	2	2	2
Other/none	3	3	5	11	16

B. Membership trends by denominational affiliation

	1952	1962	1972	1982	1992
Mainline Protestant	n.a.	45	37	32	24
Evangelical Protestant	n.a.	29	32	33	34
Catholic	22	20	24	22	24
Jewish	3	3	2	2	2
Other	n.a.	2	1	2	2
None	n.a.	1	4	9	14

SOURCE: *National Election Study* (Ann Arbor: Interuniversity Consortium for Political and Social Research, various years).

and hence answers to questions, and those without. More to the statistical point, however, were three other developments.[17]

First, there was a rising net gain for the evangelicals from familiar patterns of religious shuffling. Upwardly mobile Americans had long been more likely to move from evangelical to mainline denominations, while the more devout had been more likely to move from mainline to evangelical. The net of this balance from the 1960s swung increasingly in an evangelical direction. Beyond that, the mainline Protestant denominations were especially likely to lose their younger members, at the least during the young adult years, a tendency much more effectively countered among evangelicals. Lastly, the populations that identified with evangelical denominations were growing more indigenously—they were having more children—than those that identified with the mainline.

Yet there was more. In a development very much like the one that produced the New Politics Democrats, a major social trend that benefited the evangelical Protestants across the postwar years did *not* produce its normal countervailing tendency, at least within the first generation of partisan elites. In this, the economic growth that benefited most especially the American South but secondarily the Rocky Mountain states as the postwar years passed—these were the regions that had long been most congenial to evangelical Protestantism—did not cause a shift to mainline Protestantism within those regions as they prospered. Figure 3.10 shows the distribution of evangelical Protestants by state in the modern United States.

Such a distribution was, on its face, a picture of where evangelical elites might expect to do best (and worst) when—if—they reentered American politics. Yet all this could still in principle have produced any number of different results, from extended quiescence to expanded political liberalism. What gave it both political relevance and partisan defini-

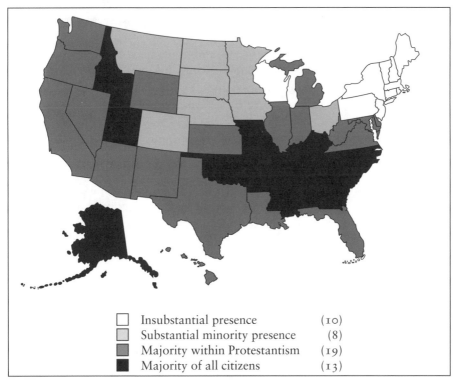

☐	Insubstantial presence	(10)
▨	Substantial minority presence	(8)
▨	Majority within Protestantism	(19)
■	Majority of all citizens	(13)

FIGURE 3.10

EVANGELICAL PROTESTANTS AS A SHARE

OF TOTAL STATE POPULATION

SOURCE: Martin B. Bradley et al., *Churches and Church Membership in the United States, 1990* (Atlanta: Glenmary Research Center, 1992), 12–36.

tion, then, was a set of associated *elite* changes, and these were to be aggressively conservative. Once more, two among them were particularly important.

The first was a movement by the late 1960s and early 1970s among conservative political strategists of no apparent religious conviction to search out new or emergent constituencies that might serve as a counterweight to the New Politics Democrats—but that might really serve to create a new Republican (and thereby conservative) majority. These individuals had practical experience in politics, and they had the desire to see evangelical Protestants play a newly active (and conservative) role in it. They just lacked the means to make that happen.

The means were instead the province of a new generation of evangelical Protestant ministers, and they were thus the key insurgent elites in the entire movement—key, at least, to its place in postwar politics. After the great split in American Protestantism, and quite apart from postwar economic trends, the evangelical denominations had needed to create their own seminaries, consciously responding to their own theological and organizational needs. By the 1970s, these seminaries were producing a generation of trained ministers who were (1) very much a part of the social base of the new, postwar, evangelical Protestantism, but (2) very much aware of the intellectual currents, albeit opposed to many of them, that were sweeping society.

They were additionally different from their nominal predecessors in possessing an expanded resource base. For if the areas of evangelical strength had benefited disproportionately from economic growth while *not* losing their upwardly mobile members, then the old income and education gaps between them and the rest of American society should have been closing, and in fact they were. As a result, the new generation of evangelical Protestant ministers were themselves increasingly suburban rather than rural, with middle- rather than working-class constituencies. Moreover, they were attuned to contemporary *technology,* especially television, where they were arguably the first generation of American religious leaders to make full and aggressive use of the medium.

They were also repelled not just by a variety of trends in American society but by the very different interpretations of these, verging on explicit endorsement, from the New Politics Democrats. Morality in public life was to be a unifying theme across all the evangelical Protestant surges, from the Great Awakening of the 1730s to the New Christian Right of the 1970s. In earlier incarnations, this had implied religious freedom, social leveling, abolitionism, and temperance. One unifying trait with modern relevance, however, was that they followed from an emphasis on personal salvation and a subsequently godly life on earth, the signature characteristics of evangelical Protestantism. Established churches, inherited titles, slavery, and drunkenness had been obvious barriers to these in an earlier day. Such wellsprings had not shifted by the late 1960s, but the institutionalized affronts to them, in the view of this new evangelical elite—the barriers to personal salvation and a godly life in our time—had changed dramatically.

Among these, the single greatest symbolic affront was probably the Supreme Court decisions removing prayer from the public schools in the early 1960s: *Engel* v. *Vitale* (370 U.S., 421, 1962), along with *Abington School District* v. *Schempp* and *Murray* v. *Curlett* (374 U.S., 203, 1963). A policy so comprehensive and an assault so explicit reached into the lives of most mass identifiers within evangelical Protestantism. By its very universality and its frontal character, it laid a groundwork that degenerative social trends could never lay.

In the demonology of governmental assaults on moral fundamentals, however, the school prayer cases were to be joined by a stream of other Court decisions, the most consequential of which was surely *Roe* v. *Wade* (410 U.S., 113, 1973). By legitimizing abortion nationwide, the decision not only increased sharply a previously proscribed activity. It also augmented the *appearance* of an increase even more, as previously private (and often illegal) abortions came into the legal public record (table 3.9, part A, p. 122).

Nevertheless, abortion remained only the most dramatic touchstone—the symbolic litmus—for a set of larger trends in American society, trends that dwarfed the impact of any (and perhaps all) Supreme Court decisions (table 3.9, part B, p. 122). And here, the perceived breakdown of the American family was the diagnostic element: the fate of the family, along with an emphasis on family protection and family values, was to be the great rallying cry through which evangelical elites mobilized their mass constituency in politics. At one end of the causal chain, the rising tide of divorce was the definitional indicator. Rising illegitimacy was then an even more pernicious product of the decline of the family. So, at the end of that causal chain, was rising crime.

The new generation of evangelical ministers did not need secular conservative strategists to call these trends to their attention, to frame them negatively, or to suggest that conservative solutions were the right ones. What such strategists could do for them was to help the evangelical ministers form local, regional, and then national linkages—networks—to pursue a reintroduction of traditional values into public life. Along the

TABLE 3.9
SOCIAL TRENDS RELATED TO "FAMILY VALUES"
IN THE POSTWAR UNITED STATES

A. The litmus test

	Number of legal abortions			Number of legal abortions
1990	1,429,577		1979	1,251,921
1989	1,396,658		1978	1,157,776
1988	1,371,285		1977	1,079,430
1987	1,353,671		1976	988,287
1986	1,326,112		1975	854,853
1985	1,328,570		1974	763,476
1984	1,333,521		1973	615,831
1983	1,268,987		1972	586,750
1982	1,303,980		1971	485,816
1981	1,300,760		1970	193,491
1980	1,297,606			

B. The degenerative trends

	1. Divorce		2. Illegitimacy		3. Crime	
	Raw number (1,000s)	Rate per 1,000	Raw number (1,000s)	Rate per 1,000	Raw number (1,000s)	Rate per 1,000
1990	1,175	4.7	1,225	43.8	12,430	66.5
1980	1,189	5.2	666	29.4	11,110	66.5
1970	708	3.5	339	26.4	5,208	34.9
1960	393	2.2	224	21.6	1,096	8.8
1950	385	2.6	142	14.1	737	7.6
1940	256	2.0	90	7.1	662	8.9

SOURCES: Abortion data from U.S. Center for Disease Control and Prevention, *Morbidity and Mortality Weekly Report,* vol. 46 (no. SS-4, 8 August 1997):49. Divorce, illegitimacy, and crime data from *Historical Statistics of the United States, Colonial Times to 1970* (Washington, D.C.: Department of Commerce, 1975), and *Statistical Abstract of the United States* (Washington, D.C.: Department of Commerce, various years). Divorce rate is calculated per total population; illegitimate birthrate is calculated per total number of unmarried women; crime rate is per total population.

way, they could also help them add techniques such as direct-mail fund raising to their arsenal, to supplement personal (and televised) theological appeals. Christopher Soper catches the absolute centrality of this new Protestant elite in responding:

Interpreting the Bible to condemn a social practice is a necessary condition for evangelical activism, but it is not a sufficient condition. Human society is full of "sins" which evangelical Christians deplore, but not all of them serve as conduits for political mobilization. Moral issues are not necessarily political ones. . . .

Evangelical leaders have an important role to play in helping to form groups. Leaders need to convince evangelicals that a social practice is sinful and that the consequences of that particular sin are grave enough to demand their political involvement. Leaders in the early temperance movement in America and Britain had the intractable problem of convincing sceptical evangelicals that there was a biblical warrant and a political necessity for temperance societies. . . . Temperance did not become a political passion until evangelicals were convinced that drinking threatened their religious goals of the conversion of the sinner and the reformation of his social world. . . .

This does not mean that any issue, given the right set of leaders, has an equal capacity to mobilize evangelicals. Evangelical theology, with its stress on personal faith and practice, leads believers to be more concerned with political issues which can be interpreted in terms of an individual's lifestyle, behavior, and morality than those issues which are corporate in nature.[18]

The result was a plethora of politically relevant organizations, all built essentially around the traditional position on cultural values. The one among them that was to bring such organizations to national prominence (and national media attention) was the Moral Majority, a nationwide network of fundamentalist Protestant ministers. But it was joined by Christian Voice, the ideological monitoring arm of the movement; by the Religious Roundtable, a coordinating body reaching out to other denominations that shared conservative theologies; and by the National Christian Action Coalition, a policy development arm. These were joined additionally by such family-oriented organizations as Concerned Women of America and Focus on the Family, which proved to have greater staying power than the first influx of more narrowly political bodies.

Given that such organizations were built on conservative social and cultural principles and that they were partly a *response* to the (liberal) social and cultural preferences of the New Politics Democrats, it might appear by hindsight that they were destined to follow an obvious partisan trajectory—into the Republican Party. Yet their social base among rank-and-file evangelicals simultaneously preferred some policy options on which the Democratic Party was arguably more representative. Moreover, specific, potentially catalytic, partisan events at first argued for a much more conditional outcome.

The initial contact for most nonevangelical Americans with evangelical Protestantism in politics was actually the election of a Democrat, Jimmy Carter in 1976, with his evident and easy public references to evangelical themes. Carter, however, proved a total disappointment to the newly formed network of evangelical Protestant ministers. In operation, on social and cultural grounds, he ran an administration built around New Politics Democrats. There were no governmental initiatives to restore the place of prayer; abortion rights were safeguarded and extended. Accordingly, it was only when Ronald Reagan made deliberate overtures to the Protestant evangelical leadership in 1980, when Democrat Carter was succeeded by Republican Reagan as president, and when Reagan spent the next eight years articulating Moral Majority themes, that the partisan die was effectively cast.

None of this came without growing pains, for a population that had disdained politics for half a century, with a mass base still lagging the national average in personal resources, and with an elite still riven by important doctrinal differences. The Moral Majority, in fact, did not survive the Reagan years. And George Bush, who did, was a quintessential mainline Protestant, leading some analysts to pronounce the demise of the New Christian Right.

However provocative, this pronouncement was also premature, for the Moral Majority was in turn succeeded by the Christian Coalition, playing the same role for the 1990s but with a broader numerical base, a more professionalized staff, and a more comprehensive political armory, both in practical techniques and in policy proposals. Founded in 1989 by the Reverend Marion "Pat" Robertson, a Pentecostal minister, but under the institutionalizing direction of Ralph Reed, an established Republican operative, the Christian Coalition was to bring the organizational voice of the evangelical Protestant elite to a new high. Like the AFL-CIO, the other postwar coordinating body that it most resembled in structural terms, the Christian Coalition was to engage actively in both electioneering and lobbying.

In operation, the organization was a curious amalgam. It claimed 1,200 chapters nationwide, with a membership of 1.7 million and a mailing list of 30 million. It had an annual budget of $20 million, and it did distribute 33 million voter guides in 1994. Much of this material, however, actually went out through 60,000 churches, and the links among its *pastors* remained the key to operational effectiveness. The key to motivating them, in turn, remained such familiar cultural concerns as opposition to abortion, along with some new additions, such as opposition to the "endorsement" of homosexuality. Its annual "Road to Victory" conferences every September were the national focus for the electioneering effort, rallying activists for a voter registration drive, then an issue awareness drive, and then a get-out-the-vote drive in their areas.

In any case, if the network had appeared defunct by the late 1980s, it appeared to be at maximum influence by 1994, when Republicans recaptured control of Congress for the first time in forty years, with the active support of the Christian Coalition. By that point, the group appeared to be a substantial faction within the state Republican parties of at least three-fifths of the states and the dominant faction within a third, though the identity of such parties inevitably shifted with changes in their state and local leaderships. Figure 3.11 (p. 126) suggests both that this strength was related to the underlying strength of evangelical Protestantism and that the localized vitality of the Christian Coalition owed something to its own organizational initiatives (or lack of same) as well.

The 1994 victory, in any event, gave increased emphasis to the national lobbying effort. The Christian Coalition had already been publishing a congressional rating system, scoring all congressmen and senators on a number of votes central to Coalition preferences and then publicizing these scores in constituencies. The 1994 result allowed them to bring some of these together in a "Contract with the American Family," which suggested both the thrust and the range of relevant proposals.[19] The result was also the single largest organized interest within the national Republican Party.

It was not, however, an interest that fit without stress. Many wealthier, more educated, more suburban, more corporate Republicans were also mainline Protestants, even seculars, and were often liberals rather than conservatives on social and cultural issues. The addition of evangelical Protestants to the national Republican coalition could thus not be accomplished without diminishing their proportionate presence and their policy preferences. In related fashion, the *extraction* of evangelical Protestants from the Democratic Party was also not unstressful, nor successful in any linear fashion. On economic rather than cultural grounds, many evangelicals still "belonged" to the Democrats, being less well-off and having more need for basic social welfare programs. They were still a crucial audience for appeals to defect from the Democratic Party, and such appeals were often successful, but evangelical Democrats did not reliably become Republicans as a result.

The evangelical Protestant elite, however, did not any longer experience these tensions. Or rather, it resolved them by emphasizing moral

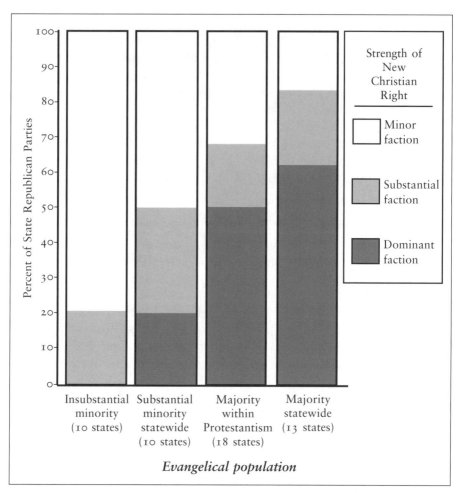

FIGURE 3.11

EVANGELICAL PROTESTANTS, THE NEW CHRISTIAN RIGHT,
AND REPUBLICAN PARTIES IN THE STATES

SOURCES: See figure 3.10; and "Who's Got the Power? Levels of Christian Right Strength in
the State Republican Party Organizations," *Campaigns & Elections*, September 1994, 22.

conservatism—social and cultural conservatism—and by giving priority to it. Their organizations reliably followed suit, and this in turn produced an institutionalized resolution. Yet in doing so, they were very much trading off one set of values within their larger constituency for another: its cultural conservatism over its economic moderation, to create a uniformly conservative presence. In this, they were the mirror image of the New Politics Democratic elite: trading off the economic moderation of *their* larger constituency for its cultural liberalism, and hence creating a uniformly liberal presence. In doing so, both were underlining the importance of elite eruptions, and elite circulations, in American politics.

Conclusion: The Circulation of Elites Revisited

> In fact, there are many cases in which conclusions drawn from residues of group-persistence (or, in other words, by "intuition") come much closer to realities than conclusions that are drawn from the combination instinct and go to make up the derivations of that pseudo-science which, in social matters, continues to be mistaken for experimental science. And, again in many cases, these latter derivations seem so harmful that the society which is not eager to decline or perish must necessarily reject them.
>
> But not less deleterious are the consequences of an exclusive predominance of Class II residues, not only in the physical arts and sciences, where their harmfulness is obvious, but in social matters as well, where it is perfectly apparent that but for the combination instinct and the use of experimental thinking, there could be no progress. So there is no stopping, either, at the extreme where Class II residues predominate; and a new oscillation sets in heading back toward the first extreme where Class I residues predominated.
>
> And so the pendulum continues swinging back and forth from one extreme to the other, indefinitely.
>
> — Pareto, *General Compendium of Sociology,* 359 [1026]

The rise and fall of partisan elites across postwar American politics did not coincide neatly with the passing of either decades or generations. Nevertheless, there were two obvious arrivals at the beginning of this period, in the immediate postwar years. These were organized labor and the Modern Republicans. And there were two obvious incarnations on the political landscape at the end of this period, at the beginning of the post–Cold War. These were the New Politics Democrats and the evangelical Protestants. If all four seem superficially unrelated, to each other and to the key elites that preceded them, all are at least united not just in embodying the overall notion of a circulation of elites but in offering all the signature characteristics for such a circulation. As it turned out, they were additionally united, in pairwise comparisons, by the way that the forces feeding into one social group also fed into another, or even by the way that the behavior of one partisan elite served partially to reshape the forces that would ultimately result in the appearance of a successor.

For example, the mass base from which organized labor had emerged was a social stratum of long standing, the industrial working class. Moreover, this was not really even expanded during the (depression) years when it began to generate a newly consequential, incipiently partisan elite. What *was* new was a vastly expanded organizational embodiment, tracing to the NLRA of 1935 and culminating in creation of the AFL-CIO (and COPE) in 1955. With it came, in a remarkably short period, a newly professionalized elite—an extensive labor bureaucracy—that seized upon the rise of unionized labor and converted it not just into an explicitly political operation but, this time, into a key component of the national Democratic coalition. In doing so, this newly ascendant elite both broadened the policy focus of labor in American politics to include social welfare issues, not just labor-management concerns, *and* guaranteed that this focus would remain central to Democratic Party appeals for another generation.

By contrast, while the social stratum that produced the Modern Republicans was also not arguably new—it had arrived in the late nineteenth century and spread in the early twentieth—it was nevertheless strikingly expanded in the late 1940s and early 1950s. In turn, this expansion brought substantive values (and policy preferences) that did distinguish it from earlier incarnations, as well as from organized labor on one side and regular Republicans on the other. Yet, unlike labor, it never produced any formal embodiment, much less an overhead agency. Instead, it percolated into politics on an individual basis, by virtue of distinctive values and by means of official party deference. Perhaps surprisingly, such an amorphous structure was not obviously a bar to influence. The nature of presidential Republicanism, and occasionally the operation of the presidency itself; the character of the Senate as a legislative institution; the lines of conflict within the Republican Party in the House; and the potential for building moderate cross-party coalitions in American politics generally: all these followed crucially from the presence of the Modern Republicans on the political landscape.

The New Politics Democrats were different yet again. Like the Modern Republicans, they issued from a vastly expanded social stratum, the nontraditional but rapidly growing stratum of white-collar (really college-graduate) Democratic Party identifiers. Like the Modern Republicans more than organized labor, these New Politics Democrats were never to have an overhead agency of any sort. On the other hand, a shifting array of issue and cause groups would prove remarkably and continually successful at pumping substance into what it meant to be a New Politics Democrat: antiwar, profeminist, environmental, and proabortion activism; opposition to social control; support of homosexual rights and lifestyles. Unlike the Modern Republicans and much more like organized labor, as a result, these New Politics Democrats were able to attempt self-consciously to take over their party, the Democratic Party, without the need for some overhead coordinating agency. In the process, they kept what were essentially *cultural* concerns at the center of American politics.

The last major concentrated elite input to postwar American politics—the last great surge of postwar elites to date—actually sprang from the group on this list least new to American politics. Indeed, while evangelical Protestantism was clearly growing again, it was not even enjoying a resurgence particularly noteworthy in historical terms. Like the Modern Republicans, the evangelical Protestant elite—the New Christian Right—did experience its resurgence under changed conditions, and with an altered programmatic core. Otherwise, however, its social base was already much more clearly formed and focused. As with unionized labor, it was the *organized* flow into politics that was important, and it was the resulting issue organizations, along with their overhead agencies—the Moral Majority and then the Christian Coalition—that were the real base for a new partisan elite. Like organized labor, the New Christian Right became the largest single organized presence within its chosen party, the Republican rather than the Democratic Party. Despite these structural similarities, it was the substance propounded by the New Politics Democrats that really served as the catalyst to draw the evangelicals back into politics: that same cluster of essentially cultural issues, the proper operative values for daily social life.

Political change is certainly evident in such a summary, change in the structural characteristics of new partisan elites and change in the policy preferences that they brought with them into politics. Yet the extent of this change is still understated by a simple compare-and-contrast approach to four key elites. For, in fact, the fortunes of each pair of postwar elites did not just feed off one another: Modern Republicans in response to the rise of organized labor, evangelical Protestants in response to the rise of New Politics Democrats. Instead, the rise (and then the fortunes) of the first pair was also intimately related to the rise (and fortunes) of the second. In this change lies more than just a difference in identity among four elite contenders. In it lies much of the central change in American politics across all the postwar years.

To be specific: the forces that created an incipient base for the New Politics Democrats, upon which they eventually capitalized under the impetus of specific events, were actually forces that were remaking organized labor at the same time. Analyses of the fortunes of union labor often focus on the declining share of the traditional workforce that a more white-collar and more highly specialized economy would leave in its hands, and the maneuvering around these trends is in fact central to any labor chronicle. But for purposes of the analysis of partisan elites, it is more important to note that these were the same forces that would eventuate in the appearance of the New Politics Democrats. Moreover, and even more to the point, they were changing *organized labor* in ways that, if anything, would integrate it, too, into the New Politics coalition.

Table 3.10 suggests, forcefully, that where "old labor" was blue collar and private sector, "new labor" was increasingly white collar and public sector. The identity of the winners in this "competition" tells that story: the National Education Association (NEA) over the United Auto Workers (UAW). So does the identity of the unions that appear only on the modern list: not just NEA, but AFT (American Federation of Teachers) and AFSCME (American Federation of State, County, and Municipal Employees). As, for that matter, does the identity of those from the old list that go *off:* UBCJ (United Brotherhood of Carpenters and Joiners), UMW (United Mine Workers of America), and ILGWU (International Ladies' Garment Workers' Union). By 1990—a remarkable statistic—only 10.8 percent of private-sector employees were unionized, but 38.7 percent of public-sector employees were.

One result was that organized labor was becoming more like the New Politics Democrats structurally. A second result was that it was becoming more like them substantively as well. New growth areas for organized labor arrived at a point in time when the New Politics Democrats were emerging to elite prominence, so getting along with the active Democratic Party meant adjusting to New Politics Democratic priorities. Moreover, new labor operatives were coming up through the same social milieu—even the same educational structure—as New Politics Democrats, and thus being exposed to the same substantive concerns. At bottom, finally, blue-collar and private-sector unions appeared to be led naturally toward social welfare issues, toward programs that would support the ordinary economic well-being of their members. Just as white-collar and public-sector unions appeared to be led naturally toward quality-of-

TABLE 3.10

THE LARGEST LABOR UNIONS — 1952 AND 1993

(MEMBERSHIP IN THOUSANDS)

1952		1993	
1. United Automobile, Aircraft and Agricultural Implement Workers Union	1,185	1. National Education Association	2,000
2. United Steelworkers Union	1,100	2. International Brotherhood of Teamsters	1,700
3. International Brotherhood of Teamsters	1,000	3. American Federation of State, County and Municipal Employees	1,300
4. United Brotherhood of Carpenters and Joiners	750	4. United Food and Commercial Workers International Union	1,300
5. International Association of Machinists	699	5. Service Employees International Union	1,000
6. United Mine Workers of America	600	6. United Automobile, Aerospace and Agricultural Implement Workers of America	862
7. International Brotherhood of Electrical Workers	500	7. International Brotherhood of Electrical Workers	845
8. Hotel and Restaurant Employees' International Alliance	402	8. American Federation of Teachers	830
9. International Ladies' Garment Workers' Union	390	9. Communications Workers of America	600
10. International Hod Carriers, Building and Common Laborers Union	386	10. International Association of Machinists and Aerospace Workers	550
		United Steelworkers of America	550

SOURCE: *The Public Perspective: A Roper Center Review of Public Opinion and Polling* 5 (July/August 1994): 9.

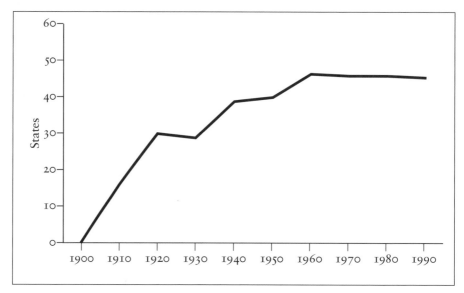

FIGURE 3.12A
PROCEDURAL REFORM AND THE SPREAD
OF PARTICIPATORY INSTITUTIONS FOR PARTY BUSINESS —
GUBERNATORIAL NOMINATIONS VIA PRIMARY ELECTIONS:
THE REPUBLICANS

SOURCE: *The Book of the States* (Lexington, Ky.: Council of State Governments, various years).

life concerns, in part because the public sector could grow only if these concerns were advanced, in part because blue-collar, private-sector unions had already helped ensure their basic economic security. In any case, these were in fact the *same* concerns motivating New Politics Democrats generally.

The evolution of partisan elites within the Republican Party was distinctly different, and it is the fate of the Modern Republicans that tells that tale. But, ironically, for the postwar elite that had always operated most informally of all those on the list, it was formal changes that proved most consequential—and most deleterious. Not that informal changes were inconsequential. At the point when the social base for the Modern Republicans was newly ascendant and notably emergent, in an explosion of middle management and the managerial suburbs, Modern Republicans were the main alternative thrust within Republicanism to the regular party. By the time the great corporations were not so obviously the story of American economic life and the suburbs were instead the story of so-

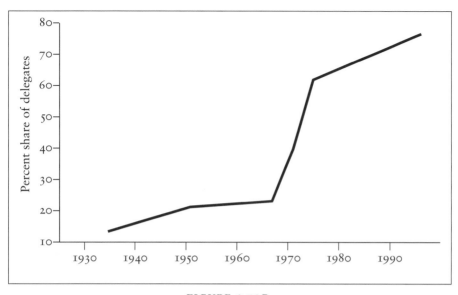

FIGURE 3.12B

PROCEDURAL REFORM AND THE SPREAD
OF PARTICIPATORY INSTITUTIONS FOR PARTY BUSINESS—
PRESIDENTIAL NOMINATIONS VIA CANDIDATE PRIMARY:
THE REPUBLICANS

SOURCES: Byron E. Shafer, *Bifurcated Politics: Evolution and Reform in the National Party Convention* (Cambridge, Mass.: Harvard University Press, 1988), 90; *Congressional Quarterly Weekly Report* 1996, various issues.

cial life for *everyone,* the main alternative to the regular party within Republicanism was the evangelical Protestants—and the remnants of Modern Republicanism were part of the regular party.

Yet central to all this was also a procedural change, for the Modern Republicans had always been dependent on deference from the official party structure, as well as on their success at the presidential level within it. As figure 3.12A (p. 132) shows, the formal means for ensuring this deference, and thus for allowing party leaders to pick Modern Republicans as candidates even when they lacked a sufficient mass base to claim nominations on their own, had been eroding at the state level for many years. After 1968—at the impetus, again ironically, of the New Politics Democrats—this ability disappeared at the presidential level as well, and with remarkable speed (figure 3.12B). With it went an important substantive, and not just structural, influence in American politics.

A tolerance for social welfare programs and an active dislike of cultural traditionalism, by an elite that had always lacked the mass base of small-business Republicanism and now lacked the base of the evangelical Protestants as well, was not a formula for success under these (nondeferential) arrangements, where the power of what became recognized as "hot button" (largely cultural) issues was evidently magnified. It was also not conceivably a formula for merging—melding—with the New Christian Right. The Modern Republicans, accordingly and over time, folded quietly into the body of their old uneasy partners, the Republican regulars. Their social base did not disappear entirely, so they did occasionally generate the individual (if increasingly idiosyncratic) Modern Republican successor. But that was all.

On the other hand, policy impacts from such changes, impressive as the changes are, were not guaranteed by the details of the change itself. Which is to say that major changes in the social structure of key partisan elites, across a major period of time, are still not the same as major impacts on the *outcomes* of public policy. In truth, it would be hard to argue that a world in which organized labor and Modern Republicans contributed the great elite infusions to the effort to shape policy conflict was a world that would handle any given issue in the same way as a world in which New Politics Democrats and evangelical Protestants contributed the major new partisan elites. But can the question of impact be taken further than that?

Surely it can also be taken to the difference in the overall agenda for political conflict, and to elite contributions to the content of that agenda. And here the difference remains striking. A large tranche of immediate postwar *partisan* conflict was over labor-management issues themselves; a huge tranche involved the social welfare issues that seemed integral to a politics formed along labor-management lines. The rise of a comprehensive labor elite was obviously central to keeping these issues at the center of American politics. While the Modern Republicans might be argued to have defined themselves in part in response to organized labor, their presence in politics was actually a further reinforcement to a concentration on these concerns.

By contrast, these issues were not central to the New Politics Democrats, born, as they were, out of civil rights, antiwar, environmentalist, and feminist conflicts. While New Politics elites were certainly not hostile to social welfare programs, neither were these a priority, especially by comparison to the cultural issues that remained central to their concerns. The evangelical Protestants then mirrored this from the other side. Like New Politics Democrats, evangelical Protestant elites attempted to add economic issues—lower taxes, a balanced budget—to their cultural and (especially) religious core. But again, *priority* was clearly on the latter, especially for the mass base and, in truth, most especially for the elites whenever they were in their sharpest conflict with New Politics Democrats.

So there was a sharply different agenda to national politics at the beginning as opposed to the end of the postwar period, and the preferences of ascendant elites were a crucial aspect of agenda change. This did not mean that many other issues were not simultaneously forced into politics by changes in the larger environment, changes that were not controlled by partisan elites of any stripe. North Korea invades South Korea; widespread rioting breaks out in American cities; OPEC induces an "oil shock" to the economy; AIDS surfaces as a major menace to public health: these issues were not the preferred policy focus for any of these elites and were certainly not the product of their individual agendas. Yet even here, four key elites could have been expected to approach each of these concerns in a different and distinctive manner, so their presence did powerfully affect the way in which such definitionally "extraneous" political issues were addressed.

Still, there are caveats. First and foremost, an agenda is not legislation. Indeed, organized labor elites in the 1950s, like evangelical Protestant elites in the 1990s, would themselves have emphasized how limited and frustrating their actual policy successes had been.[20] Setting an agenda for conflict is a task that an emergent elite has a fair chance of accomplishing. Seeing it converted into law involves that elite in negotiations—or contests—with all the other elite claimants, ascendant or receding, where the outcome is not nearly so obvious.

Which leads on to a second caveat: key insurgent elites were not the elite universe, not by a long shot. Other elites were propelling (or sustaining) other items on the agenda, and they were prevailing (or retreating) on all such items in ways that affected their ultimate legislative fate. The particular interpretation of the circulation of elites used here, for example, leads away from two other obvious and hugely influential sets of specialized partisan actors: the southern Democrats and the regular Republicans. Or rather, what it really does is treat them as established context rather than operational focus. Likewise, the particular *periodization* used here leads away from a lesser but still important partisan infusion falling between these two pairs during the postwar years, that of black Democrats.

This is not the place to tell these other stories, although elements of the first two have surfaced in constructing the ones that had to be told. Nevertheless, the success of organized labor and the Modern Republicans, both in imposing an agenda and in securing policy details, was heavily influenced by the behavior of the southern Democrats and the regular Republicans—just as the success of the New Politics Democrats and evangelical Protestants was heavily influenced by details of the *evolution* of the southern Democrats and regular Republicans, by the time the former became major forces on the political scene.

Still, with these caveats entered, the share of the story of postwar American politics captured by this particular focus on the circulation of elites remains impressive. The postwar period has not proved lacking in major candidates for elite influence on American politics. Indeed, four bracket this period in a major way. As a result, the entire structure of specialized political actors—especially, for these purposes, partisan political elites—is not lacking in major transformations either. There are some structural similarities between elites at the beginning and end of the postwar years, but even these are mixed differently. Otherwise, the difference in social identity and substantive focus is large indeed.

An analytical focus on these elites does provide a further discipline. From one side, their social base, leadership component, and distinctive values require specific attention. From the other side, the roots and products of these elements require specific attention as well. The first demands a cross-sectional focus. The second demands a longitudinal focus. By the same token, application of this analytic focus to these specific elites does at least touch upon the main postwar alternatives, both for alternative partisan elites and for alternative policy preferences. If such a focus does not present these alternatives in the same detail, there must be some backdrop and some foreground to any analysis.

Under a focus that offers *this* backdrop and *this* foreground, the differences in the partisan character of postwar politics remain striking. Its structure is as different as organized labor, Modern Republicans, New Politics Democrats, and evangelical Protestants. Its substance is as different as social welfare, labor relations, alternative lifestyles, and traditional values. Pareto, perhaps inevitably, would have found such differences to be important, to be inherent, and to be constantly undergoing change:

> In the economic system, the nonlogical element is relegated entirely to tastes and disregarded, since tastes are taken as data of fact. One might wonder whether the same thing might not be done for the social system, whether we might not relegate the non-logical element to the residues, then take the residues as data of fact and proceed to examine the logical conduct that originates in the residues. That would yield a science similar to pure, or even to applied, economics. But unfortunately, the similarity

ceases when we come to the question of correspondences with reality.

The hypotheses that, in satisfying their tastes human beings perform economic actions which may on the whole be considered logical is not too far removed from realities, and the inferences from those hypotheses yield a general form of the economic phenomenon in which divergences from reality are few and not very great, save in certain cases (most important among them the matter of savings). Far removed from realities, instead, is the hypothesis that human beings draw logical inferences from residues and then proceed to act accordingly. In activity based on residues human beings use derivations more frequently than strictly logical reasonings, and therefore to try to predict their conduct by considering their manner of reasoning would be to lose all contact with the real.

— Pareto, *Compendium of General Sociology,* 287 [831]

Acknowledgments

Kurt Strovink began the research on which this chapter is based; Brian Bell filled several crucial holes along the way; and Robert McMahon did the vast bulk of the supportive digging. Robert, in particular, was central to its tables. Steve Moyle then did the graphics work to bring them to life. Elaine Herman converted all this into an actual document, and Maureen Baker managed the total process. I also benefited particularly from focused conversations with David Kennedy of Stanford University, David Magleby of Brigham Young University, and Steven Gillon and Daniel Howe of Oxford University. I thank them all, even as I absolve them of any errors in presentation or argument.

Notes

1. In our time, such elites also acquired that essential badge of newness and consequence, the cover story on national news magazines. For the most recent example, see "America's Christian Crusader," *Time,* 15 May 1995, along with its cover story: Jeffrey H. Birnbaum, "The Gospel According to Ralph: Reed's Burgeoning Christian Coalition Evokes Zeal and Fear as It Mobilizes to Dominate the Political Center," 26–33.

2. Originally published as Vilfredo Pareto, *Trattato di Sociologia Generale,* 3 vols. (Florence: Barbera, 1916). The version used here is Pareto, *Compendium of General Sociology,* abr. Giulio Farina, trans. Elizabeth Abbott (Minneapolis: University of Minnesota Press, 1980). This version provides the original section numbers to go with its editing and abridgement, so that the citation for this quote about the "heterogeneousness of society"—and the form

followed throughout—is Pareto, *Compendium of General Sociology,* 271 [791], where 271 is the page from the abridgement/translation, and 791 is the original section number.

3. The historical literature on American labor and unionization is less useful for subsequent analysis than it might be, since so much of it is written from the perspective of what "should have happened" or "did not happen." But a straightforward general history is Philip Taft, *Organized Labor in American History* (New York: Harper and Row, 1964); and an extremely helpful interpretive overview is Robert H. Zieger, *American Workers, American Unions, 1920–1985* (Baltimore: Johns Hopkins University Press, 1986). On the legal framework, see Milton Derber and Edwin Young, eds., *Labor and the New Deal* (Madison: University of Wisconsin Press, 1957); along with William E. Forbath, *Law and the Shaping of the American Labor Movement* (Cambridge, Mass.: Harvard University Press, 1991). See also Irving Bernstein, *Turbulent Years: A History of the American Worker, 1933–1941* (Boston: Houghton Mifflin, 1969).

4. Michael Barone, *Our Country: The Shaping of America from Roosevelt to Reagan* (New York: Free Press, 1990), 100.

5. Both citations are from Vivian Vale, *Labour in American Politics* (London: Routledge and Kegan Paul, 1971), 34. More generally, see Louis S. Reed, *The Labor Philosophy of Samuel Gompers* (New York: Kennikat Press, 1966).

6. For the evolution of the law, see Harry A. Millis and Emily C. Brown, *From the Wagner Act to Taft-Hartley: A Study of National Labor Policy and Labor Relations* (Chicago: University of Chicago Press, 1950); and R. Alton Lee, *Truman and Taft-Hartley: A Question of Mandate* (Lexington: University of Kentucky Press, 1966). Among postwar investigations of labor that include the story of unification are Vale, *Labour in American Politics;* Graham K. Wilson, *Unions in American National Politics* (New York: St. Martin's Press, 1979); and Joseph C. Goulden, *Meany* (New York: Atheneum, 1972). More generally, see Derek C. Bok and John T. Dunlop, *Labor and the American Community* (New York: Simon and Schuster, 1970); Robert Price, *Profiles of Union Growth: A Comparative Statistical Portrait of Eight Countries* (Oxford: Basil Blackwell, 1980); and Thomas A. Kochan, Harry C. Katz, and Robert B. McKersie, *The Transformation of American Industrial Relations* (New York: Basic Books, 1986). See also Bennett M. Berger, *Working-Class Suburb: A Study of Auto Workers in Suburbia* (Berkeley: University of California Press, 1960).

7. Especially helpful in constructing the overall picture are Alfred D. Chandler Jr., *The Visible Hand: The Managerial Revolution in American Business* (Cambridge, Mass.: Harvard University Press, 1977); *Masters to Managers: Historical and Comparative Perspectives on American Employers,* ed. Sanford M. Jacoby (New York: Columbia University Press, 1991); *Postwar Economic Trends in the United States,* ed. Ralph E. Freeman (New York: Harper and Brothers, 1960); *The American Economy in Transition,* ed. Martin Feldstein (Chicago: University of Chicago Press, 1980); and Edwin M. Epstein,

The Corporation in American Politics (Englewood Cliffs, N.J.: Prentice Hall, 1969). See also John H. Bunzel, *The American Small Businessman* (New York: Knopf, 1962); and John Kenneth Galbraith, *The New Industrial State* (Boston: Houghton Mifflin, 1967).

8. Social scientists, too, turned to the question of whether a "new American" was emerging to go with all of this. Those who said yes included David Riesman, with Nathan Glazer and Reuel Denny, *The Lonely Crowd: A Study of the Changing American Character* (New Haven: Yale University Press, 1950); and William H. Whyte Jr., *The Organization Man* (New York: Simon and Schuster, 1956). Those who said no included David M. Potter, *People of Plenty: Economic Abundance and the American Character* (Chicago: University of Chicago Press, 1954); and Seymour Martin Lipset, *The First New Nation: The United States in Historical and Comparative Perspective* (New York: Basic Books, 1963).

9. William H. Chafe, *The Unfinished Journey: America since World War II,* 2d ed. (Oxford: Oxford University Press, 1991), 117. See also Kenneth T. Jackson, *Crabgrass Frontier: The Suburbanization of the United States* (New York: Oxford University Press, 1985).

10. Useful overviews of the situation within the national Republican Party include George H. Mayer, *The Republican Party, 1854–1964* (New York: Oxford University Press, 1964); Charles O. Jones, *The Republican Party in American Politics* (New York: Macmillan, 1965); Stephen Hess and David S. Broder, *The Republican Establishment: The Present and Future of the G.O.P.* (New York: Harper and Row, 1967); A. James Reichley, *The Life of the Parties: A History of American Political Parties* (New York: Free Press, 1992). But see especially Nicol C. Rae, *The Decline and Fall of the Liberal Republicans: From 1952 to the Present* (New York: Oxford University Press, 1989).

11. Particularly useful on the population bulge is Richard A. Easterlin, *Birth and Fortune: The Impact of Numbers on Personal Welfare* (New York: Basic Books, 1980); on the student "shock troops," James Miller, *Democracy Is in the Streets: From Port Huron to the Siege of Chicago* (Cambridge, Mass.: Harvard University Press, 1994); and on the New Politics coalition, with apologies, Byron E. Shafer, *Quiet Revolution: The Struggle for the Democratic Party and the Shaping of Post-Reform Politics* (New York: Russell Sage Foundation, 1983). The larger framework gets serious attention in Allen J. Matusow, *The Unraveling of America: A History of Liberalism in the 1960s* (New York: Harper and Row, 1984). See also Daniel Bell, *The Coming of Post-Industrial Society: A Venture in Social Forecasting* (New York: Basic Books, 1973); and the special issue "Integrating the Sixties: The Origins, Structures, and Legitimacy of Public Policy in a Turbulent Decade," *Journal of Policy History* 3, no. 1 (1996).

12. Among many, see George E. Mowry, *The Era of Theodore Roosevelt, 1900–1912* (New York: Harper and Row, 1958); William L. O'Neill, *The Progressive Years: America Comes of Age* (New York: Dodd, Mead, 1975); and Arthur S. Link and Richard L. McCormick, *Progressivism* (Arlington Heights,

Ill.: Harlan Davidson, 1983).

13. Pieces of this story are everywhere, but these works are especially helpful: Betty Glad, *Jimmy Carter: In Search of the Great White House* (New York: Norton, 1980); Theodore H. White, *America in Search of Itself: The Making of the President, 1956–1980* (New York: Harper and Row, 1982); Nelson W. Polsby, *Consequences of Party Reform* (Oxford: Oxford University Press, 1983); Jeane J. Kirkpatrick, *The New Presidential Elite: Men and Women in National Politics* (New York: Russell Sage Foundation, 1976); Warren E. Miller and M. Kent Jennings, *Parties in Transition: A Longitudinal Study of Party Elites and Party Supporters* (New York: Russell Sage Foundation, 1986). See also Byron E. Shafer and William J.M. Claggett, *The Two Majorities: The Issue Context of Modern American Politics* (Baltimore: Johns Hopkins University Press, 1995).

14. Alan J. Ware, *The Breakdown of Democratic Party Organization, 1940–1980* (Oxford: Oxford University Press, 1985), 241–42. See also David R. Mayhew, *Placing Parties in American Politics: Organization, Electoral Settings, and Government Activity in the Twentieth Century* (Princeton: Princeton University Press, 1986).

15. For example, from the Christian Coalition web page: Gary Thomas, "Unions Spending Big Money to Sway Elections," www.cc.org/unions.html, 10 July 1996, noting, "Big labor's agenda includes far more than the minimum wage and other work-related issues—and it often goes against profamily goals."

16. Especially helpful on the historical evolution are C.C. Goen, *Revivalism and Separatism in New England, 1740–1800* (New Haven: Yale University Press, 1988); Stephen Marini, *Radical Sects in Revolutionary New England* (Cambridge, Mass.: Harvard University Press, 1982); Whitney Cross, *Burned-Over District: The Social and Intellectual History of Enthusiastic Religion in Western New York, 1800–1850* (Ithaca, N.Y.: Cornell University Press, 1950); Nathan O. Hatch, *The Democratization of American Christianity* (New Haven: Yale University Press, 1989); Richard J. Carwardine, *Evangelicals and Politics in Antebellum America* (New Haven: Yale University Press, 1983); Lawrence W. Levine, *Defender of the Faith: William Jennings Bryan, the Last Decade, 1915–1925* (New York: Oxford University Press, 1975). See also Sydney E. Ahlstrom, *A Religious History of the American People* (New Haven: Yale University Press, 1972); William G. McLoughlin, *Modern Revivalism: Charles Grandison Finney to Billy Graham* (New York: Ronald Press, 1959); Mark A. Noll, ed., *Religion and American Politics: From the Colonial Period to the 1980s* (New York: Oxford University Press, 1990).

17. The theological explanation is addressed centrally in Dean M. Kelley, *Why Conservative Churches Are Growing* (New York: Harper and Row, 1972); but see also Jeffrey K. Hadden, *The Gathering Storm in the Churches* (Garden City, N.Y.: Doubleday Anchor, 1969). By far the most careful and comprehensive statistical treatment is Andrew M. Greeley, *Religious Change in America* (Cambridge, Mass.: Harvard University Press, 1989). On other aspects

of the larger development in the late twentieth century, see George M. Marsden, *Fundamentalism and American Culture* (New York: Oxford University Press, 1980); James Davison Hunter, *American Evangelicalism: Conservative Religion and the Quandary of Modernity* (New Brunswick, N.J.: Rutgers University Press, 1983); Kenneth D. Wald, *Religion and Politics in the United States,* 2d ed. (Washington, D.C.: CQ Press, 1992); A. James Reichley, *Religion in American Public Life* (Washington, D.C.: Brookings Institution, 1985); and the special issue "Religion in America Today," *Annals of the American Academy of Political and Social Science* 480 (July 1985). See also Ralph Reed, *Active Faith: How Christians Are Changing the Soul of American Politics* (New York: Free Press, 1995).

18. J. Christopher Soper, *Evangelical Christianity in the United States and Great Britain: Religious Beliefs, Political Choices* (Basingstoke: Macmillan, 1994), 55–56.

19. These were the ten planks: (1) Religious Equality Amendment; (2) Education; (3) School Choice; (4) Parental Rights Act; (5) Tax Relief for Families; (6) Restoring Respect for Human Life; (7) Encouraging Contributions to Private Charities; (8) Restricting Pornography; (9) Privatizing the Arts; (10) Crime Victim Restitution. See " 'Contract with the American Family,' " *Congressional Quarterly Weekly Report,* 20 May 1995, 1449.

20. For a contemporary example, see David Hosansky, "Christian Right's Electoral Clout Bore Limited Fruit in 104th," *Congressional Quarterly Weekly Report,* 2 November 1996, 3160–62.

4

Party Organizations,
1946–1996

John F. Bibby

For observers of American political parties, the 1990s are an era filled with paradoxes. Few, however, are as puzzling as the one involving the organizational character of those parties: the weakened state of the party in the electorate coexisting with strengthened party organizations, particularly at the national level—organizations that have become integral to implementing *national* electoral strategies. It is as if the immediate post–World War II era, of a relatively strong party in the electorate along with weak organizations operating in a confederate structure, had been turned on its head. This analysis describes the changing nature of party organizations in the United States since 1945, seeks explanations for the paradoxical state of American parties, and considers the implications of major change in American party organizations.

In V.O. Key's well-known tripartite conception of party, the party organization was viewed as an essential element, coequal to the party-in-the-electorate and the party-in-government.[1] In giving the organizational element of the party prominence, Key was confirming the importance for both electoral and governmental systems that he and a veritable honor roll of scholars before and since have documented—Ostrogorski, Michels, Duverger, Schlesinger, Wilson, Mayhew. For each of them, the state of the party organization *mattered*, for candidate selection, for campaign operation, for election outcomes, and for ultimate governance.

In tracing the changes in American party organizations since the end of World War II, this analysis focuses on the regular, legally recognized, organizational units of the parties, including national committees, congressional and senatorial campaign committees, and state central committees. From the beginning, however, it must be noted that concentrating on the official organizational units of the party does not capture the full scope of effective "party organization." When an interest group has permeated the boundaries of the party and taken on such tasks as voter mobilization and campaign advertising, for example, it stretches credulity to consider it as somehow independent of, much less outside, the party organizational orbit. Similarly, when there are reliable cadres of campaign consultants that work exclusively for one party, they must realistically be considered an essential organizational resource.

The party organization thus encompasses an array of allied organizations and individuals that work with the party in achieving its principal goal: winning elections. As such, the party organization can be likened to a network of regular party organizations, allied groups, and active individuals involved in electoral politics.[2] In addition to the regular party, these allied organizations and individuals include interest groups, campaign consultants, candidate organizations, and fund raisers. They will receive some attention in each of the major sections of this chapter, and more as our discussion approaches the present.

The trends in party organization identified in this analysis include heightened definition and institutionalization, integration among party units at the national and state/local levels, centralization of influence within national organizations, service provision to partisan candidates, as well as conscious reinforcement of ideological/issue-oriented bases for participation by party activists. These patterns of party organizational development reflect, most centrally, a process of adaptation to an increasingly candidate-centered politics. As a result of this adaptation process, the party organizations have increasingly adopted the role of campaign intermediaries that facilitate the activities of their candidates, while neither controlling the nomination of these candidates nor actually running their general election campaigns.

While the parties' adaptation to candidate-centered politics has brought significant changes in party organization, which are described in this chapter, it must also be recognized that the trend toward candidate-centered campaigns has been of long duration. Party organizations in the United States have long been forced to operate in an antiparty and individualistic culture. Thus the direct primary, a Progressive era reform, deprived party organizations of their most important power, the making of partisan nominations for public office; in the process, the primary assured candidate domination of parties instead.[3]

In this light, the much-heralded presidential nominating reforms initiated by the Democrats in the 1960s, which did severely weaken the influence of party leaders over candidate selection, should not be seen as something strikingly new. As Leon Epstein reminds us, the post-1968 reforms may have been triggered by a specific reform movement, yet they were also the "product of long-standing and distinctively American developments fostering candidate-centered politics."[4] American party organizations operate in a unique environment since, as Epstein further notes:

> Everywhere outside the United States, party organizations, at one level or another but usually local or regional, control the bestowing of their party labels; that is to say, dues-paying party members or their chosen executive committees select (nominate) candidates.[5]

Unlike other western democracies, the United States largely lacks a regularized, dues-paying, party organizational membership. American parties are thereby deprived of an element of legitimacy in candidate selection that is operative in, for example, Britain.[6] Only in America do laws give candidate selection over to voters whose partisan commitment is no more than the legal requirement for participation in the primaries. Thus in a striking example of America's exceptionalism, party organizations have been weakened and the motivation for individuals to become regular and active party members has been reduced.

Party Organizations in the Immediate Post–World War II Era

Although survey research has demonstrated the vitality of the party in the electorate during the late 1940s and 1950s, this period was *not* a golden age of party organizations. Instead, it was a time when the Republican and Democratic National Committees (RNC and DNC) possessed little power; when congressional and senatorial campaign committees had limited resources with which to assist candidates; when state organizations were relatively uninstitutionalized and lacked significant influence in all but a small number of states with long-standing, traditional, machine-type structures; when even true urban machines were showing signs of decline; and when, in much of the country, local organizations, where they existed, were underfunded and understaffed.

National Party Organizations

National committees.—By the 1930s, both the RNC and DNC had become institutionalized, with permanent headquarters in Washington, year-round professional staffs of 75 to 100 persons, and annual budgets in excess of $1 million.[7] Presidential campaigns were run out of national committee headquarters, with the chair of the committee having been designated either by the presidential nominee following the national convention or by an incumbent president. Yet the definitive analysis of the operation of the national committees of the 1950s still aptly characterized it as "politics without power" and the national chairmanship as a job "of uncertain dimensions, dimly and distortedly perceived by party enthusiasts and the public, but nevertheless one from which great accomplishments were expected although it had almost no traditional or regular support."[8] Institutionally, the committees possessed only a small repository of power, in the management of national conventions.[9]

This DNC/RNC weakness derived from the lack of any reliable base of support. Committee members—a national committeeman and woman from each state—were essentially *ambassadors* from their state organizations, although even as ambassadors they often lacked a defined and influential place within their home-state party structures. Until 1952, when the RNC began to incorporate state chairs into the committee structure, state party chairs were not even members of the national committees. It took another generation, until the post-1968 reforms, before state chairs became members of the DNC. This vigorously confederative membership structure meant that the national committees were unrepresentative in the extreme of their own electoral and officeholding strength. The committees therefore lacked the legitimacy to engage in policymaking, as Epstein has duly noted: "A body in which, for example, North Dakota Democrats had as many votes as New York Democrats was not likely to exercise much power, nor did any expect it to do so."[10]

Also fundamental to the weakness of the national committees was their dependence on state parties for financial support. Unlike today, the national committees lacked independent sources of revenue. With limited financial resources and a reliance on other levels of the party for financial support, the national committees were not able to engage in state and local party-building activities or to support candidates within the states except occasionally in a minor way. During the immediate postwar era, national party organization was thus clearly confederate in character, with power flowing from state parties to the national level. As Alexander Heard observed in his classic study of campaign finance of this period:

The financial dependence of the national units of party organization on units at other levels is symptomatic of the general distribution of power and activity throughout the parties. Not even in the Republican Party, with its finance committee system sponsored from the top, does the national leadership have an independent source of funds sufficient for its purposes.[11]

Congressional and senatorial campaign committees. — Just as national committees of the immediate postwar era were a pale shadow of their current counterparts, the Hill committees of today, with their multi-million-dollar budgets, advanced technology housed in modern office buildings, diverse professional staffs, and candidate recruitment and support operations, bear scant resemblance to those of the late 1940s and early 1950s. Hugh Bone reports that the Democratic Congressional Campaign Committee (DCCC) then "had only about five on its staff and has been crowded into a single room in the basement of the House Office Building."[12] It had no field staff to assist its candidates and was not in a position to provide assistance in the preparation of campaign literature or advertising.

Campaign support, when it was forthcoming, was primarily in the form of financial contributions. The modestly financed and staffed National Republican Congressional Committee (NRCC) was able to provide some money to candidates, along with limited assistance on campaign literature and media advertising. The small-scale nature of both House committee operations is revealed by the fact that the DCCC spent only $57,050 in 1952, while the NRCC made expenditures of $1.7 million. The senatorial campaign committees were also modest operations, with staffs of four to five persons that channeled funds in limited amounts to individual candidates. The Democratic Senatorial Campaign Committee (DSCC) did not even maintain a year-round office until 1952. In that year, the DSCC made expenditures of only $84,482 and its GOP counterpart spent $781,558.[13]

Nevertheless, the four Hill committees jealously defended their independence from encroachment by the national committees. Thus, in 1951, when RNC chairman Guy Gabrielson sought to consolidate research and publicity staffs of the Hill committees with those of the national committee, congressional and senatorial committees actually vetoed the plan.[14] There are likewise well-documented conflicts during the 1950s between the congressional Democrats and the DNC over which element of the party should be developing party policy.[15]

State Party Organizations

State central committees. — Traditional state party organizations capable of controlling nominations, running campaigns, and utilizing (and depending upon) various forms of patronage and corporate support reached their high-water mark around 1900.[16] It should be noted, however, that while hierarchical state organizations flourished in places like New York, Pennsylvania, Rhode Island, Maryland, West Virginia, Michigan, North Dakota, and Wisconsin, they were by no means universal. Even in the heyday of the traditional state party machine, many of the states had weak state organizations.

Genuine, traditional, state party machines, in any event, had largely passed from the scene by the 1920s, except for such stray survivors as those of Connecticut and Virginia. Progressive reforms early in this century had undermined the bases of power for these organizations, not just by instituting the direct primary system for nominations but by establishing civil service systems that severely limited patronage and enacting corrupt practices laws that cut off some sources of financing. By the end of World War II, the Republican and Democratic state party organizations possessed only vastly reduced influence over nominations, and they gradually lost the ability to direct state-level campaigns.[17]

While no thoroughgoing inventory of the status of state parties in the immediate post–World War II period was ever conducted, available evidence suggests a widespread pattern of organizational atrophy. Key, for example, concluded that most state central committees "are virtually dead," with only a few having "continuing staffs active in the business of the party." He lamented the "grave shortcomings" of these parties in "the development, grooming, and promotion of candidates for statewide office."[18] In the South, he judged that "most of the time party machinery is an impotent mechanism dedicated largely to the performance of routine duties. It has few functions that lend it prestige or power. . . . Party organization as such plays no significant role and the locus of its control may be of no great moment."[19]

Corroboration of Key's observations is found in surveys conducted by the RNC and DNC. A 1957–58 DNC survey revealed only twenty-one Democratic state committees that employed full-time professional staff. In 1961, only thirty-six of the GOP state committees had a permanent headquarters with at least one paid professional staff member; as late as 1960–64, 17 percent of state chairs operated out of their homes or businesses without the benefit of party headquarters.[20] Clearly, the notion that state party organizations of the postwar era were as strong as, or even stronger than, those of the 1990s, is largely myth. There were exceptions, but they were exceptions created in large part by special conditions: John Bailey's Democratic organization in Connecticut did not have to contend with the direct primary until 1955, and the Byrd Democratic organization of Virginia thrived on unusually low voter turnout.[21]

State legislative campaign committees. —Standard elements in the party organization at the state level in at least forty states since the late 1980s have been campaign committees in both chambers of the state legislatures.[22] These organizations have become the principal party organizations engaged in providing both financial and technical/professional support for legislative candidates. This now-crucial element in the organizational structure of the state parties was simply not present during the immediate postwar period. Instead, to the extent that party assistance was provided to legislative candidates, it came from local parties or state central committees.

Local Party Organizations

Machines: declining or absent. —Like the traditional state party organization, the machine style of organization at the local level rose to prominence in the nineteenth century and diminished in the twentieth. As David Mayhew notes, however, urban machines continued to function in the late 1940s and did not begin to slope off until the 1950s.[23] The traditional local organization (that is, the machine) was characterized by a substantially independent power base, organizational autonomy, longevity, hierarchical leadership, control over nominations, and reliance on material incentives rather than purposive incentives for engaging people in its operational work and support. This type of local organization has provided the basis for an academic and popular literature rich in romance and nostalgia, as the real and fictionalized exploits of Chicago's Richard J. Daley and Boston's James Michael Curley are told and retold.

But, in fact, county and city parties have not been characterized by this style of organizational politics in most of the country. Mayhew's survey of local parties identified only thirteen states that in 1960 could be characterized as home to predominant traditional party organizations. The machine was never a nationwide phenomenon, being largely absent from the western, Deep South, Plains, and northern tiers of states. Instead, the traditional organization tended to be concentrated in the Middle Atlantic region and in states settled early in the Ohio and Mississippi valleys—a geographic distribution that casts doubt on two commonplace generalizations about American politics.

The first of these inaccurate generalizations is that the machine phase was a natural but temporary stage in the political development of cities. The second is that there was a link between machines and large immigrant populations. Of course, in many places, immigrants did provide an ingredient for machine building. Yet many certifiable machine cities

—Cincinnati, Memphis, Kansas City, New Orleans, Indianapolis, and Louisville—were hardly the ones most affected by waves of European immigration.

The New Deal of Franklin Roosevelt's Democratic administration had important consequences for urban politics and for Democratic organizations in particular. In the short run, it tended to strengthen Democratic city machines, as federal relief money was distributed in a manner that shored up old organizations and actually helped build new ones in places like Pittsburgh, Providence, and Scranton. But in the long run, the New Deal had a weakening effect, as it undermined the patronage base of local party organizations. The new social insurance programs were largely insulated from patronage and served as models for later grant-in-aid programs as well as vanguards for professionalism in state and local government. Until the New Deal era, urban machines had come in both Democratic and Republican varieties, but they had become an almost exclusively Democratic phenomenon by the 1950s.[24]

Real local organizations.—An additional organizational change in the Democratic Party was the emergence of unions as a source of support, upon which the party came to rely. Led by the CIO, labor unions supplied campaign funds to Democratic candidates, mobilized voters at election time, and sought to influence public opinion. An important organizational element was thus added to Democratic Party structure.[25] By assisting with—and in some instances taking over—the performance of party functions, unions (and later, other allied groups) gave the Democrats an organizational structure that differentiated it from the GOP.

The focus of much academic and journalistic attention on the effectiveness of selected urban machines, such as the Daley organization in Cook County, has tended to obscure basic features of 1940s and 1950s party organization at the local level. In most places, it was volunteer based, rather than professional and full-time. The normal mode of operation featured looseness, flexibility, informality, and improvisation. Most importantly, it was characterized by "organizational slack" and the tendency of activists to perform at a minimum level of efficiency.

In Wayne County, Michigan (Detroit), during 1956, only 38 percent of the Democratic precinct leaders and 22 percent of Republicans performed critical vote-mobilization tasks (registration, house-to house canvassing, election-day roundup) for the party.[26] In a 1960s four-state study, only in New Jersey did a majority of state legislators mention the party as having sponsored their careers; and in Ohio, California, and Tennessee only one-fourth said the party played this role.[27] Republican organizational weakness in the cities was particularly striking. The RNC reported in 1961 that 10,000 precincts, or about 30 percent of the total in fourteen major cities, were *unmanned*.[28]

Nationwide surveys of task performance by county parties in 1964 provide further evidence of organizational slack. Approximately 60 percent were engaged in registration drives, publicizing party and candidate activity, raising money, and arranging campaign events.[29] Samuel Eldersveld therefore has concluded that it should not be assumed that " 'in the past' local parties were extremely efficient. They may have been so in such machine oases as Chicago or Philadelphia or Jersey City, but *normally the level of efficiency in task performance had always been low.*"[30]

The research of Alan J. Ware and James Q. Wilson confirms the decline of traditional party organizations in urban areas, as material rewards were less and less available for distribution by party leaders, and participation in party activities increasingly became based on solidary and purposive incentives. More and more participation occurred within reform and amateur clubs and candidate organizations, where followers had to be content with either "the fun of the game, the sense of victory, or devotion to the cause."[31]

Summary of Salient Features, Post-World War II

Confederate structure lacking integration. — The national committees were rigorously confederate in terms of their membership, powers, and bases of support. The RNC and DNC depended on the state parties for financial support and as a result had scant influence (much less control) over their state and local affiliates. The party organization was, therefore, lacking in direction and leadership from the national level, and vertical party integration was effectively absent. The parties were decentralized organizationally, with the national nominating conventions in effect assemblies of state and local parties. Decentralization and weak integration also characterized relations between the national committees and the Hill committees, which guarded their separate status jealously.

Generally weak organizations at the state level. — Although the national committees had, by the end of World War II, achieved elements of institutionalization—year-round headquarters, professional staffing, a division of labor—state parties in most of the states were relatively uninstitutionalized, as well as being organizationally weak. Some still operated out of the homes and/or offices of the state chairs, and their level of campaign activity was generally low. One cause of this weakened status of state organizations was the direct primary, which encouraged personal candidate organizations. Another was the decline in interparty competition within the states, which rendered party organizational support for candidates less important.[32]

Local parties: urban Democratic machines and general organizational slack.—The urban machine continued to exist in many places after 1945, though it had become an almost exclusively Democratic phenomenon, due to forces unleashed by the New Deal. Machine-style politics, however, was anything but the norm locally, where 70 percent of elections were conducted on a nonpartisan basis. Most local organizations did engage in party building and candidate-support activities, but these organizations were operated in an improvising mode by volunteers and were characterized by organizational slack.

Organized labor becomes an element in the Democratic structure.—By the late 1940s, the Democratic Party had become heavily dependent on organized labor to perform voter-mobilization tasks and provide other forms of assistance to its candidates. This was the major semi-integrated interest group in party affairs at the time. Indeed, no other would attain the scope of organized labor among the Democrats in the years to follow, though many more would come to share pieces of the same function, and in both parties.

The Evolution of a Candidate-Centered Politics

Parties in the 1990s are nothing if not testimonies to organizational durability and adaptiveness in the face of strong competitive and antiparty forces in the political environment. Developments pushing the country toward a candidate-centered system of politics intensified during the 1960s and 1970s, yet party organizations adapted to the sea changes and found an important niche for themselves in the electoral process. They became, in effect, major and institutionalized *service providers* to "their" candidates. On the other hand, as mentioned previously, this process of adaptation to candidate-centered forces in American politics has itself been a long-term and evolving dynamic.

Party organizations of the 1990s, in any event, have little in common with the mass parties that developed in the 1830s and that, in their "golden age," during the latter half of the nineteenth century, were capable of controlling nominations and mobilizing masses to win elections. The party organizations of today neither control nominations nor run campaigns. Yet in spite of having lost these important functions, party organization in the late twentieth century is characterized by an impressive degree of centralization (at least for U.S. parties!) and by heightened integration between national and state units.

This organizational structure at the national and state levels has taken on the role of a professional service provider and resource mobilizer for individual candidates. Party organizations have established for themselves a significant role in the electoral process while retaining the affiliation of ambitious candidates still in need of the nomination of a major party.[33] Nevertheless, these invigorated party organizations do not signify even a shifting back toward that previous "golden age." For these are party organizations that have also *shed* some traditional party functions as they have adapted to a candidate-centered environment.

Social Change and Party Organization

Candidate-centered politics has deep roots in the American experience. —Early nudges away from a party-centered politics and toward a more candidate-centered politics occurred late in the nineteenth century, with adoption of the Australian ballot—printed ballots provided by the government rather than by the parties—and the secret ballot.[34] This process was accelerated by the Progressive movement early in this century, which caused state laws to be enacted that imposed a regulatory regime on parties and gave them a status not unlike that of public utilities.[35] That is, parties were given special rights under the law (e.g., ballot access) because they were deemed to perform some essential public service. But in return, parties were subject to state regulation of their internal structure and practices, of campaign spending, and, most important, of their nominating procedures.

By imposing the direct primary on parties, the Progressive movement gave American politics a candidate-centered quality and bestowed further special advantages on incumbent officeholders.[36] Key places great and far-reaching emphasis on the debilitating impact of the direct primary for party organizations:

> [The direct primary] created circumstances that made difficult the maintenance and operation of statewide party organization. The new channels to power placed a premium on individualistic politics rather than on the collaborative politics of party.[37]

Interestingly, the presidential nominating process remained an anomaly up until the post-1968 reforms, in the sense that state and local party leaders maintained a dominating influence. Unlike nominations for state and congressional offices, which were achieved in most places through voter mobilization by the personal organizations of the candidates, presidential nominees were the choice of an assembly of state and local party leaders.[38] But even while this anomalous system survived into the 1960s, there were indications that it, too, was moving toward a plebiscitary system, as the nonpartisan demands of presidential office became more salient and as the power of state and local parties declined.

Thus presidential primaries had already become an important part of almost every serious presidential nominating campaign in the 1940s and 1950s, as with Dewey in 1948, Eisenhower and Kefauver in 1952, and Stevenson in 1956. A further early indicator of the trend toward candidate-centered politics was the substantial campaign role accorded the Citizens for Eisenhower organization in 1952. This was not an official GOP operation, but an attempt to mobilize voters outside the regular party structure. As with the role of labor unions among the Democrats, Citizens for Eisenhower broadened the operational character of "the party organization" among Republicans.

Institutionalizing the candidate-centered system.—In the 1960s and 1970s, there was a coming together of a variety of forces that institutionalized this candidate-centered party system. Prominent agents of party change were the decline of the party in the electorate, party rules reforms and a subsequent change in the legal status of national party organizations, organization-building strategies adopted at the national level, a revolution in party fund raising plus new federal rules governing campaign finance, advances in the technology of campaigning that spawned an expansion of the campaign consultant industry, and the activism and proliferation of nonmaterialist interest groups.

Although the combined impact of these forces pushed party organizations into the background of campaigns, of elections, and of voter perceptions, parties managed to retain an important role as providers of critical campaign resources. Other than party organizations, only superrich activists—Perots, Kennedys, Rockefellers—or mass movement leaders could provide campaign resources to candidates equal to those that the parties could still offer.[39]

The decline of the party-in-the-electorate.—There is abundant empirical evidence that partisanship declined as a basis for voter choice during the 1960s and 1970s. W. Phillips Shiveley's study of presidential elections showed that from 1840 until 1960, change in the vote from one election to the next primarily reflected differential mobilization of each party's identifiers, rather than the conversion of voters from supporting one party to supporting the other.[40] Beginning in the 1960s, however, such conversion had become the principal force causing interelection vote shifts. This change was attributed primarily to the ability of nominees to appeal directly to the public and to woo voters away from the opposition. Similarly, at the congressional level, Alford and Brady found that until 1960 there was no systematic personal advantage in incumbency, but that after 1960 there was a sustained advantage to incumbency, and it was of equal importance to partisanship.[41]

The post-1960 era has also been characterized by a sharp increase in split-ticket voting in presidential, Senate, and House elections.[42] These voting patterns in federal elections are consistent with Martin Wattenberg's (1990) findings, which show that in the 1960s and thereafter, fewer voters expressed any likes or dislikes of the parties, thus indicating a decline in the *relevance* of parties in voter choice.[43] Voters were apparently responding to the candidates themselves much more than previously.

Formal Change and Party Organization

Democratic Party rules changes: a plebiscitary system and nationalization. —Reacting to the disastrous and tumultuous 1968 Democratic National Convention, the Democratic Party then embarked on a process of reform that transformed presidential nominating politics. In this process, after the recommendations of the McGovern-Fraser and successor reform commissions had been implemented, the influence of party organizational leaders was severely reduced.[44] Because one of the unintended consequences of the reforms was a proliferation of presidential primaries, the nominating process became highly participatory, media oriented, and based on the candidate preferences of voters.

While the immediate impetus for change in the delegate selection process arose within the Democratic Party, Democratic reforms had a spillover effect on the Republican Party. State legislatures, in revising their statutes to bring them into conformity with national Democratic Party rules, frequently adopted the same or similar rules for both Democrats and Republicans. As a result, the number of Republican presidential primaries also proliferated after 1968. While differences remain in the national party rules of the two parties concerning presidential nominating procedures, both parties operate within basically the same system, in which the influence of party leadership has greatly diminished.

Nominations are no longer made by a convention of state and local party leaders, nor are they made by a regularized national party membership in anything like the European sense.[45] In the post-1968 system, candidates can bypass the party organizational leadership entirely, seeking delegate support in public presidential primaries and in an open caucus system. Indeed, the practical politics of presidential nominations dictates that every presidential aspirant create an independent, national, and personal campaign structure.[46]

A second major consequence of Democratic Party reforms was a nationalization of party rules and a strengthening of the legal status of national party organizations. On their face, the Democratic reforms allowed the national Democratic Party to assert authority over the selection of national convention delegates within the states. Yet this also constituted a major and significant departure from the traditional confederate structure of parties in the United States. Through rigorous enforcement of its delegate selection rules, the national Democratic Party forced a massive restructuring of the rules governing its state affiliates.

The legal status of the national party was further strengthened by a series of decisions from the U.S. Supreme Court, which upheld the principle that national party rules take precedence over state statutes and over state party rules in matters pertaining to delegate selection (*Cousins* v. *Wigoda*, 419 U.S. 477 [1975]; *Democratic Party of the United States* v. *Bronson C. LaFollette*, 449 U.S. 897 [1981]). Austin Ranney concluded that the power conferred on the national Democratic Party by rules changes and judicial decisions was so sweeping that the national party's legal authority had reached "its highest peak since the 1820s."[47]

The Democratic Party Charter, adopted in 1974, further proclaimed the supremacy of the national party. It required state parties in instances of conflict between national party rules and state laws to take "provable positive steps to bring such laws into conformity and to carry out such other measures as may be required by the National Convention or the Democratic National Committee." The charter explicitly moved away from a confederate structure by changing the composition of the Democratic National Committee and making it more representative. Instead of the traditional pattern of state equality of representation on the committee, the size of state delegations to the DNC was based on state population and presidential voting records.

Reform Republican-style: nationalization by other means. —Throughout the decades-long process of reform within the Democratic Party, the GOP remained essentially unreformed, with its confederate legal structure intact. While the Democrats were imposing an elaborate set of rules on their state parties, the national Republican Party did not seek to assert the legal authority over its state parties that judicial rulings now bestowed on it. Instead, the national party maintained a permissive attitude toward its state-level affiliates. Unlike the Democrats, the GOP had no rules prohibiting open presidential primaries, requiring proportional representation and/or equal division of the sexes in state delegations, or setting time limits within which the delegate selection process had to occur.

In 1974 the RNC explicitly rejected a proposal that would have authorized the committee to review affirmative action plans of state parties, even though the proposal conferred no enforcement power on the RNC.[48] Further evidence of the party's commitment to maintenance of its confederate legal structure was its continuing adherence to the principle of state equality in representation on the RNC and on all convention committees. As with the Democrats, however, a process of party nationalization has been occurring within the GOP, though it has come about through means other than rules reform.

The Republican path toward party reform and toward strengthening the power of the national party occurred instead through a process of organization building. Taking advantage of the national party's pioneering (and highly successful) efforts to raise large sums of money via direct mail and large givers in the early 1960s, the RNC under the leadership of Chairman Ray C. Bliss (1965–69), and more aggressively under Bill Brock (1977–81), undertook a large-scale program of providing a wide array of services to its state and local organizations. Among the programs initiated by Brock and expanded by his successors were (1) assistance in building professionalized staffs and in fund-raising operations; (2) financial and technical assistance to state legislative candidates; (3) issues research; (4) computer and data-processing assistance; (5) consulting services for redistricting; and (6) campaign management training.[49]

These were efforts designed to make state parties more helpful to candidates at the state level. The RNC programs to strengthen state parties operated in a manner similar to the federal government's grant-in-aid system, in that before state parties could receive aid, they frequently had to accept conditions, albeit flexible ones, imposed by the national party.[50] In the process, state parties were professionalized and gained enhanced candidate-support capabilities. But they also became increasingly dependent on the national party for the resources essential for organizational maintenance and for participating in their own state-level campaigns.

Although it was the GOP, with its superior financial resources, that initially developed an array of programs to aid state parties and their candidates, the national Democratic Party then consciously copied the Republican example during the 1980s, in yet another example of the way in which a candidate-centered politics draws adaptations from both the parties. While its level of aid to local parties has consistently lagged behind that of the Republicans, the process of organizational revitalization has created a more centralized party structure for the Democrats as well.

Financial Change and Party Organization

National fund raising: national parties as mobilizers of campaign resources. — National party fund raising has undergone a veritable revolution in terms of the amounts of money collected and in the direction of flow for intraparty funds. In the post–World War II years, the national committees largely depended on state parties for funds, and hence were not in the business of providing either money or services in any significant way to their state affiliates. The fund-raising operations of the congressional and senatorial campaign committees during this period were modest, and their expenditures were correspondingly low. In 1952, for example, the combined congressional and senatorial campaign committees for the Republicans spent less than $2.5 million, and for the Democrats less than $150,000.[51]

Beginning in the 1960s, the Republicans led the way in exploiting fund-raising potential of direct-mail solicitations, and in ensuing years they have outpaced the Democrats in raising party money. The national-level committees of *both* parties have, nevertheless, increased their funding and expenditures to unprecedented levels. Republican committees raised $443.5 million and Democratic committees raised $305.3 million in 1995 and 1996.[52] This independent fund-raising ability has enabled them to adapt to candidate-centered politics by providing campaign services to candidates in a major way, as with the DNC's $44 million advertising budget in support of President Clinton's reelection.[53]

Development by the national parties of a multimillion-dollar fund-raising capacity has occurred within the context of changes in the Federal Election Campaign Act (FECA), changes that have encouraged parties to play an enlarged role as a mobilizer of resources for their candidates. The FECA limits for coordinated expenditures are higher than for direct contributions to congressional and senatorial campaigns, and it is in coordinated expenditures that the greatest growth has occurred in "hard money" for national parties—funds raised and spent in accord with the FECA restrictions.

Coordinated expenditures give the congressional and senatorial campaign committees greater leverage over a candidate's campaign than is derived from direct contributions. By controlling expenditures "on behalf of" candidates, the national party committees gain greater influence over the campaigns per se.[54] Using their substantial fund-raising ability, the national-level party committees have also developed a direct "service vendor" capacity that enables them to provide a wide array of campaign services and expertise to their candidates at reasonable prices (e.g., media production, issues research, fund-raising assistance, and campaign management).

One of the most far-reaching additional effects of the FECA was its provisions encouraging the formation of political action committees (PACs). Although PACs are rightfully seen as potential competitors for influence with party organizations, the parties have also themselves adapted to the PAC phenomenon by aggressively assuming the function of brokers and intermediaries in raising campaign money, "by cueing, channeling, and funneling" PAC and other money to worthy candidates. As Frank Sorauf and Scott Wilson have observed, "in these activities the party committee is neither the source nor the final spender of that money, but mere mobilizing of money has become a major part of the parties' enhanced role in campaigns."[55]

"Soft money" and party integration. — "Soft money," money raised outside the restrictions of the FECA, which cannot be contributed to (and spent directly in support of) federal candidates, has been raised in massive amounts since the 1980s, primarily by the national party organizations. Thus, in 1995 and 1996, national-level Republican committees raised $141.2 million in soft money, a 224-percent increase over 1991 and 1992, and Democratic committees likewise raised $122 million, an increase of 237 percent over 1991 and 1992.[56] A portion of this soft money is used for general party-building activities by the national party organizations. But substantial amounts of these funds are channeled to state parties for spending on general party overhead, voter registration, get-out-the-vote drives, and state and local campaigns—activities that are at least technically not in direct support of federal campaigns.

The ability of the national party committees to raise and allocate soft money has greatly expanded the role of these committees in electoral politics. Not surprisingly, in allocating soft money, national party units do so in a manner that supports party-building activities in states that are crucial to national strategy in presidential, Senate, and House elections. In addition to national-to-state transfers of soft money designed to implement national campaign strategies, the national-level committees of the parties also transfer soft money to state and local candidates—$5.9 million by the National Republican Senatorial Committee and $2.8 million by the Democratic Senatorial Campaign Committee in 1995 and 1996.[57]

Transfers of soft money, like coordinated expenditures and other forms of national aid to state parties, have resulted in a heightened level of intraparty integration as well as a nationalizing of party campaign efforts that constitutes a change of major proportions in the American party system. While the flow of resources to state parties has strengthened the capacity of many of these units to provide a higher level of service to their candidates, they have at the same time become increasingly dependent on the largess of the national party. In the process, they have lost some of their traditional autonomy.

As Heard accurately observed in 1960, "any changes that freed the national party committees of financial dependence on state organizations could importantly affect the loci of party power" and enable the parties to develop "a more cohesive operational structure."[58] The conditions that Heard projected into the future have now been fulfilled, and the national party organizations have been strengthened in their campaign roles, while state parties have been integrated into national campaign strategies directed by national party organizations.

Operational Change and Party Organization

New campaign technologies and professional management. —Campaigns for president, Congress, governor, and many state legislative seats increasingly utilize the latest and most sophisticated campaign techniques and technologies. To a limited degree, party organizations are able to provide campaigns with essential campaign services. But even in their currently expanded service mode, this party role in campaigns is restricted. In 1992 the party share of campaign costs for House campaigns was 9 percent, compared to the 50–70 percent totals that characterize party dominance of campaign finance in European democracies.[59] For those services and resources that are not available from the party, candidates find it necessary to hire their own professional campaign consultants, for polling, developing and placing media advertising, targeting direct mail, getting out the vote, and managing the campaign.

The candidates' need for surrogates to replace the old-style machines and face-to-face campaigns has thus spawned a major industry, the professional campaign consulting firm.[60] The consultants are loosely affiliated with the parties, in the sense that most work almost exclusively for one party's candidates. But they still work primarily for *candidates,* not parties, and hence tend to reduce the party role in campaigns and reinforce the tendency toward individual-centered politicking. Even in this area, however, the party organizations at the national level have demonstrated some adaptive qualities. The national-level committees of both parties have periodically maintained a stable of loyalist consultants on retainer, for example, so that they were available for dispatch to campaigns that needed special expertise.

The rise of citizen organizations. —As the incentives for political participation have become increasingly less dominated by material rewards, citizen groups concerned about quality-of-life issues have played an increasingly important role in campaigns. To win nominations, candidates have been pressured by (and have sought to woo) environmental, feminist, gay, antiabortion, Christian Right, and gun-owner groups. While these groups tend to ally themselves with one or the other of the major parties, their devotion to a cause means that they focus their attention on candidates and their issue positions and that they operate with substantial autonomy from the parties.[61] Such groups are interested principally in gaining the ear of the candidates and, through them, influencing public policy. The importance of these groups in nominating and general election campaigns does force candidates and parties to seek their support, but they remain outside the regular organizational structure of the party and constitute another force creating a candidate-centered politics.

Party Organizations in the 1990s

American party organizations of the 1990s display characteristics that would be unfamiliar to expert observers or practical operatives of the immediate post–World War II years. The workings of national committees can hardly be described now as "politics without power." The Hill committees are no longer small-scale dispensers of money and campaign services. State parties, unlike Key's less-than-flattering portrait of the 1950s, are functioning statewide operations with professional staffing. National and state parties are now integrated to an unprecedented degree in carrying out national campaign strategies. And urban machines have largely passed from the scene. There is, however, substantial continuity between the late 1940s and 1990s at the local level, in the sense that understaffed volunteer organizations still carry out traditional campaign-related activities.

Legal and Practical Nationalization of Party Organizations

Since 1945, political parties have undergone dramatic changes in their legal status, changes that have nationalized the organizations and conferred on them additional constitutional rights. Party organizations have also derived some benefits from the changes in the FECA, although the act simultaneously unleashed a major competitor to party influence, the PAC.

Nationalization of the organizational structure. — The Democratic reform movement began the shift in which the national party organizations gained formal, legal supremacy over state legislatures and state parties in matters of delegate selection. Yet this assertion of national party authority was then confirmed by the Supreme Court. As a result, the DNC was able to enforce vigorously a set of codified rules on state governments and state parties. The development, adoption, and implementation of reforms in the Democratic Party, which has been described in detail by Byron Shafer, reflected the power of a "Washington-based staff acting on behalf of a nationally oriented political movement."[62]

The Court-endorsed strengthening of the national parties and the nationally mandated reforms initiated by the Democratic Party stripped residual powers away from state and local party leaders. It was no longer possible for a party organization to control or even decisively influence the presidential nominating process. Candidate-centered politics was confirmed at every level as the new order of the day.[63] The Democrats also made their organizational structure more national in character, through a party charter that eliminated the principle of state equality in the composition of the DNC. This party nationalization process, via rules changes backed up by Supreme Court decisions, has largely bypassed the (unreformed) Republican Party. Still, the precedents developed during the Democratic reform process stand available for GOP use, should future conditions so dictate.

Rights of free association for state parties. — The grounds on which the national party organizations gained stronger legal standing derived from the Court's granting them expanded rights of free association under the First Amendment. The Court found that a party organization enjoys a "constitutionally protected right of political association" (*Cousins* v. *Wigoda,* 419 U.S. 477, at 487 [1975]), and that in effect this right can override the policy concerns of state governments. Although the Court's broad conception of associational rights for the parties was initially used to assert national party primacy over state laws and state party rules, subsequent decisions have also granted these rights to state parties. As a result, the legal standing of state parties has been strengthened too, and some state regulations of parties have been struck down as violations of the First Amendment.

Thus, in 1986, the Court ruled that Connecticut could not prevent voters registered as independents from voting in a Republican primary, if the state GOP wanted to allow independents as well as registered Republicans to do so (*Tashjian* v. *Connecticut,* 479 U.S. 20 [1986]). This decision was followed by one that threw out a California law banning party organizations from making preprimary endorsements, limited the length of state party chairs' terms, and required the state chairmanship to be rotated every two years between residents of northern and southern regions of the state (*Eu* v. *San Francisco Democratic Central Committee,* 109 S.Ct. 1013 [1989]).

Although these cases have given state parties a degree of freedom from state regulation that they have not enjoyed since the reforms of the

Progressive era swept the nation, it is unlikely that the most significant regulation of state parties will be abolished. The direct primary, for example, which has contributed so much to America's particular brand of parties, remains so ingrained in the political culture that there is no likelihood of party organizations being able to free themselves from its yoke.

Federal Election Campaign Act and party organizations.—In providing for public funding of presidential candidates, the FECA reinforced and codified a candidate-centered type of politics, providing that public funds would go, not to political parties, but to the presidential candidates. Each candidate is thus required to set up a central campaign committee, which accepts all contributions or federal subsidies and makes expenditures. This system builds into the law a view that party organizations are "separate from and ancillary to candidates' campaign organizations."[64]

Although expenditure and contribution limits in the FECA have restricted the direct involvement of party organizations in federal campaigns and encouraged the creation of PACs, the FECA, as interpreted by the courts, does provide some benefits to parties. These include (1) authorization of campaign spending by national committees in presidential elections—$11.5 million in 1996; (2) authorization to engage in coordinated expenditures, which in the case of senatorial candidates enables parties to play a significant campaign role; (3) permission for individuals to contribute $20,000 in "hard money" per year to national committees; (4) public funding of national conventions; (5) and permission for the use of "soft money" to fund party building activities and issue advocacy—advertisements that do not contain "express advocacy" of the election or defeat of a federal candidate. These latter now constitute multimillion-dollar ways for parties to avoid some of the expenditure and contribution limits of the law.

Even the FECA provisions for public funding of presidential candidates have *some* positive implications for parties. The law defines a major party as one receiving 25 percent of the vote in the last presidential election and makes candidates of such parties eligible for the full quota of public funding. Given the remote possibility of a situation in which either the Democrats or Republicans fail to win 25 percent of the vote, it would appear that both parties have an assured future with a federal subsidy for their presidential campaigns.

In a decision that could dramatically increase the role of political parties in campaigns, a divided Court in 1996 ruled that a state party organization could engage in unlimited independent expenditures on behalf of federal candidates (*Colorado Republican Committee* v. *Federal Elec-*

tion Commission, 1996). This decision, which gives state parties the same right to engage in independent expenditures as the Court had previously granted to interest groups and individuals, provides party organizations with an opportunity to participate on a large scale in federal elections. The door could be opened wider for party organizations to fund federal campaigns if the Court later rules that limits on party coordinated expenditures are unconstitutional.

Institutionalized Service to Candidates by the National Party

The National Committees.—The change in the national committees can be readily detected just by comparing their modern office buildings on Capitol Hill, brimming with large professional staffs and the latest hi-tech equipment, to the rather shabby and spartan rented quarters they maintained in downtown Washington as late as the mid-1960s. With the ability to raise massive amounts of money—through direct-mail prospecting, soliciting big givers, and putting the arm on unions, corporations, and other groups for soft money—the national committees have become relatively autonomous bureaucracies in the business of aiding candidates, especially presidential candidates, as well as state and local party organizations. The national committees in the immediate postwar years were, it is true, like their present-day counterparts in being primarily chairman-dominated, Washington-based, staff operations. But they lacked the resources to play the kind of role in electoral politics and in the affairs of the state parties that has now become institutionalized.

A prominent example of the electoral role that a national committee can now play is the $20 million "issues advocacy" campaign by the DNC through television advertising from the fall of 1995 to the spring of 1996, a campaign designed to bolster President Bill Clinton's standing with the public in the run-up to the 1996 elections. The DNC's role as a service agency to the president's reelection campaign has been dramatically demonstrated in Bob Woodward's report that Clinton personally supervised the content of the advertisements that the DNC ran on his behalf.[65] The RNC also engaged in a more limited "issues advocacy" effort on behalf of its nominee, Bob Dole.[66]

The national committees also work to support their national candidates more generally, principally by transferring funds and providing technical expertise to their state parties; in the process, they have achieved an unprecedented degree of leverage over these state affiliates. This is now true even of the DNC, which initially lagged behind the RNC in developing the resources essential for engaging in this type of activity. In the 1990s, however, under the leadership of Chairman Ron Brown, the DNC strongly supported and encouraged the creation of "Coordinated Campaign" structures in the states, to serve a broad range of candidates with such services as voter registration, voter-list development, get-out-the-vote drives, polling, targeting, media purchasing, and scheduling. Coordinated campaigns were funded with contributions from the DNC, state parties, candidates, state legislative campaign committees, and key Democratic constituency groups such as organized labor.

The RNC has supported similar programs in recent election years, though the Republican activities tend to operate primarily through state party organizations and rely much less heavily on assistance and cooperation from allied groups. The scope of these integrated national-state efforts at voter mobilization is extensive, as the RNC's "Victory '96" illustrates. This direct voter-contact program was funded with $15.3 million in RNC funds and $48.3 million in state party money.[67] It included candidate-specific mail; slate mail, 84.8 million pieces of targeted mail; absentee ballots; voter-identification phone calls; advocacy calls; turnout calls, 14.5 million calls to Republican households; volunteer phone centers; and collateral materials.

In effect, what has been occurring through national committee transfers of funds and assistance programs for state parties is that the national party has been using its superior resources and legal authority to nationalize campaign efforts and integrate the national and state parties in an unprecedented manner. National money and resources tend to flow to state parties in conformity with the *national* party's campaign strategy and priorities (and in presidential election years, with the strategy and priorities of the presidential nominees). State parties are thereby being integrated into a national campaign structure in presidential, House, and Senate campaigns.

Thus, in an effort to skirt restrictions imposed by the FECA, the DNC during 1995 and 1996 transferred large sums of money to state parties, which in turn paid for television advertising developed and placed in the media by the DNC's media production company. The RNC indicated that it, too, funneled money to its state parties to purchase television advertising developed under the auspices of the national party. Both the DNC and RNC also directed large givers to send their contributions to state parties in states deemed to be of crucial importance by national party strategists.[68]

Another recent example of this pattern of integrating state parties into the national campaign occurred in Florida. In an effort to cause the Clinton campaign some discomfort in the spring of 1996, the RNC's communications director developed a newspaper ad critical of President Clinton's judicial appointments. Space for the ad, which received widespread news coverage, was then purchased by the Florida State GOP so that it would run simultaneously with the president's arrival in the state.[69] Coordinated activities of national and state organizations such as these blur the distinction between national and state organizations, as nationally funded state parties engage in party building activities and issues advocacy that help federal as well as state-level candidates.

For the state parties, the benefits of national largess can be substantial—more professional staffing, hi-tech equipment, and expanded and updated voter lists. Yet there is also a price: support granted in one election cycle can be withdrawn in the next, depending on the national party's priorities. In addition, state parties are becoming increasingly dependent on their national organizations for the resources they need to help their own state candidates.

The congressional and senatorial campaign committees. — At the national level, the traditional division of labor between the national committees and the campaign committees on the Hill has been maintained. In this division, the national committees focus principally on presidential campaigns and on assisting state·parties as they are integrated into national campaign strategy. The congressional and senatorial committees are then engaged principally in assisting their own candidates. This activity, however, does require considerable cooperation and joint activity with the national committees and state parties, as the Hill committees transfer soft money to the latter.

As the main party vehicles for campaign spending on senatorial and congressional candidates, the Hill committees actually deliver the bulk of the campaign services the parties provide.[70] As table 4.1 (p. 166) demonstrates, the spending levels for contributions and coordinated expenditures are substantial. Such totals, however, are not the whole story. On top of these "hard money" expenditures, the Hill committees engage in even larger "soft money" spending—in excess of $24 million by the Democratic senatorial and congressional committees and more than $53 million by their Republican counterparts in 1995 and 1996.[71] Also, these committees are actively engaged in candidate recruitment, while the candidates' need for costly campaign services provides the Hill committees with the opportunity to become an important part of subsequent campaigns. Finally, to close the circle, their ability to provide these services is, of course, tied to the committees' ability to raise money in large amounts.

The array of services provided to candidates targeted for assistance includes campaign management, polling, issue and opposition research, campaign communications, and fund raising. As noted earlier, the Hill

TABLE 4.1

TOTAL PARTY CONTRIBUTIONS AND COORDINATED
EXPENDITURES FOR HOUSE AND SENATE CANDIDATES,
1980–96

Election	Democratic committees	Republican committees
1980	$ 2,895,711	$11,813,833
1982	4,591,141	19,330,201
1984	5,440,322	17,359,766
1986	10,082,244	17,439,176
1988	11,244,145	17,798,882
1990	10,070,048	13,620,066
1992	19,742,102	26,421,677
1994	23,799,217	23,198,460
1996	17,424,542	21,985,180

SOURCE: Norman J. Ornstein, Thomas E. Mann, and Michael J. Malbin, comps., *Vital Statistics on Congress, 1997–1998* (Washington, D.C.: CQ Press, 1998), 106–7.

committees have become major mobilizers of nonparty campaign resources (from PACs, wealthy individuals, and incumbent senators and representatives) for their candidates. As channelers and mobilizers of campaign money, the Hill committees provide their candidates with the knowledge and tools to raise PAC money. In addition, the committees try to manipulate the informational environment in which PACs make their contributions.[72] As a result of their activities, candidates and their aides rank Hill committees ahead of other local, state, *and national* party organizations and ahead of PACs, unions, or other groups, in terms of providing essential professional services. The Hill committees' services continue to be doled out on the basis of electoral criteria—competitiveness of the constituency and chances of victory—and not on the basis of candidate ideology.[73]

Unofficial party and allied groups. — A party's organizational resources, in their totality, involve more than the formal, legally constituted party organizations, such as the national, Hill, and state committees. In operational fact, these resources go on to include *other organizations* on which the party relies for electoral services. These unofficial party units, along with the Washington-based "think tanks," have proliferated since the 1980s and constitute important organizational resources for the parties. A prominent example is the Democratic Leadership Council and its "think tank" affiliate, the Progressive Policy Institute, which has been a source of policy initiatives used by Democratic candidates. A counterpart, major source of policy resources utilized by GOP campaigners is the conservative Heritage Foundation.

Allied interest groups also supplement the activities of the party organizations. In the 1995–96 election cycle, there was an unprecedented level of such activity by allied interest groups, especially through advertising on issue advocacy and through independent expenditures. The AFL-CIO alone allocated $53.5 million to defeating incumbent Republican members of Congress. Other Democratic allies, led by Citizen Action, a loose coalition of liberal organizations including environmentalists, gun-control advocates, and women's groups, launched a $7 million drive consisting of ads, mailings, and phone calls blasting the GOP on environmental and education issues; the Sierra Club spent $6.5 million on issue ads and voter guides. This spiraling level of campaign activity by groups allied with the Democrats, of course, sparked a counterattack from groups with Republican ties, such as the U.S. Chamber of Commerce, Americans for Tax Reform, and the Christian Right.[74]

When, as in 1996, the AFL-CIO conducts a $35 million advertising and grassroots campaign nationwide, aimed at helping the Democrats retake control of the House of Representatives, no line drawn around "the party organization" can be entirely sensible.[75] More specifically, when, as in Oregon's 1996 special Senate election, the Democratic nominee is aided by a variety of liberal interest groups engaged in the traditional party-type functions of door-to-door canvassing, phone banks, direct mail, and neighborhood rallies, while the GOP candidate receives similar assistance from a similar array of groups on the political right, that line remains blurred in application.[76]

A particularly revealing instance of the close ties that can exist between parties and their interest-group allies concerns Americans for Tax Reform, which made 4 million phone calls and mailed 19 million pieces of mail critical of Democrats in 1996. Much of this activity was financed with $4.6 million from the RNC.[77] Similarly, Ralph Reed, executive director of the Christian Coalition, was part of an organizational coordinating structure that met weekly in the office of the RNC chairman to plot Republican strategy in 1996.[78]

Although allied groups are an increasingly important campaign resource for the parties and their candidates, these partisan allies are nonetheless formally autonomous and do have their own agendas. They do not even uniformly and reliably coordinate their activities with the candidates or parties they are seeking to assist. Thus the *Washington Post* reported that in Pennsylvania's 21st District during a twenty-hour period in 1996, there was a barrage of 500 television ads by such groups as the American Hospital Association, the AFL-CIO, Citizen Action, and the conservative Citizens for a Republic Education Fund. Much of this advertising came without advance knowledge or involvement of the candidates.[79]

In addition to organizational allies on whom the parties and their candidates rely, political consultants with close ties to the party organizations constitute a further generic party resource. An example of the extent to which allied groups, consultants, and candidate organizations can be linked in a party *network* can be found in New Jersey. There, housed in one office building, is a complex and interlocking set of political organizations all geared to assisting Republican candidates. These include the Committee for Responsible Government, a PAC dominated by Republican Governor Christine Whitman, which gives money to candidates in New Jersey and around the country; a political consulting firm headed by an individual who is the political director of Whitman's PAC; and four other political consulting, advertising, accounting, and graphic design/ printing companies with interlocking and overlapping leadership structures and ties to the PAC.[80]

State Parties and State Services

Judged by measures of institutionalization and bureaucratization, the state party committees are organizationally stronger than they were in the 1950s and early 1960s. Virtually every state party now has a permanent headquarters. Increasingly, party headquarters are housed in modern office buildings packed with computer hardware, telephone banks, and printing facilities. Professional staffing is now the norm, with almost all state parties having either a full-time chairman or an executive director.[81] Budgets have increased substantially, with multimillion-dollar expenditures now commonplace, as the parties have developed regularized fundraising programs. The New York State Republican Committee, for example, raised $4.4 million during the first six months of 1996.[82] In contrast, Heard reported in 1960 that one-third of the GOP state parties and nearly all of the Democratic parties had failed to set up centralized fund-raising operations.[83]

State central committees. — With a more assured financial base and a more bureaucratized organizational structure, the state parties are now able to engage in an expanded array of both party building and candidate-support activities. This active role of the state parties in providing assistance to their candidates is shown in table 4.2, which reports the results of surveys of state committees conducted in the 1980s and 1990s. These surveys also reveal one of the distinctive differences *between* the

TABLE 4.2

CAMPAIGN ASSISTANCE TO CANDIDATES
PROVIDED BY STATE PARTIES
(IN PERCENTAGES)

Type of assistance provided to candidates	Republican state parties	Democratic state parties
Financial contributions to:		
gubernatorial candidates	81	54
congressional candidates	71	55
state legislative candidates	95	52
local candidates	39	23
Fund-raising assistance to:		
state candidates	96	63
congressional candidates	63	30
Voter registration drives	73	81
Public opinion polling	78	50
Media consulting	75	46
Campaign seminars/training	100	76
Coordinating PAC contributions	52	31

SOURCES: *The Transformation of American Politics: Implications for Federalism* (Washington, D.C.: Advisory Commission on Intergovernmental Relations, 1986), 115; A. James Reichley, *The Life of the Parties: A History of American Political Parties* (New York: Free Press, 1992), 390.

parties, in that Republican state parties tend to be more active in supporting candidates than are the Democrats. A countervailing interparty difference involves the greater reliance of Democratic state parties on allied groups for assistance in carrying out party activities (see table 4.3, p. 170).

It should be clear, however, that while the state parties are organizationally stronger and provide a broader array of campaign services than in the past, their role in campaigns is supplementary to that of their candidates' own *personal* organizations. The job of the party organization is normally to provide technical services—training, advertising, polling, voter-list development, get-out-the-vote efforts—as well as money and volunteers. For example, in 1988, the Florida GOP had a $200,000 program that involved sending instructions on how to obtain an absentee ballot to one million likely GOP voters.[84]

The adoption of an expanded candidate-service role by invigorated state parties does, at the same time, reveal the limits of their influence. Although they are now more institutionalized and bureaucratic, these orga-

TABLE 4.3

STATE CHAIRS REPORTING THAT THE PARTY
AND ITS CANDIDATES RECEIVED SIGNIFICANT LEVELS
OF SUPPORT FROM EXTRAPARTY ORGANIZATIONS
(IN PERCENTAGES)

Type of organization	Democratic	Republican
Mentioning no extraparty organization	0	33
Mentioning a party auxillary group	0	15
Mentioning a business, farm, or professional organization	11	48
Mentioning a social action group	37	7
Mentioning a teachers' group	41	4
Mentioning a labor union	89	4

SOURCE: Cornelius P. Cotter, James L. Gibson, John F. Bibby, and Robert J. Huckshorn, *Party Organizations in American Politics* (New York: Praeger, 1984), 138.

nizations can rarely control nominations, and they still do not run the campaigns of their nominees. Even the most party-oriented candidates view party services as supplementary to those developed within their own organizations—witness the observations of Representative David Price (D-N.C.), a former state party chairman, who actively involved the party organization in his campaigns:

> Neither my recognition among party activists nor my wider exposure as a party spokesman gave me anything approaching a decisive edge in the Democratic primary.... [The] nomination was not within the power of the state, or national, party organizations to deliver. I and my fledgling campaign team, including many active local Democrats, were largely on our own in pursuing it.... While my campaign thus evidenced relatively strong participation by ... party organizations, it could not ... be judged a party-centered campaign.[85]

Patronage, one of the traditional bases of organizational strength for the state party, has now been sharply reduced, even in states where more traditional party organizations survived into the 1980s. In a series of decisions beginning with *Elrod* v. *Burns* (1976) through *Rutan* v. *Republican Party* (1990), the Supreme Court severely limited the ability of public officials to hire personnel on the basis of "party affiliation and support." Instead, the ground troops of the state parties have become volunteers recruited principally on the basis of issues and ideology, not on the basis of material incentives and party loyalties.

While traditional patronage jobs have lost much of their role in party maintenance, other types of preferment remain important. Gubernatorial appointments to state boards and commissions with jurisdiction over professional licensing, highways, banking, environmental and recreational policy, hospitals, universities, and historical/cultural activities will still be desired by people seeking policy influence, public recognition, public service, and material gain. Politics also intrudes into state decisions regarding contracts, bank deposits, economic development, and the purchase of services. These types of preferment are useful principally as a means of raising money for the party and candidates, however, and do not produce campaign workers the way the old-style organizations did.[86]

State legislative campaign committees. — Although the congressional and senatorial campaign committees have a long history, dating arguably to 1866, the development of counterpart organizations within state legislatures is primarily a post-1960s phenomenon. The emergence of state legislative campaign committees as the principal party support for legislative candidates was a response to the need by legislators for additional campaign assistance—in the face of rapidly escalating campaign costs, intensifying competition for control of state legislative chambers, rising uncertainty about election outcomes, and legislative professionalism among career politicians. The strongest legislative campaign committees thus developed in states with strong levels of interparty competition, high campaign costs, weak state central committees, and professionalized legislatures. By extension, legislative campaign committees were least likely to develop in the South, where Democratic electoral dominance was pervasive and the GOP often failed to contest large numbers of seats.[87]

Legislative campaign committees led by incumbent legislative leaders who have the clout to raise large campaign war chests have even become, in some places, the strongest party organization in the state, as in New York and Illinois. Accordingly, these campaign committees are much more than incumbent-protection institutions. They tend to follow a strategy similar to that of the Hill committees in Washington. That is, their focus is on achieving or maintaining chamber control, with resources concentrated on marginal incumbents, competitive challengers, and open seats.[88]

Unlike the situation with state central committees, in which the Republicans tend to have the advantage in organizational strength, Democratic legislative campaign committees do not operate at a disadvantage. This counterbalancing appears to stem from the Democrats' majority status in most state legislatures since the 1970s. They have, therefore, been able to use incumbency and the power that goes with chamber control to raise large amounts of money for their candidates. Like the Hill committees, they are heavily involved in recruiting candidates and providing them with technical services. As the chief of staff of the Ohio Senate Republican Caucus described his operation, "We are a full-service operation for individual campaigns."[89] That is, the campaign services were geared to the needs of individual candidates, not unlike the way a consulting firm would provide its services. Likewise, the former speaker of the Wisconsin Assembly, Democrat Tom Loftus, described his campaign committee as follows:

> We raised [money] to help Democrats running in marginal seats. In most cases we recruited the candidate. We provide training through campaign schools. We provide personnel and logistical support, issue papers, press releases, speakers for fund-raisers, fund-raisers themselves, and phone banks; we pay for a recount if it's a close race; we pay for the lawyer if it goes to court; if they have kids, we pay for the babysitter.... We do everything a political party is supposed to do.[90]

Although shared goals, party loyalty, and personal associations encourage an element of cooperation and coordination between legislative campaign committees and state central committees, legislative campaign committees tend to operate with autonomy.[91] They are run by legislative leaders, and they service primarily the agendas and priorities of legislators, especially gaining control of legislative chambers. This gives them a high degree of independence from the agendas of the state central committees and from the campaign operations of gubernatorial, senatorial, congressional, and presidential candidates.

Such committees are thus not involved in general party building, as are most state central committees. Nor do they tend to be closely linked to local party organizations, which were traditionally considered important participants in legislative elections. Recruitment and campaign priorities are set on a statewide basis by legislative leaders and not in consultation with local party officials. And since the campaign committees focus their activities on a relatively few districts, most local party leaders have little contact with legislative campaign committee personnel. Even in districts in which the campaign committees are active, they normally engage in little joint activity with local party organizations. As a result, the development of strong legislative campaign committees has brought few benefits to local party units.[92]

Local Parties and Local Services

The remnants of traditional urban machines do survive in several cities, as in Philadelphia, Chicago, and Albany. In a few places, moreover, newly professionalized and effective organizations are thriving: a prominent example is the Republican Party of Nassau County (Long Island), New York. Most members of the party executive committee in Nassau are reported to hold patronage positions in county government; the county chairmanship is a full-time, paid position; the local party raises more money than the state central committee, owns a three-story headquarters building, and even operates its own printing plant and artists' studio; and it makes extensive use of pollsters. As a partial result, the Nassau County party has emerged as a kingmaker in state GOP politics.[93] Another professionalized but nonpatronage-based local organization is the Santa Clara County Republican Party (California), which has a paid executive director, a headquarters complete with computerized volunteer and voter lists, and a sophisticated system for reaching voters.[94]

Local party committees. —These well-organized local party organizations, however, are not the norm—far from it. In most other places, local party organizations are essentially volunteer operations, have low levels of expenditure, and remain relatively underdeveloped in terms of such indicators of institutionalization and bureaucratization as paid staff, formal budgeting, and maintenance of year-round offices. Yet it is worth recalling, as surveys of local party organizations have demonstrated, that this lack of bureaucratic development does not represent an organizational decline from some previously high level of structural strength.[95]

The pattern of candidate-centered politics that characterizes campaigns for federal and statewide offices also characterizes local campaigns, including state legislative campaigns. That is, the candidates do not rely principally on local party organizations to facilitate and promote their races for office. This does not mean, however, that local parties are inactive. They are most important in terms of recruiting volunteers and getting voters to the polls, least important in terms of creating and maintaining a campaign infrastructure through fund raising and campaign management. Whereas the Republicans have demonstrated an advantage in organizational strength at the levels of the national committee and of state central committees, surveys of local parties reveal no distinct advantage for either party. The types of assistance provided to legislative candidates, however, do differ between the parties, with the Republicans more inclined to give money to candidates and the Democrats more apt to conduct registration drives, buy radio/television time, coordinate PAC activity, and conduct get-out-the-vote drives.[96]

Further evidence of continuity in party organizational maintenance and activity at the county level was revealed in the nationwide study of county parties in the 1992 presidential campaign by Paul Allen Beck and his associates. This study demonstrated that national party communications to local parties, attempts to integrate these units into national campaign efforts, and presidential candidate visits to a county did stimulate a high level of local party campaign activity. As a result, Beck and associates concluded that "there is a vibrant party campaign at the grass roots."[97]

The enhanced level of intraparty integration between the national party committees and state committees is now also in evidence in national-local and state-local party relations. The national committees, particularly the RNC, have programs designed to strengthen their local affiliates, and the emergence of soft money, raised at the national level and then channeled to state and local parties in accordance with a national campaign strategy, has also encouraged the integration of local parties into the national and state party structure.[98] Similarly, county leaders report increased levels of assistance coming from the state parties for financial recordkeeping, computer services, research, office space, staffing, candidate recruitment, and both operating and campaign expenses. Finally, there has been a growth in joint state-local party activities, such as developing lists of contributors, raising funds, recruiting people for government appointments, getting out the vote, and registering voters.[99]

Conclusions

Party Organizations as Activist Networks

In the post-1960s era, party organizations in the United States have changed from being loose confederations of state and local associations that mobilized local electorates, into national entities that direct resources, recruit candidates, and supply expertise.[100] The state parties have become an integral part of these national entities, as they have simultaneously been strengthened through national party money and expertise. To a significant extent, the national party organizations rely on direct-mail solicitations of funds to underpin all this activity, solicitations that are most effective when the addressees have ideological views of politics or strong commitments to particular issues. With coaching from their national parties, state parties have learned to make similar appeals.

These fund-raising techniques reflect another emerging characteristic of American party organizations. Increasingly, they are becoming networks of "issue-based participatory activists."[101] The influence of the Christian Right within Republican organizations is but one manifestation of this pattern; the influence of pro-choice, gay rights, environmental, and affirmative action supporters within the Democratic Party are others.[102] The source of this trend, toward party organizations based on issue-oriented activists, can be found in a series of complex interacting forces: the emergence of a range of specific cultural issues such as abortion, women's rights, environmental concerns, law and order, and gay rights; broad sociological and economic trends, such as rising levels of educational attainment, reduced blue-collar employment, and increased numbers of white-collar workers; plus, surely, the simple decline in the availability of patronage as an incentive to participate in politics.[103]

Evidence of the extent to which parties are becoming networks of issue activists can be seen in the gap between the issue or ideological positions of delegates to national conventions versus rank-and-file party voters.[104] Thus, in 1992, one could find almost no antiabortion delegates among the state delegations to the Democratic convention, while the pro-choice minority at the Republican convention felt constrained to hide its preferences. This dramatic issue divide occurred in spite of the fact that surveys show the abortion issue to split the mass voter base of each party almost identically.[105]

Similarly, surveys of persons participating in presidential nominating politics through attendance at state party caucuses and conventions clearly show that the bulk of these party participants "have a pronounced ideological tilt to them, far more so than primary voters or party identifiers."[106] Liberals and moderates have become an exceedingly rare commodity among GOP caucus/convention attenders; the center of gravity among Democratic caucus/convention participants is just as clearly on the liberal side. State party convention delegates show a similar strong propensity for interest-group involvement, with the Democrats manifesting higher levels of participation in educational, social issue, and environmental organizations than their Republican counterparts.[107]

Issue-based groups are also becoming well ensconced in the organizational structure of the regular party. *Campaigns and Elections* reported in 1994 that the Christian Right was the dominant faction in eighteen state Republican organizations and had substantial influence in thirteen others.[108] Evidence of this influence was on display at the 1997 meeting of the RNC when Ralph Reed, executive director of the Christian Coalition, played a major role in engineering the third-ballot switch of votes by more than thirty Religious Right committee members, a switch that boosted Colorado businessman James Nicholson to the RNC chairmanship.[109]

The increasing involvement of individuals whose motivation to participate in party politics is derived not from material rewards such as patronage but from ideological and issue concerns is creating conflicts not just between rank-and-file party voters and their organizational activists, but between officeholders and the party organization as well. Indeed, there is an almost schizophrenic party structure emerging in some jurisdictions. That is, elected officials, who need broad social support in order to win, exist side-by-side with a growing body of organizational activists concerned mainly about ideology and principles.

The conflicts inherent in this mix were apparent, for example, within the Minnesota GOP in 1994. A Republican state convention, dominated by the Religious Right, endorsed one of their own for the gubernatorial nomination over the incumbent (moderate) Republican governor, Arne Carlson. Carlson, nevertheless, went on to defeat the organization's choice by an overwhelming margin in the primary and then to win the general election by a comfortable margin. To the extent that party organizations increasingly become networks of issue activists, conflicts such as the one in Minnesota, featuring elected officials *versus* the party organization, are likely to proliferate and intensify. There is a further organizational problem in the fact that the loyalties of issue-oriented activists tend to be stronger toward their preferred candidates than toward their political parties.[110] In the process and perhaps paradoxically, activist-dominated party organizations are likely to widen the policy differences between the Republican and Democratic parties.

Party Organizations as Resource Mobilizers

American electoral politics in the 1990s, when compared to that of the years that followed World War II, is more ideological. It is more capital-intensive, money and electronic communications having replaced the voter-mobilizing activities of patronage and membership-based party organizations. And it is clearly more expensive. Undergirding much of these changes are a weakening of party ties among voters; a growth of ideological and issue-oriented groups, intent on having an electoral and policy impact; advances in campaign technology; changes in formal public policy regarding parties and PACs; and internal party reforms, in the realm of both rules and activities. The result is the emergence of a candidate-centered style of politics, the principal structural components of which are "aggressive, self-propelled candidate organizations."[111]

In the face of the challenges posed by these forces of change, party organizations have neither fallen into disarray nor withered. In one sense, they show heightened strength and vitality. They now demonstrate greater professionalism among their leaders and staffs. They possess higher levels of financing, particularly at the national level. They show increased intraparty integration, as state and local party units have become essential elements in implementing national electoral strategies. And they feature a heightened concentration of power in national party organizations. These are parties capable of providing significant levels of assistance to their nominees, thereby becoming major players in electoral politics.

Nevertheless, party organizations in the 1990s are *not* parties of the traditional variety, in the sense that they control nominations, run campaigns, or even directly contribute the largest share of funds for those activities. These party organizations serve their candidates by mobilizing and channeling the resources needed for successful campaigns. They are instrumental organizations geared to winning general elections for party standard-bearers whom they had only a modest role, if any, in selecting. Thus, by the traditional criteria of party strength, today's national and state party organizations appear weak. Just as by other standards—professionalism, bureaucratization, resource development, and internal integration—the national and state organizations show renewed strength.

Local parties, finally, offer yet a different contrast. The traditional machine style of organization has indeed withered. But most *county* organizations, in fact, have *continued as they were* in the 1950s and 1960s—as understaffed, underfunded, organizationally slack, volunteer operations engaged in traditional voter-mobilization activities.

Throughout this analysis of party organizational changes between 1945 and 1996, the central theme has been that party organizations have *adapted* to the challenges of candidate-centered politics and that in the process they have become stronger entities at the national and state levels than they were in the immediate post–World War II years. The national party organizations in particular have become major participants in electoral politics; with their massive resources, they have achieved a degree of intraparty integration and centralization that was unheard of in the 1940s through the 1960s. Analyses that would downplay the consequence of this development, on the other hand, still sometimes assert that such adaptation has amounted to little more than the transformation of parties into "super PACs," that the resulting party organizations have in essence ceased to be "real political parties."

This line of argument ignores one of the basic differences between party organizations and PACs or large interest groups, even those of the broadest consequence, such as the AFL-CIO. Party organizations at the national and state levels still operate in a more comprehensive manner than any PAC or interest group—in gathering resources, in allocating and targeting the distribution of those resources, in recruiting candidates, and in integrating a network of affiliates and allied interests into campaign structures intended to benefit candidates. In terms of the comprehensiveness of their activities and efforts at coordination, there is no PAC in the American political system that is the match of the Democratic and Republican organizations.

This is not to deny that the post-1960s era is characterized by candidate-centered politics. But the scope of national party activities—fund raising, candidate and state-party assistance, soft money transfers, and issue advocacy—has become so massive that these party units also appear to constitute a modest *countervailing force* to candidate-centered politics. Presidential campaigns are now heavily reliant on the RNC and DNC; House and Senate campaigns in competitive constituencies similarly depend on at least an allocation of national party resources; even gubernatorial races in key states benefit substantially from national party largess.

Lastly, while the organizations of the two major parties are unrivaled in the scope and comprehensiveness of their operations, they are also quite different from each other. The evidence is overwhelming that the Republicans have been more effective in harvesting the money needed to play a major campaign role, by providing technical and financial assistance to candidates and state affiliates. At the same time, as the 1996 campaign illustrates, the Democrats remain able to do a superior job of utilizing the resources of allied groups, to offset the party-based strengths of the GOP.

These fundamental differences, of course, expose differing vulnerabilities for the parties. For Republican organizations, the key vulnerability is simply their dependence on *money* as the basic resource. A downturn in the party's electoral fortunes, or a major change in campaign finance legislation, could undermine the GOP organization in a major way, and quickly. At the same time, defections by allied interest groups, or legislation that would effectively restrict, in particular, the use of union dues for political communications and political organizing, could severely harm the Democratic Party, which depends so heavily on organized-group assistance.

At the same time, the significant differences that exist between Republican and Democratic organizations should not obscure the extent to which the two organizations are becoming more alike. For example, the Democrats have demonstrated, in recent years, a prodigious ability to raise money and have thereby succeeded in erasing some of the financial edge enjoyed by the Republicans. Conversely, the Republicans have found powerful allied interests in, for example, the Religious Right and small-business organizations, groups prepared to supplement party activities in ways not unlike organized labor's role in Democratic politics. Beyond all that, the organizations of both parties are increasingly dominated by issue-oriented activists.

Future Directions

The strengthening of party organizations, particularly at the national and state levels, means that some modification is in order for the widely accepted assertions about the minimal role of party organizations in electoral politics. James Q. Wilson, for example, in his classic study of political organizations published in 1974, observed that parties were "more important as labels than as organizations" and that their chief effect on election outcomes was as "an organizing principle to enable voters to identify with various candidates."[112] Parties have certainly retained some role as an organizing principle for voters, though they probably now succeed in this at a reduced level of impact. Conversely, they have become significant contributors to candidates organizationally, where they previously played a reduced role there.

As they have done in previous eras of change, party organizations since World War II have again demonstrated their durability, resiliency, and adaptiveness. This adaptation to a heavily candidate-centered environment should *not* be seen as essentially a post-1960s development: roots for the development of a politics that is more candidate-centered than that of other Western democracies lie deep in America's history and culture. In this historical light, the parties' adaptation to candidate-centered politics is in reality a continuation of a long-term process, one that has only accelerated since the mid-1960s.

One of the most striking features of the structure of party organizations at the end of the current century is the extent of intraparty integration and centralization of power at the national level. This is a change of major proportions in the American party system. A serious observer of American political parties can no longer assert, as V.O. Key did in the leading parties text for two decades after 1945, that "no nationwide organization exists.... Rather, each party consists of a working coalition of state and local parties."[113] The national party units now use and work through state and local parties on a regular basis, to implement *national* electoral strategies, and they exert a strong influence over their state and local affiliates through the allocation of resources.

That said, a truly nationalized party structure shows no real likelihood of developing in the United States. Too many impediments to such a structure are too firmly embedded in the political system. The constitutional barriers that federalism and separation of powers impose to such structure, for example, remain substantial. The party-fragmenting and party-weakening nomination processes are now an even more ingrained part of the political system. The cultural bias against parties—at the least, a strong cultural *suspicion* of parties—is reflected in campaign finance statutes at the federal level and in many state statutes that provide public support to candidates and not to parties.

It is well within the bounds of possibility, moreover, that public policy toward parties will change again, in ways that would undermine the power of national party units. This could occur, for example, if future reforms were to eliminate or severely restrict the flow of soft money within the party structures. It should also be kept in mind that the share of candidate campaign expenditures contributed by party organizations remains low—less than 10 percent in House and Senate races—and that, ultimately, candidates are still personally responsible for putting together the financing *and organization* needed to win elections.

A speculative issue in this evolution concerns the converse potential for party-centered *governance* to develop in coming decades because of the enhanced party role in candidate recruitment and campaign support. If the role of party organizations in these crucial aspects of an office-holder's career were to continue to grow, it is at least conceivable that party organizations might be able to impose a higher degree of discipline on the public policy decisions of officeholders.

At present, however, such a development seems less likely. The party organizations continue to dispense support to candidates based on electoral criteria like competitiveness—"winability"—not on programmatic criteria like loyalty to party doctrines. In addition, officeholders continue to show substantial independence, especially in responsiveness to their individual constituencies. Whatever the governance implications of the post-1960s type of party organization, then, it is clear that these parties have now institutionalized a candidate support role for themselves, one that makes them major participants in electoral politics and is simultaneously consistent with a system of candidate-centered politics.

Notes

1. V.O. Key Jr., *Politics, Parties, and Pressure Groups,* 5th ed. (New York: Crowell, 1964), 164.

2. Mildred A. Schwartz, *The Party Network: The Robust Organization of Illinois Republicans* (Madison: University of Wisconsin Press, 1990), 4–5.

3. Joseph A. Schlesinger, "The New American Party System," *American Political Science Review* 79 (December 1985): 1155.

4. Leon D. Epstein, *Political Parties in the American Mold* (Madison: University of Wisconsin Press, 1986), 108.

5. Leon D. Epstein, "Overview of Research on Party Organizations," in *Machine Politics, Sound Bites and Nostalgia*, ed. Michael Margolis and John Green (Lanham, Md.: University Press of America, 1993), 2–3.

6. Leon D. Epstein, "Changing Perceptions of the British Party System," *Political Science Quarterly* 109 (Special Issue, 1994): 487.

7. Cornelius P. Cotter and John F. Bibby, "Institutional Development of Parties and the Thesis of Party Decline," *Political Science Quarterly* 95 (Spring 1980): 4.

8. Cornelius P. Cotter and Bernard Hennessy, *Politics without Power: The National Party Committees* (New York: Atherton Press, 1964), 103.

9. Hugh A. Bone, *Party Committees and National Politics* (Seattle: University of Washington Press, 1958), 203.

10. Epstein, *Political Parties in the American Mold*, 204.

11. Alexander Heard, *The Costs of Democracy* (Chapel Hill: University of North Carolina Press. 1960), 289.

12. Bone, *Party Committees and National Politics*, 130.

13. Ibid, 145, 148.

14. Ibid., 151.

15. Philip A. Klinkner, *The Losing Parties: Out-Party National Committees, 1956–1993* (New Haven: Yale University Press, 1995).

16. David R. Mayhew, *Placing Parties in American Politics* (Princeton: Princeton University Press, 1986), 224.

17. The postwar years saw Rhode Island and Connecticut, two traditional organization states, adopt the direct primary, leaving Indiana (which adopted the primary to nominate statewide candidates in 1976) as the lone holdout for statewide nominations. Malcolm E. Jewell, *Parties and Primaries: Nominating State Governors* (Lexington: University of Kentucky Press, 1984), 12.

18. V.O. Key Jr., *American State Politics* (New York: Knopf, 1956), 271.

19. V.O. Key Jr., *Southern Politics in State and Nation* (New York: Knopf, 1949), 387, 392.

20. Cornelius P. Cotter, James L. Gibson, John F. Bibby, and Robert J. Huckshorn, *Party Organizations in American Politics* (New York: Praeger, 1984), 12–13, 15.

21. Mayhew, *Placing Parties in American Politics*, 225.

22. Daniel M. Shea, *Transforming Democracy: Legislative Campaign Committees and Political Parties* (Albany: SUNY Press, 1995), 17.

23. Mayhew, *Placing Parties in American Politics*, 22–25.

24. Ibid., 323–24.

25. Ibid., 324–25; Byron E. Shafer, "Partisan Elites, 1946–1996," chap. 3 of this book.

26. Samuel J. Eldersveld, *Political Parties in American Society* (New York: Basic Books, 1982), 147.

27. John C. Wahlke, Heinz Eulau, William Buchanan, and Leroy C. Ferguson, *The Legislative System* (New York: Wiley, 1962), 92.

28. John F. Bibby, *Republicans and the Metropolis: The Role of National*

Party Leadership (Chicago: Center for Research in Urban Government, Loyola University, 1967), 8.

29. Cotter et al., *Party Organizations in American Politics,* 54; Paul Allen Beck, "Environment and Party: The Impact of Political and Demographic Characteristics on Party Behavior," *American Political Science Review* 68 (September 1974).

30. Samuel J. Eldersveld, "The Party Activist in Detroit and Los Angeles: A Longitudinal View, 1956–1980," in *Political Parties in Local Areas,* ed. William Crotty (Knoxville: University of Tennessee Press, 1986), 108; emphasis added.

31. Alan J. Ware, *The Breakdown of Democratic Party Organization, 1940–1980* (Oxford: Oxford University Press, 1985); and James Q. Wilson, *Political Organizations,* rev. ed. (Princeton: Princeton University Press, 1995), 115.

32. Schlesinger, "The New American Party System," 1160–62.

33. John H. Aldrich, *Why Parties? The Origin and Transformation of Political Parties in America* (Chicago: University of Chicago Press, 1995), 273.

34. Schlesinger, "The New American Party System," 1155–56.

35. Epstein, *Political Parties in the American Mold,* chap. 6.

36. Schlesinger, "The New American Party System," 1156.

37. Key, *American State Politics,* 169.

38. Epstein, *Political Parties in the American Mold,* 203.

39. Aldrich, *Why Parties?* 273.

40. W. Phillips Shively, "From Differential Abstention to Conversion: A Change in Electoral Choice, 1864–1988," *American Journal of Political Science* 36 (May 1992).

41. John R. Alford and David W. Brady, "Personal and Partisan Advantage in U.S. Congressional Elections, 1846–1986," in *Congress Reconsidered,* 4th ed., ed. Lawrence C. Dodd and Bruce I. Oppenheimer (Washington, D.C.: CQ Press, 1989).

42. Harold W. Stanley and Richard G. Niemi, *Vital Statistics on American Politics,* 5th ed. (Washington, D.C.: CQ Press, 1995), 136.

43. Martin Wattenberg, *The Decline of American Political Parties, 1952–1988* (Cambridge, Mass.: Harvard University Press, 1990).

44. Byron E. Shafer, *Quiet Revolution: The Struggle for the Democratic Party and the Shaping of Post-Reform Politics* (New York: Russell Sage Foundation, 1983).

45. Epstein, *Political Parties in the American Mold,* 208.

46. Byron E. Shafer, *Bifurcated Politics: Evolution and Reform in the National Party Convention* (Cambridge, Mass.: Harvard University Press, 1988), 79.

47. Austin Ranney, "The Political Parties: Reform and Decline," in *The New American Political System,* ed. Anthony King (Washington, D.C.: American Enterprise Institute, 1978), 230.

48. John F. Bibby, "Party Renewal in the National Republican Party," in *Party Renewal in America: Theory and Practice,* ed. Gerald M. Pomper (New York: Praeger, 1980).

49. Ibid.; Klinkner, *The Losing Parties.*

50. Epstein, *Political Parties in the American Mold,* 223.

51. Bone, *Party Committees and National Politics,* 148.

52. Federal Election Commission, "Political Parties Fundraising Hits $881 Million," Press Release, Washington, D.C., 1997.

53. Ruth Marcus and Charles R. Babcock, "The System Cracks under the Weight of Cash," *Washington Post,* 9 February 1997, A20.

54. Frank J. Sorauf and Scott A. Wilson, "Political Parties and Campaign Finance: Adaptation and Accommodation to a Changing Role," in *The Parties Respond: Changes in American Politics and Campaigns,* 2d ed., ed. L. Sandy Maisel (Boulder, Colo.: Westview Press, 1995), 239.

55. Ibid., 242–43.

56. Federal Election Commission, "Political Parties Fundraising Hits $881 Million."

57. Blaine Harden and Charles R. Babcock, "Senate Campaign Cash Diverted to NY GOP," *Washington Post,* 19 February 1997, A1.

58. Heard, *The Costs of Democracy,* 294.

59. Sorauf and Wilson, "Political Parties and Campaign Finance," 239.

60. Larry J. Sabato, *The Rise of Political Consultants: New Ways of Winning Elections* (New York: Basic Books, 1981).

61. Jeffrey M. Berry and Deborah Schildkraut, "Citizen Groups, Political Parties, and the Decline of the Democrats," paper presented at the annual meetings of the American Political Science Association, Chicago, 1995.

62. Epstein, *Political Parties in the American Mold,* 210.

63. Ibid., 211–12.

64. David E. Price, *Bringing Back the Parties* (Washington, D.C.: CQ Press, 1984), 243.

65. Bob Woodward, "Clinton Called Shots for Party Ad Blitz," *Washington Post,* 25 June 1996, A1, A8.

66. Ruth Marcus, "A Vote-for-Dole Ad by Another Name," *Washington Post,* 1 June 1996, A1, A10.

67. Republican National Committee, *1996 Chairman's Report* (Washington, D.C.: Republican National Committee, 1997), 9–10.

68. Ruth Marcus, "DNC Finds Easy Way to Save 'Hard Money,'" *Washington Post,* 1 July 1996, A4; Ira Chinoy and Dan Morgan, "DNC Donors Also Gave to State Groups," *Washington Post,* 26 January 1997, A1, A8.

69. Dan Balz, "'Team GOP' Tunes Up Message Machinery," *Washington Post,* 26 May 1996, A18.

70. Paul S. Herrnson, *Congressional Elections: Campaigning at Home and in Washington* (Washington, D.C.: CQ Press, 1995), 84.

71. Federal Election Commission, "Political Parties Fundraising Hits $881 Million."

72. Herrnson, *Congressional Elections,* 94.

73. Ibid., 81–83.

74. Marcus and Babcock, "The System Cracks Under the Weight of

Cash," A21.

75. Ibid.

76. Thomas B. Edsall, "Candidate's Backers Hope to Make Oregon a Liberal Proving Ground," *Washington Post,* 27 January 1996, A3.

77. Marcus and Babcock, "The System Cracks Under the Weight of Cash," A21.

78. Balz, " 'Team GOP' Tunes Up Message Machinery," A18.

79. Guy Gugliotta and Ira Chinoy, "Outsiders Make Erie Ballot a National Battle," *Washington Post,* 10 February 1997, A1, A10–A11.

80. Brett Pulley, "At One Office, Intricate Links in New Jersey's GOP Funds," *New York Times,* 8 July 1996, A1, A9.

81. Cotter et al., *Party Organizations in American Politics,* 16–19; A. James Reichley, *The Life of the Parties: A History of American Political Parties* (New York: Free Press, 1992), 391–92; John F. Bibby, "State Party Organizations: Coping and Adapting," in Maisel, *The Parties Respond.*

82. Clifford J. Levy, "Pataki and GOP Report Surge in Raising Funds," *New York Times,* 16 July 1996, A12.

83. Heard, *The Costs of Democracy,* 218–22, 228–29.

84. Charles R. Babcock, "Parties Rack Up Six-Figure Gifts of 'Soft Money,' " *Washington Post,* 28 September 1992, A15.

85. David E. Price, *The Congressional Experience* (Boulder, Colo.: Westview Press, 1992), 140–41.

86. Reichley, *The Life of the Parties,* 385.

87. Anthony Gierzynski, *Legislative Campaign Committees in American States* (Lexington: University of Kentucky Press, 1992), 11–14; Shea, *Transforming Democracy;* Alan Rosenthal and Cindy Simon, "New Party or Campaign Bank Account? Explaining the Rise of State Legislative Campaign Committees," *Legislative Studies Quarterly* (1995):248–68.

88. Jeffrey M. Stonecash and Sara Keith, "Maintaining a Political Party: Providing and Withdrawing Campaign Funds," *Party Politics* 2 (1996): 313–28; Gierzynski, *Legislative Campaign Committees in American States,* 71–91.

89. "Guru in Ohio," *Congressional Quarterly Weekly Report,* 4 November 1989, 2979.

90. Tom Loftus, "The New 'Political Parties' in State Legislatures," *State Government* 58 (1985): 108.

91. Frank J. Sorauf, *Inside Campaign Finance: Myths and Realities* (New Haven: Yale University Press, 1992), 120.

92. Shea, *Transforming Democracy,* chap. 7.

93. Dan Barry, "Republicans on Long Island Master Science of Politics," *New York Times,* 8 March 1994, A15; Tom Watson, "All Powerful Machine of Yore Endures in New York's Nassau," *Congressional Quarterly Weekly Report,* 17 August 1985, 1623–25.

94. David S. Broder, "Ground War Heating Up in California," *Washington Post,* 10 September 1988, A16.

95. John P. Frendreis, Alan R. Gitelson, Gregory Fleming, and Anne

Layzell, "Local Political Parties and Legislative Races," in *The State of the Parties,* ed. Daniel M. Shea and John C. Green (Lanham, Md.: Rowman and Littlefield, 1995); Cotter et al., *Party Organizations in American Politics;* James L. Gibson, John P. Frendreis, and Laura L. Vertz, "Party Dynamics in the 1980s: Change in County Party Organizational Strength, 1980–1984," *American Journal of Political Science* 33 (February 1989).

96. Frendreis et al., "Local Political Parties and Legislative Races," 139–43.

97. Paul Allen Beck, Audrey Haynes, Russell J. Dalton, and Robert J. Huckfeldt, "Party Effort at the Grass Roots: Local Presidential Campaigning in 1992," paper presented at the annual meetings of the Midwest Political Science Association, Chicago, 1994, 14.

98. John F. Bibby, "Political Parties and Federalism: The Republican National Committee Involvement in Gubernatorial and Legislative Elections," *Publius* 9, no. 1 (1979); Bibby, "Political Parties Trends in 1985: The Continuing but Constrained Advance of the National Party," *Publius* 16, no. 1 (1986); Beck et al., "Party Effort at the Grass Roots."

99. Gibson et al., "Party Dynamics in the 1980s," 76.

100. Wilson, *Political Organizations,* xiii.

101. Byron E. Shafer, ed., *Postwar Politics in the G-7: Orders and Eras in Comparative Perspective* (Madison: University of Wisconsin Press, 1996), 36.

102. Clyde Wilcox, *Onward Christian Soldiers: The Religious Right in American Politics* (Boulder, Colo.: Westview Press, 1996); Shafer, "Partisan Elites."

103. Shafer, *Postwar Politics in the G-7,* 34; Shafer, "Partisan Elites."

104. Shafer, *Bifurcated Politics,* 100–107; Warren E. Miller and M. Kent Jennings, *Parties in Transition: A Longitudinal Study of Party Elites and Supporters* (New York: Russell Sage Foundation, 1988), chap. 9.

105. Shafer, *Postwar Politics in the G-7,* 36.

106. William G. Mayer, "Caucuses: How They Work, What Difference They Make," in *In Pursuit of the White House: How We Choose Our Presidential Nominees,* ed. William G. Mayer (Chatham, N.J.: Chatham House, 1996), 133.

107. John G. Francis and Robert C. Benedict, "Issue Group Activists at Conventions," in *The Life of the Parties: Activists in Presidential Politics,* ed. Ronald B. Rapoport, Alan I. Abramowitz, and John McGlennon (Lexington: University of Kentucky Press, 1986), 105–110.

108. Wilcox, *Onward Christian Soldiers,* 75–77.

109. David S. Broder, "Two Called to Serve," *Washington Post,* 29 January 1997, A21.

110. Warren E. Miller, *Without Consent: Mass-Elite Linkages in Presidential Politics* (Lexington: University of Kentucky Press, 1988), chap. 2.

111. Mayhew, *Placing Parties in American Politics,* 331.

112. Wilson, *Political Organizations,* 95.

113. Key, *Politics, Parties, and Pressure Groups,* 315.

5

Mass Partisanship,
1946–1996

WILLIAM G. MAYER

hatever their other sources of power, however strong their organizational capacity, political parties in a democracy must have some capacity to shape and influence voting behavior. Access to money and technology, plus a lengthy list of well-developed policy proposals, are useful assets for a party to possess. They may even be a sufficient source of political power for an interest group or a think tank. But all of the distinctive functions served by *political parties* depend ultimately on their capacity to elect public officials. Thus, any attempt to examine the interconnection of parties and political change must ultimately come to terms with mass partisanship: with the relationship between political parties and the ordinary voter.

Because parties are so centrally connected with voting, mass partisanship is also probably the best-documented and most-studied aspect of the American party system. Thanks to the efforts of a number of polling organizations—in particular, the Center for Political Studies at the University of Michigan—we possess an unusually rich and continuous set of indicators of partisan attitudes and behaviors within the American public over most of the last half century. Accordingly, after an introductory discussion of the nature and characteristics of mass partisanship, this chapter examines five different measures of that concept, along with the changes that took place in them between 1952 and 1996.

The general picture, it soon becomes clear, is that American mass partisanship has declined over the past fifty years, though some dispute remains as to how large that decline has been and how to interpret it. A final section discusses these changes against the background of other major developments in postwar American politics, assessing the place of mass partisanship in this larger fabric of political change.

The Nature of Mass Partisanship

The term *partisanship* is used throughout this chapter in a deliberately broad way, to characterize the relationship between two important actors in the world of electoral politics: political parties and voters. Long before the advent of survey research, it was clear to even the most casual observer of American politics that parties had a major influence on how most citizens voted.[1] When voting behavior emerged as a significant subject for academic inquiry, the crucial question was not, "Do parties affect voters?"—they obviously do—but, "*How* do parties affect voters?"

Exactly what kind of relationship connected voters to their favorite political party? It was clear from the outset that this relationship was not one of explicit membership in a formal organization. Highly structured, mass membership parties thrived in many European democracies, but not in the United States. Instead, the tie had to be of a less tangible, more psychological character. But what did parties "look like" in the mind of the average voter?

The Michigan Model

The first major answer to this question was developed during the 1950s by a group of scholars at the University of Michigan. The most complete presentation of their position appears in the classic 1960 book by Campbell, Converse, Miller, and Stokes, *The American Voter*.[2] According to the Michigan school, American mass partisanship did not have a great deal of substantive intellectual or policy content. Instead, voters were connected to political parties primarily by an "affective" or emotional tie.

Both halves of this portrait are worth noting. On the one hand, *The American Voter* did not offer an especially exalted view of the political sophistication of the typical citizen. The vast majority of the electorate did not possess developed ideologies or well-integrated political opinions; by and large, they lacked even the minimum requisites for issue voting; in particular, few were able to say where the parties stood on the most important issues of the day. And yet, those obstacles notwithstanding, most voters did think of themselves as either Democrats or Republicans, and that identification appeared to play a central role in shaping their other political opinions and behaviors, especially the way they voted on election day. As Campbell et al. explained their theory:

> Generally this tie is a psychological identification, which can persist without legal recognition or evidence of formal membership and even without a consistent record of party support. Most Americans have this sense of attachment with one party or the other. And for the individual who does, the strength and direction of party identification are facts of central importance in accounting for attitude and behavior.
>
> In characterizing the relation of individual to party as a psychological identification we invoke a concept that has played an important if somewhat varied role in psychological theories of the relation of individual to individual or of individual to group. We use the concept here to characterize the individual's affective orientation to an important group-object in his environment. Both reference group theory and small-group studies of influence have converged upon the attracting or repelling quality of the group as the generalized dimension most critical in defining the individual-group relationship, and it is this dimension that we call identification.[3]

The Michigan view of partisanship has often been compared with the way that most people develop and maintain a commitment to a particular religious denomination.[4] But a better analogy might be to say that the Michigan scholars saw the relationship between a voter and his favorite party as very much like the relationship between a sports fan and his or her favorite team. Though sports metaphors are overused in contemporary American politics, in this case the comparison can be illuminating:

• By and large, a young person growing up in Chicago or Boston does not become a fan of the Cubs or the Red Sox as the result of a careful, deliberate, rational weighing of the alternatives. Indeed, most people never make any conscious decision about rooting for a particular sports team. Instead, they grow up in an environment where the Red Sox are "the good guys" and the Yankees are "the enemy," and over time gradually come to absorb the same outlook. And so it seemed to be with political parties. By growing up in a family where the Democrats were the heroes of a typical political drama and the Republicans were the villains, young people learned to view politics from the same basic perspective. In the end, they developed a set of emotional reactions to the two major parties that did not have a great deal of issue content behind them. Perhaps the key piece of evidence underlying this part of the Michigan theory was the finding that the single strongest predictor of an individual's current party identification was the partisanship of his or her parents. To a remarkable extent, partisanship seemed to be passed on from parents to children.

• Once a person becomes a fan of a sports team, however, that allegiance quickly comes to serve as a dominant cue for interpreting events and situations. Given a close play at the plate, the verdict of most fans about whether the base runner is safe or out depends on what team the runner belongs to. In an analogous way, party identification provides an important lens through which partisans see and interpret the world of politics, and thus it heavily shapes the judgments they render about particular candidates and controversies. Should Richard Nixon be impeached? Is Jimmy Carter a strong leader? Is Dan Quayle qualified to be president? On all these issues (and literally hundreds of others), the single best predictor of an individual's opinion was his or her partisanship.

• Finally, just as a lifelong Red Sox fan did not suddenly start rooting for the Yankees, so too did a person's partisanship tend to be an enduring commitment. At both the aggregate and the individual level, party identifications seemed impressively stable—a good deal more stable than ideology, issue opinions, or voting behavior. Indeed, almost like a habit, party identifications actually grew stronger over time. The longer people identified with a party, the stronger their reported sense of attachment to it became.

An Alternative Approach

The affective model of party identification dominated academic voting studies for almost three decades. In the mid-1970s, however, a number of scholars—most notably, Morris Fiorina—began to enunciate a different concept of partisanship, one that portrayed it as a more rational and cognitive phenomenon.[5] In brief, Fiorina depicted party identification as a kind of "running balance sheet" of each voter's experiences and evaluations about how the parties had previously performed in government.

In this view, a voter born in 1930 would, by the 1990s, have strong personal memories of almost half a century of partisan and political history. He might give the Democrats credit for leading the country through the Great Depression and World War II, but blame them for postwar inflation and the stalemated war in Korea. He might have positive personal memories of both Eisenhower and Kennedy, while remaining uncertain what they had accomplished in policy terms; he might have considerably more negative assessments of Johnson and Nixon; and so on.

If this voter's net evaluation of all these experiences showed the Democrats performing significantly better than the Republicans, then he or she became a Democrat. If other people felt that their needs and values had been better served by Republican policies, they developed an identification with the Republican Party. Fiorina's model of party identification thus placed great emphasis on so-called *retrospective* voting issues: on the impressions and evaluations that voters had developed by observing how each party had handled its prior governmental responsibilities. Other scholars accorded a larger role to a party's current stands on questions of policy and ideology.[6] Details aside, the revisionist theories of party identification generally agreed on three main points:

1. Party identification was not only, or even primarily, an emotional attachment. It also had a significant rational component. In particular, party labels served as a kind of informational shortcut that helped voters make sense of the complicated world of electoral politics. Instead of having to learn about the specific policy stands of dozens of individual candidates for state and federal office, a voter could infer a great deal about a candidate's likely behavior in office simply by knowing his party affiliation.[7]

2. Thus, party identifications also had *political* content. They were not just a function of psychological and sociological processes occurring within the family and other primary groups. They also reflected important experiences and expectations about ideology, policy, and governmental performance.

3. Finally, the revisionist perspective saw party identifications as significantly more malleable than the Michigan model: party identifications could and did change. Put another way, partisanship was not just something that caused other political attitudes and behaviors. It also responded to a wide variety of political stimuli. In Fiorina's words, "There is an inertial element in voting behavior [i.e., party identification], but that inertial element has an experiential basis; it is *not* something learned at mommy's knee and never questioned thereafter."[8]

Over the past ten or fifteen years, the revisionist theory of party identification has probably had more impact than the Michigan model on those political scientists doing work in the subfield of parties and elections. Yet there have been, to date, remarkably few attempts to compare and test the two models against one another. The problem is simply stated: there are relatively few issues on which the models offer clearly divergent predictions. One general example can illuminate the problem.

As we have just seen, one of the key pieces of empirical support for an affective model of partisanship was the finding that most people identified with the same party their parents did. Within the framework of the Michigan model, such a pattern was said to show that party identifications were acquired primarily through the processes of familial socialization. But it is equally possible to absorb these facts within the constraints of Fiorina's theory. Parents, after all, generally pass on a large number of social and demographic attributes to their children: race, religion, educational attainment, socioeconomic status, region of residence, and so forth. To the extent that these attributes help shape a person's political values and perspectives, it would not be surprising to find that parents and children also reach similar conclusions when evaluating party performance.

From the 1880s through the 1950s, for example, several successive generations of white southerners identified overwhelmingly with the Democratic Party. From the perspective of the Michigan model, this was because party allegiances forged during the Civil War and Reconstruction were simply passed, via socialization, from one generation to the next. Yet the rational-cognitive school might reply that white southerners joined the Democratic Party because they approved of its stands on the issues, especially racial issues, and that the intergenerational continuity is explained by the fact that white southern parents tended to pass on their issue positions to their white southern children.

Perhaps the clearest difference between the two theories, as I have just indicated, concerned the extent to which party identifications are changeable in the short run. Yet even this distinction starts to blur on closer examination. On one hand, the authors of *The American Voter* never claimed that party identifications were perfectly stable.[9] On the other hand, Fiorina's model suggests that, except for very young voters, a running tally of party evaluations should not be expected to change very rapidly. So when analysis of panel surveys showed that party identifications were pretty stable but did exhibit some variation over time, it was not immediately clear which theory was supported.[10]

Mass Partisanship in the 1950s: An Overview

What was the state of American mass partisanship in the late 1940s and early 1950s? While a detailed analysis of the data will be postponed for a few pages, the general picture is readily summarized in advance: in the immediate postwar years, partisan attachments seem to have meant a good deal to the average American. This point should not be overstated.

As several historians have noted, American political parties as an influence on the electorate probably reached their strongest point in the late 1800s. Compared with that time period, the parties of the 1940s and 1950s were, as evidenced by available measures, already a good deal weaker.[11] From the perspective of the 1990s, however, one is more impressed by how strong the parties remained.

To begin with, about 75 percent of Americans had a party identification. That is to say, they willingly labeled themselves either Democrats or Republicans. The "independent" appellation, for all its popularity in our civics rhetoric, was chosen by only about a quarter of the adult population. As we later see, a number of political scientists have recently argued that many contemporary independents are actually hidden, or "closet," partisans. What is noteworthy about the 1950s, however, is that few Americans apparently felt the need to mask their partisanship: the vast majority openly admitted to having a party allegiance, without any further prompting.

Moreover, between 1952 and 1964—in what Philip Converse has accurately called "the steady-state period"[12]—the level of American mass partisanship was impressively *stable*. Year in and year out, regardless of the election results, an average of about 36 percent of Americans said they were strong partisans; about 38 percent were weak partisans; and 22 percent were independents. (The other 3–4 percent of the population were apolitical or considered themselves members of some minor party.)

Equally striking is the way that partisanship structured voting behavior throughout the ballot. If a person could be persuaded to vote for the presidential candidate of a particular party, there was at least an 80 percent chance that he would vote for the senatorial and congressional candidates of the same party. About 70 percent also voted a straight ticket for state and local offices.

There is a famous anecdote from this period—sufficiently famous that I have heard three different cities claimed as its place of origin—that summarizes the conventional wisdom about how most voters behaved and, hence, about how election campaigns were run. The story is about a candidate chosen by a big-city Democratic machine for some local office like county assessor or district attorney. Midway through the campaign, the candidate begins to notice that the local organization is working very hard to get votes for Franklin Roosevelt, but it does not seem to be doing anything at all for him. So he complains to the boss, and the boss says to him,

> "You ever notice how, when a big boat pulls into a dock, the water in its wake drags a lot of trash in behind it?"

"Yeah."

"Well, Roosevelt's the boat and you're the trash."

The 1952 survey of American voters, the first of the National Election Studies, can be used to make the same point statistically. In the 1952 survey there were 262 strong Democrats who voted in the November election, and 219 of them (84 percent) voted for the Democratic presidential candidate, Adlai Stevenson. There were also 200 strong Republicans, 197 of whom (98 percent!) voted for the GOP nominee, Dwight Eisenhower. Thus, of all the strong partisans in the 1952 survey who cast a presidential ballot, 90 percent (416 of 462) remained loyal to the standard-bearer of their party.

This behavior was underpinned by a slightly paradoxical set of opinions and perceptions within the general public. As we have already seen, most Americans had no difficulty saying that they considered themselves Democrats or Republicans. According to a different sequence of questions, which asked respondents what they liked and disliked about the parties, about 40 percent of Americans expressed a positive attitude toward one party and a negative attitude toward the other, while another 20–25 percent liked their own party and were neutral about the opposition. At the same time, however, only about 50 percent claimed to see any important differences between the parties. Much as the Michigan scholars had claimed, the strong emotional reactions to the parties held by most Americans were not necessarily buttressed by substantive political content.

Finally, party regularity at the ballot box produced an assumption of unified party government: whatever party won the presidency would also claim a majority of seats in the House and Senate. Between 1896 and 1954, the United States encountered divided partisan control of the national government for a total of only eight years. And in every case, the division was brought into being by a midterm election and was resolved in the next presidential voting. Indeed, so rare was divided government during this era that when the Democrats unexpectedly lost control of Congress in 1946, Democratic Congressman J. William Fulbright issued a highly publicized recommendation that President Truman should appoint a Republican as Secretary of State and then resign from the presidency, thereby allowing that Republican to succeed to the Oval Office.[13]

Five Measures of Mass Partisanship

As noted earlier, there is probably no aspect of American political parties that has been measured as regularly and systematically as mass partisanship. Surveys of party elites or party organizations are hard to come by, but American voters are, if anything, oversurveyed. For academic voting analysts in general, and for this chapter in particular, the most important surveys are the American National Election Studies (ANES), conducted in 1952 and then every two years since 1956 by the Survey Research Center and the Center for Political Studies at the University of Michigan.

Unfortunately for the formal parallelism of this book, reliance on the Michigan election surveys means that we do not have data for the first six years of the period we are examining. Yet there is no reason to think that the general picture of partisan change presented here would be very different if the ANES surveys had commenced a few years earlier; as the following analysis shows, the major break-point appears to come later. In compensation for those few missing observations, then, we acquire a data source of immense richness and reliability. Specifically, five different measures of American partisanship that have been included in the National Election Studies on a regular basis will carry the analysis here.

Party Identification

The most frequently used measure of mass partisanship—indeed, it is probably the single most-analyzed question in all of political science—is party identification. For the benefit of those who have managed to remain uninitiated, the standard ANES party identification question set is listed at the top of table 5.1.

Initially, almost all research on the strength of American party identifications used this sequence of questions to divide respondents into three major categories: "strong partisans" (including both strong Republicans and strong Democrats), "weak partisans" (again, Republicans and Democrats), and "independents." That is to say, those respondents who said they were Democrats or Republicans were further subdivided according to whether their professed attachment to the party was strong or weak. Those respondents who initially declined a party identification were lumped together into a single category, as independents.[14]

This classification scheme, which might be called the "traditional definition" of party identification, yields the data shown in part A of table 5.1. The forty-four years spanned by these figures appear to divide into four major subperiods. First comes the "steady-state period," from 1952 through 1964. Shortly after the 1964 election, however, the public's attachment to both major parties began to unravel. The decline took place over a period of about ten years, ending in 1972 or 1974. In all, the number of strong partisans fell by about 10 percent, while the number of independents increased by perhaps 15 percent. Up to this point, the story

TABLE 5.1

STRENGTH OF AMERICAN PARTY IDENTIFICATION,
1952–96

- "Generally speaking, do you usually think of yourself as a Republican, a Democrat, an Independent, or what?"
- (**If Republican or Democrat**) "Would you call yourself a strong Republican/Democrat or a not very strong Republican/Democrat?"
- (**If Independent or Other**) "Do you think of yourself as closer to the Republican or Democratic party?"

A. *Traditional definition*

	Strong partisans	*Weak partisans*	*Independents*
1952	35	39	22
1956	36	37	23
1958	38	39	19
1960	36	38	23
1962	35	39	21
1964	38	38	23
1966	28	43	28
1968	30	40	29
1970	29	39	31
1972	25	39	35
1974	26	35	36
1976	24	39	36
1978	23	37	37
1980	26	37	35
1982	30	38	30
1984	29	35	34
1986	28	37	33
1988	31	31	36
1990	30	34	35
1992	29	32	38
1994	31	33	35
1996	32	35	33
1952–56–60 average	36	38	23
1988–92–96 average	31	33	36
Change	−5	−5	+13

Continued . . .

TABLE 5.1 — CONTINUED

B. Revised definition

	Strong partisans	Weak partisans	Independent leaners	Pure independents
1952	35	39	17	6
1956	36	37	15	9
1958	38	39	12	7
1960	36	38	13	10
1962	35	39	13	8
1964	38	38	15	8
1966	28	43	16	12
1968	30	40	19	10
1970	29	39	18	13
1972	25	39	22	13
1974	26	35	22	15
1976	24	39	21	14
1978	23	37	24	14
1980	26	37	22	13
1982	30	38	19	11
1984	29	35	23	11
1986	28	37	21	12
1988	31	31	25	11
1990	30	34	24	11
1992	29	32	27	12
1994	31	33	24	10
1996	32	35	24	9
1952–56–60 average	36	38	15	8
1988–92–96 average	31	33	25	11
Change	−5	−5	+10	+3

SOURCE: *National Election Study* (Ann Arbor: Interuniversity Consortium for Political and Social Research, various years).

is probably a familiar one, even to fairly casual observers of American politics.

The early 1970s, in particular, witnessed the publication of a huge spate of books and articles declaring that American political parties were in decline, maybe even already dead.[15] What has received substantially less attention is the trend since the mid-1970s. All the gloomy prophecies notwithstanding, party identifications stopped falling after 1974 and, beginning in 1982, even enjoyed a small increase. This resurgence, which appears most clearly in the proportion of strong partisans, did not undo all the damage the parties had suffered between 1964 and 1974, but it did make clear that the obituaries were premature—and that political parties had a good deal more resilience than they were often given credit for.

According to an important recent study, however, the data just discussed overstate the magnitude of party decline, precisely because the traditional definition of party identification treated independents as a single undifferentiated category. Further analysis has suggested that this was probably an inaccurate assumption, for most of those who initially said that they were independents admitted, when asked, that they felt closer to one party than to the other. And these "independent leaners," as they came to be called, turned out to behave much more like traditional party identifiers than like the "pure independents," who denied feeling closer to either party. A group of scholars centered at the University of California at Berkeley maintained, therefore, that the growing number of "independents" recorded by the traditional definition of party identification actually included a large number of "closet partisans."[16] In consequence, the Berkeley group argued for a four-category classification system for measuring the strength of party allegiances: strong partisans, weak partisans, independent leaners, and pure independents. These data are shown in part B of table 5.1.

At one level, this "revised definition" of party identification produces the same pattern as the more traditional classification: American mass partisanship stayed constant between 1952 and 1964, declined between 1964 and 1974, and then exhibited a modest increase in the early to mid-1980s. Yet the magnitude of the antipartisan swing, measured this way, was considerably smaller. Where the traditional definition had suggested a 15-percentage-point increase in the number of independents, the revised data showed an increase only about half that size. And where the original classification had painted a picture in which almost 40 percent of the American public were floating free of party attachments, the revised definition showed only a distinct minority to be truly independent: about 14 percent in the mid-1970s, about 11 percent in more recent surveys.

Party Identification and the Vote

The influence of party identifications on voting behavior can weaken in two distinct ways. On the one hand, as we have just seen, more and more Americans can perceive themselves as independent of, or less firmly attached to, partisan moorings. Strong partisans become weak partisans; weak partisans and independent leaners turn into pure independents. But a second possibility also exists: even among those who continue to think of themselves as Democrats or Republicans, that identification simply ex-

TABLE 5.2

PROPORTION OF PARTY IDENTIFIERS VOTING
IN ACCORD WITH THEIR IDENTIFICATION,
1952–96

A. *Presidential elections*

	Strong partisans	*Weak partisans*	*Independent leaners*
1952	90	74	74
1956	91	75	82
1960	94	77	87
1964	94	72	84
1968	89	68	67
1972	84	64	74
1976	93	75	78
1980	88	71	61
1984	92	79	87
1988	95	76	86
1992	90	65	67
1996	95	76	72
1952–60 average	92	75	81
1988–96 average	93	72	75
Change	+1	−3	−6

Continued . . .

erts less influence on their voting behavior. Put another way, the recent uptick in the number of strong partisans is of little help to the parties if more and more of these partisans end up deserting their party's candidates on election day. In short: do people who call themselves partisans actually *vote* partisan?

The data needed to answer this question are shown in table 5.2. For each of three offices—the presidency, the Senate, and the House of Representatives—the table shows the percentage of strong, weak, and independent-leaning partisans who voted in accord with their reported party identifications. For presidential balloting, the clear moral of these data is the continuing vitality of party identifications as a force in the voting booth. Though partisan defections increased somewhat during the turbulent elections of 1968 and 1972, party voting has enjoyed a nice recovery in more recent years, especially 1984 and 1988. In 1992 the presidential candidacy of Ross Perot made sizable inroads into the ranks of weak partisans and independent leaners. But even with the Perot vote taken

TABLE 5.2 — CONTINUED

B. *U.S. Senate elections*

	Strong partisans	Weak partisans	Independent leaners
1952	88	81	69
1956	93	84	75
1960	94	82	87
1964	91	78	74
1968	88	75	60
1972	84	70	69
1976	89	73	69
1980	88	73	66
1984	87	75	71
1988	85	74	72
1992	87	73	75
1996	90	82	69
1952–60 average	92	82	77
1988–96 average	87	76	72
Change	−5	−6	−5

C. *U.S. House elections*

	Strong partisans	Weak partisans	Independent leaners
1952	91	82	72
1956	95	87	84
1960	91	85	78
1964	93	76	76
1968	89	75	71
1972	88	78	76
1976	87	73	72
1980	82	71	69
1984	87	68	68
1988	83	76	75
1992	86	74	71
1996	92	75	73
1952–60 average	92	85	78
1988–96 average	87	75	73
Change	−5	−10	−5

SOURCE: *National Election Study* (Ann Arbor: Interuniversity Consortium for Political and Social Research, various years).

into account, the average rate of party loyalty over the last three presidential elections may actually have increased among strong partisans and declined only slightly among both weak and independent partisans.

On the other hand, party identifications have held up less well as a guide to voting in Senate elections. For each category of partisan, there is a clear if modest increase in the rate of defection. In the 1952–60 period, about 92 percent of strong partisans voted for their party's nominee to the U.S. Senate. In the 1988–96 period, this fell to 87 percent. An even greater erosion is visible in the data on House voting, as shown in part C of table 5.2 (p. 199). Weak partisans seem to have been especially prone to desertion in congressional elections; where the average loyalty rate for this group was once 85 percent, it had dropped to 75 percent by the 1988–96 period.

Overall, the results in table 5.2 appear to support several major conclusions. First, party identifications remain a very important influence on vote choice. At least 85 percent of strong partisans can be counted on to support their party's candidate, regardless of the office at stake. Even among weak partisans and independent leaners, party loyalty in the voting booth rarely dips below 65 percent. That said, it is also clear that party identifications do not count for as much as they did four or five decades ago. Yet in an era when it is often claimed that parties are being undermined by the mass media and issue voting, the data also show, paradoxically, that rates of party loyalty have declined least in the media-intensive, issue-rich environment of presidential elections. The erosion of party voting is considerably more pronounced in Senate and House elections, in which media coverage is generally far more limited (especially on television) and in which voters are much less likely to possess the knowledge requisite for most forms of issue voting.

Likes and Dislikes about the Parties

Another frequently used source of evidence about trends in American mass partisanship comes from a series of open-ended questions in which respondents are asked to evaluate the Democratic and Republican parties. Generally placed near the beginning of the ANES surveys in presidential years, the four questions read as follows:

- Is there anything in particular that you like about the Republican Party? (What is that?)
- Is there anything in particular that you don't like about the Republican Party? (What is that?)

- Is there anything in particular that you like about the Democratic Party? (What is that?)
- Is there anything in particular that you don't like about the Democratic Party? (What is that?)

The great advantage of these questions is that they allow respondents to evaluate the parties in whatever terms they choose, instead of reacting to a set of issues and categories created by survey designers. Respondents can talk about broad ideological themes, specific policy issues, past party performance in office, records for helping or hurting various group interests—or they can reply that there is, in fact, nothing that they like or dislike about a particular party. For each of the four questions, interviewers and coders are allowed to record up to five distinct answers,[17] thus providing a rich portrait of public attitudes toward the two major parties.[18] The great disadvantage of this measure, unfortunately, is that its administration was changed crucially halfway through the postwar period. Since this measure has received considerable attention elsewhere, it should be examined here as well—but as we later see it is probably not a very reliable indicator of changes in postwar partisanship.

When using these questions as an indicator of partisanship, survey analysts have typically begun by dividing respondent attitudes toward each party into three major categories. "Positives," as the name implies, are those who say that they like more things about a party than they dislike; these are respondents for whom the number of distinct positive comments exceeds the number of distinct negative comments. "Negatives," of course, are people whose net attitude toward a particular party is unfavorable, who provide the interviewer with more dislikes than likes. "Neutrals," finally, are respondents who do not, on balance, express either a positive or a negative attitude toward a party. For the analysis that follows, it is important to recognize that one can get classified as a neutral in two major ways. One is to express an equal number of likes and dislikes for a party: for example, three positive comments about the Democrats and three negative comments. The second and vastly more common route to neutrality is to provide what is sometimes called a "no content" response, where the respondent tells the interviewer that there is nothing he likes or dislikes about a party. Taking into account each respondent's view of both parties, then, produces a sixfold classification of the electorate:

- positive-positives (who have positive views of both parties)

- positive-neutrals (who have a positive view of one party and a neutral view of the other)
- positive-negatives
- neutral-neutrals
- negative-neutrals
- negative-negatives

It is these data, shown in table 5.3, that provide the key piece of evidence for one of the most influential recent assessments of trends in American mass partisanship. The major problem facing contemporary American parties, according to Martin Wattenberg, who first elaborated the trend, is not that people actively dislike them but that they no longer see them as meaningful or relevant.[19] Where parties were once a central element in the way most Americans looked at politics, today they occupy a considerably more marginal position. Translated in terms of the variables and categories just described, the argument is not that voters are increasingly negative about the parties, just that they are increasingly *neutral*.[20]

The problem in this analysis, and its measure, is simply stated. After increasing slightly between 1952 and 1956, the proportion of respondents who had nothing good or bad to say about either party stayed essentially constant between 1956 and 1968, never falling below 13 percent and never rising above 17 percent. And then, between 1968 and 1972, the number of "no content" respondents almost doubled, jumping from 14 percent to 26 percent. Since 1972, the number of such responses has again stayed fairly stable, going up a bit in 1976 and 1980 but then declining marginally over the next four elections.

How should one explain this pattern? The decline in party identification was a ten-year affair, beginning sometime after the 1964 election and finally cresting in about 1974. The causal agents associated with the hypothesis of growing neutrality—namely, political leadership and the mass media—have been operating for an even longer period. Yet after making allowance for sampling error, it is unclear if any increase in "no content" responses occurred outside of the 1968–72 window. All of this suggests a second interpretation: what was taken initially for an increase in public apathy toward the parties was actually a subtle but important change in the ANES survey instrument.

From 1952 through 1968, the interviewing form simply listed this question and then provided several blank lines on which the interviewer could write down responses. Beginning in 1972, however, the first sentence was converted into an explicit screening question. That is, the sur-

TABLE 5.3
TRENDS IN PUBLIC LIKES AND DISLIKES OF THE MAJOR PARTIES, 1952-96

| | Positive-positive | Positive-neutral | Positive-negative | Neutral-neutral | | | Neutral-negative | Negative-negative |
				(no likes or dislikes)	(equal likes and dislikes)			
1952	6	18	50	10	3		10	4
1956	9	23	40	13	3		9	3
1960	8	24	41	16	1		7	2
1964	5	21	38	17	3		11	4
1968	4	17	38	14	3		14	10
1972	4	15	30	26	3		13	8
1976	4	13	31	29	3		12	8
1980	5	18	28	34	2		9	5
1984	4	18	32	33	2		8	3
1988	7	18	34	28	2		8	4
1992	3	13	34	29	2		12	5
1996	5	15	34	27	2		10	6

SOURCE: *National Election Study* (Ann Arbor: Interuniversity Consortium for Political and Social Research, various years).

NOTE: Figures in any single year may not sum to 100 percent due to rounding.

vey form now instructed the interviewer to go on to the next question if the respondent said "no" or "don't know." Under the original format, it seems likely that a significant number of respondents who replied in hesitant or uncertain terms were asked the accompanying probe: "What is that?" Since 1972, however, such respondents have been coded as "don't knows" and thus as "no content" responses.

The increase in "no content" responses may not be entirely an artifact of changes in survey methodology. The new question format appears to explain most of the change, but a small part of the shift—a few percentage points—may reflect a real alteration in public opinion. The important points are that any real change in American attitudes was probably a good deal smaller than these data on likes and dislikes would suggest and that the actual increase in partisan neutrality does not take us very far as a description or explanation of recent changes in mass partisanship.

Perceptions of Party Difference

Mass partisanship is not just a matter of feelings and emotions, but of perceptions and beliefs. While the "likes/dislikes" data offer one perspective on the cognitive side of American partisanship, a more direct measure is provided by a question that has been included in most (though not all) of the ANES presidential-year surveys: "Do you think there are any important differences in what the Republican and Democrats stand for?"

As the data in table 5.4 indicate, in both 1952 and 1960, when almost 75 percent of Americans readily identified themselves as either Democrat or Republican, only 50 percent claimed to see any important differences between the parties. This figure jumped to 59 percent in 1964, when one candidate (Barry Goldwater) went out of his way to emphasize his ideological distinctiveness. But this increased perception of party differences proved temporary; in the next three presidential elections, the public was once again evenly split on the matter. In 1980, however, the number of Americans seeing important differences between the parties rose to about 60 percent, and it has remained at this new level in every succeeding presidential election. In other words, the 1964 level of partisan polarization, once thought to be quite exceptional, has now become the norm in American politics.

While the trend is clear, it is considerably more difficult to say whether the data in table 5.4 represent good news or bad for the political parties. During the 1950s and parts of the 1960s, there were frequent complaints that American parties were ideologically flaccid and programmatically irresponsible: both the Democrats and the Republicans encom-

TABLE 5.4

PERCEPTION OF PARTY DIFFERENCES, 1952–96

- "Do you think there are any important differences in what the Republicans and Democrats stand for?"[a]

	Yes	No	Don't know
1952	50	41	9
1960	50	43	6
1964	59	41	–
1968	52	48	–
1972	46	44	10
1976	47	42	10
1980	58	34	8
1984	62	30	8
1988	60	35	6
1992	60	35	5
1996	64	34	1
1952–60 average	50	42	8
1988–96 average	61	35	4
Change	+11	−7	−4

SOURCE: *National Election Study* (Ann Arbor: Interuniversity Consortium for Political and Social Research, various years).

a. Wording varied slightly from year to year. In 1952 the question was, "Do you think there are any important differences between what the Democratic and Republican parties stand for, or do you think they are about the same?" In 1968, "Do you think there are any important differences between the Republican and Democratic parties?" In 1964 and 1968 the ANES coding system did not distinguish between "no" and "don't know" responses.

passed too many different opinions and viewpoints, they seemed much more concerned with winning elections than with implementing policies, and in the end there really was not much difference between them.

Today, ironically, one hears a great deal of the opposite criticism: the parties are too far apart, both are controlled by ideological zealots and extremists, neither represents the needs and preferences of the mainstream "sensible center." However interpreted, it is difficult to square these data with the argument that the public increasingly sees party labels as meaningless and irrelevant.

Straight-Party Voting versus Split-Ticket Voting

Whether self-described partisans vote in accord with their partisan identification and whether people cast straight-party or split-ticket votes are two forms of political behavior that are often treated as virtually identical. But on a conceptual level, at least, the two are quite distinct. Voters can, after all, temporarily defect from their chosen party and still cast a straight ticket. The key question is whether, having deserted their party for one office, they go on to abjure that party in every other election on the ballot. A lesser difference between partisanship and straight-ticket voting concerns the applicability of these notions to independent voters. Independents are, by definition, incapable of casting a vote in accord with (or against) their party identification, but they are capable of voting a straight-party ticket.

Beyond those immediate distinctions, the two forms of behavior have very different implications for leading normative accounts of mass democracy. None of the great expositors of the theory of party government ever expected, required, or even recommended that there be large numbers of psychologically committed party loyalists who would vote for a party's candidates year in and year out, *regardless* of who the candidates were or what they stood for. To the contrary, responsible party government rests on the assumption that not everyone's vote is rigidly determined, that at least some votes are available to the party that has performed well in office or that offers a particularly good set of policy proposals.

Split-ticket voting, by contrast, does pose a problem for many theories of party government. As more and more people vote for, say, a presidential candidate of one party and a congressional candidate of another, it becomes progressively more difficult to hold either party responsible for the final performance of government.[21] Thus the level of and trend in split-ticket voting merit separate examination.

One measure of this phenomenon is, by now, quite well known. Table 5.5 shows the percentage of congressional districts that had *split outcomes*: that is, districts that elected a representative from one party even as they cast a plurality of their presidential votes for a candidate from a different party. As these data make clear, by the late 1940s, supposedly a time of strong and stable partisanship, split-party outcomes were already a good deal more common than they had been at the beginning of the twentieth century, rising from about 5 percent in the earlier period to about 20 percent in 1948 and 1952.[22] During the past fifty years, however, the number of split-party results has ratcheted up another notch. In only three of the nine presidential elections since 1964 have more than 70 percent of congressional districts produced a unified partisan verdict. In 1972 and 1984, about 45 percent of all districts supported a presidential candidate from one party and a congressional candidate from the other.

TABLE 5.5

SPLIT-PARTY OUTCOMES IN PRESIDENTIAL AND
CONGRESSIONAL ELECTIONS, 1900–1996

	Number of districts with split results	*Percentage*
1900	10	3.4
1904	5	1.6
1908	21	6.7
1912	84	25.2
1916	35	10.5
1920	11	3.2
1924	42	11.8
1928	68	18.9
1932	50	14.1
1936	51	14.1
1940	53	14.6
1944	41	11.2
1948	90	21.3
1952	84	19.3
1956	130	29.9
1960	114	26.1
1964	145	33.3
1968	139	32.0
1972	192	44.1
1976	124	28.5
1980	143	32.8
1984	190	43.7
1988	148	34.0
1992	100	23.0
1996	110	25.3

SOURCE: 1900–1992 data taken from Norman J. Ornstein, Thomas E. Mann, and Michael J. Malbin, comps., *Vital Statistics on Congress, 1995–1996* (Washington, D.C.: CQ Press, 1996), 70. Figures for 1996 provided courtesy of Norman Ornstein.

NOTE: Before 1952, complete data are not available for all congressional districts.

Though the results in table 5.5 have important implications for the conduct of American national government, they are not necessarily a good indicator of individual behavior. In a congressional district with an approximately equal number of Democrats and Republicans, it would require only a very small number of ticket splitters to produce a narrow Republican plurality for one office and a narrow Democratic victory for the other. Perhaps, then, the pattern we have just observed has more to do with the declining sectionalism in American politics than with any real or significant changes in split-ticket voting.

The data in table 5.6, by contrast, are all direct measures of individual voting behavior. The first two columns in the top half of the table show the level of split-ticket voting in presidential and congressional elections: the percentage of voters in the ANES surveys who report voting for a presidential candidate from one party and a congressional candidate from another.[23] The next four columns report similar results on the frequency of split-ticket voting in senatorial and congressional elections, and then for all three types of federal elections together (presidential, senatorial, and congressional). The final element of table 5.6 is a question that appeared regularly in the National Election Studies between 1952 and 1984, asking if the respondent had voted a straight ticket for state and local offices.

Of all the data examined in this chapter, those in table 5.6 probably offer the most depressing news for both the Democratic and Republican parties. Where split-ticket voting once characterized only a small minority of Americans, it has become, over the past half-century, a dramatically more common form of behavior. In the elections of 1952, 1956, and 1960, about 85 percent of all those who cast both a presidential and a congressional vote were straight-ticket voters. Indeed, 80 percent or more voted for the same party in all three kinds of federal elections. Beginning in 1964, however, split-ticket voting started to increase, soaring to particularly high levels in 1968 and 1972. In the latter year, only 70 percent of the electorate voted for a presidential and congressional candidate of the same party, and just 57 percent cast a straight-party vote for all three federal offices.

The good news for the parties is that the problem has not gotten any worse since 1972. The proportion of straight-party votes has fluctuated over the last six presidential elections, but does not show any long-term decline. The bad news is that, unlike some of the other data series we have examined, neither is there any evidence that straight-ticket voting is starting to make a comeback. The levels of straight-ticket voting in 1988 and 1992 are almost identical with those that existed in 1976 and 1972, respectively.

Before moving on, one final issue connected with straight-party and split-ticket voting needs to be addressed. The assumption that guides most investigations into ticket splitting—including this one—is that change in this form of behavior tells us something significant about change in voter *attitudes*. This need not always be the case, however; ticket splitting may

TABLE 5.6

FOUR SURVEY MEASURES

OF STRAIGHT-TICKET VERSUS SPLIT-TICKET VOTING

(IN PERCENTAGES)

	Presidential-congressional		Senatorial-congressional		Presidential, senatorial, and congressional	
	Straight ticket	Split ticket	Straight ticket	Split ticket	Straight ticket	Split ticket
1952	87	13	90	10	83	17
1956	85	15	89	11	80	20
1960	85	15	90	10	83	17
1964	85	15	82	18	74	26
1968	74	26	77	23	64	36
1972	70	30	75	25	57	43
1976	73	27	74	26	62	38
1980	65	35	69	31	53	47
1984	74	26	80	20	65	35
1988	74	26	73	27	62	38
1992	64	36	75	25	57	43
1996	76	24	81	19	69	31
1952–60 average	86	14	90	10	82	18
1988–96 average	71	29	76	24	63	37
Change	−15	+15	−14	+14	−19	+19

(**Asked only of voters**): "How about the elections for other state and local offices—did you vote a straight ticket or did you vote for candidates from different parties?"[a]

	Straight ticket	Split ticket			Straight ticket	Split ticket
1952	74	26		1968	52	48
1956	71	29		1970	48	52
1958	69	31		1972	42	58
1960	73	27		1974	39	61
1962	58	42		1980	41	59
1964	60	40		1982	45	55
1966	50	50		1984	48	52

SOURCE: *National Election Study* (Ann Arbor: Interuniversity Consortium for Political and Social Research, various years).

a. Wording varied slightly from year to year. From 1956 to 1964, the question read, "How about the elections for state and local offices ...." In 1970, "Did you vote for other state and local offices?" [**If yes**] "Did you vote a straight ticket, or did you vote for candidates from different parties?"

rise or fall for reasons that have nothing to do with the partisan allegiances felt by the voters. There is considerable evidence, for example, that the level of party loyalty shown in the voting booth is affected by the type of ballot a state uses and whether it facilitates or discourages straight-ticket voting.[24] Since this question is directly addressed in chapter 6 of this volume, I limit myself here to examining a second possibility: that recent changes in ticket splitting are actually a reflection of changes in *candidate* behavior.

Suppose, in particular, that there was during this same period a large increase in the number of uncontested congressional elections. In that case, many highly partisan voters might not be able to cast a straight-ticket vote simply because their party did not field a congressional candidate in their district. In fact, however, just the opposite is true. As the data in table 5.7 demonstrate, the past fifty years actually witnessed a substantial decline in the number of uncontested congressional elections. In the elections of 1952, 1956, and 1960, an average of 81 congressional districts had only one major-party candidate.[25] But this fell to an average of 49 uncontested seats in the elections of 1964 through 1980 and then, after increasing somewhat in 1984 and 1988, plummeted to only 33 in 1992 and 20 in

TABLE 5.7

UNCONTESTED CONGRESSIONAL ELECTIONS,
1952–96

	Number of congressional districts with only one major-party candidate listed on the ballot
1952	92
1956	71
1960	79
1964	42
1968	47
1972	54
1976	51
1980	54
1984	67
1988	81
1992	33
1996	20

SOURCES: Based on data from Congressional Quarterly, *Guide to U.S. Elections*, 3d ed. (Washington, D.C.: CQ Press, 1994); and *Congressional Quarterly Weekly Report*, 15 February 1997, 447–55.

1996. In short, the recent increase in ticket-splitting occurred at a time when the option of casting a straight-party vote was gradually being extended to a larger and larger proportion of the electorate.

Summing Up: Mass Partisanship in the 1990s

The results of this analysis are summarized in table 5.8 (p. 212). For each of the variables discussed in the preceding section, table 5.8 shows the average figure for the first three presidential elections covered by the National Election Studies (1952, 1956, and 1960), the average figure for the three most recent presidential elections (1988, 1992, and 1996), and the change over time.[26] Individually, these results describe the situation in the 1990s. Collectively, they have two further things to say about the character of political change in our time.

The Five Indicators, a Half-Century Later

For all the twists and turns in these data, the general trend is immediately clear: party loyalties and allegiances, however conceptualized and measured, are weaker today than they were in the days of Harry Truman and Dwight Eisenhower. With the single exception of the question asking respondents if they see important differences between the parties—a problematic measure of party strength, since it does not index affection for either party—every indicator in table 5.8 shows a decline in American mass partisanship.

The measures offer rather different verdicts, however, as to how large that decline has been. In presidential voting, the drop in party loyalty is barely noticeable. Especially in the two traditional categories of party identifiers, strong and weak partisans, the percentage who voted in accord with that identification in the late 1980s and early 1990s compares quite favorably with the level of party loyalty in the 1950s. If the Berkeley analysis is correct, underlying party identifications have also survived quite well: the proportion of strong partisans has fallen by only about 5 percentage points; there has been a 3-point increase in the number of true independents.

But other indicators paint a much bleaker portrait of the parties' predicament. If party voting has held up well in presidential elections, it has declined more substantially in Senate and, especially, House elections. Over and above all this, there is the dramatic fall-off in straight-ticket voting. In the 1980s and 1990s, candidates for local office could no longer count on being "dragged in" by a big vote for their party's presidential candidate. Only about 60 percent of all voters preferred the same party's

TABLE 5.8

CHANGES IN MASS PARTISANSHIP: A SUMMARY
(IN PERCENTAGES)

	1952–60 average	1988–96 average	Change
Party identification: traditional definition			
Strong partisans	36	31	−5
Weak partisans	38	33	−5
Independents	23	36	+13
Party identification: revised definition			
Strong partisans	36	31	−5
Weak partisans	38	33	−5
Independent leaners	15	25	+10
Pure independents	8	11	+3
Party loyalty in presidential elections			
Strong partisans	92	93	+1
Weak partisans	75	72	−3
Independent leaners	81	75	−6
Party loyalty in Senate elections			
Strong partisans	92	87	−5
Weak partisans	82	76	−6
Independent leaners	77	72	−5
Party loyalty in House elections			
Strong partisans	92	87	−5
Weak partisans	85	75	−10
Independent leaners	78	73	−5
Percentage seeing important differences between the parties	50	61	+11
Percentage of split-party outcomes, presidential and congressional elections	25	27	+2
Straight-ticket voting			
Presidential-congressional	86	71	−15
Senatorial-congressional	90	76	−14
Presidential, senatorial, and congressional	82	63	−19

candidates for all three federal offices, and less than half voted a straight ticket in state and local races.

How did we get from there to here? Again, the indicators tell somewhat different stories. In the data on split-party outcomes in presidential and congressional elections (see table 5.5, p. 207), one could make the case that the crucial break with partisan tradition actually took place in 1956. In Eisenhower's second run for the White House, almost 30 percent of all congressional districts voted for a presidential candidate of one party and a congressional candidate from the other. In almost every other case, however, the decline in American mass partisanship seems to have been confined to a rather narrow time span: from about 1964 to 1974. In the two decades before that, partisanship was in a high and stable "steady state." In the two decades since then, partisanship has fluctuated a good deal but shows no further signs of long-term, sustained decline.

So the good news for American political parties is that their standing with the mass electorate is no longer falling. Though each new election seems to bring a chorus of woeful declamations about the collapse and disintegration of the American party system, the best description of mass partisanship over the past quarter century is not decline, but stability. The bad news is that there is little evidence that the parties have regained any of the ground they lost.

Considered in isolation, the changes in mass partisanship that occurred between 1964 and 1974 might be interpreted as only a temporary and transitional phenomenon. In particular, several accounts of the party realignment process postulate that partisan attachments will decline somewhat as a party system ages, until they are revived and reinvigorated by the next realignment.[27] Yet that clearly is *not* what occurred during the period we are examining here. The decline in mass partisanship seems, by every indication, to be a lasting one. Though the past decade or two have witnessed striking indications of growth and renewal in party organizations and partisan behavior in Congress, there is little evidence to suggest that these developments have been matched by a revival of mass partisanship.

Mass Partisanship and Political Change

What does mass partisanship tell us about the larger fabric of political change in the United States? Political parties, I have long believed, are an interesting and fruitful subject for academic research for two reasons: they are an important independent variable, and they are a good dependent variable. That is to say, a nation's party system has a significant role in shaping how the larger political system functions—but the parties are also a very telling *reflection* of that system and its history, substantive concerns, and political divisions.

The decline in mass partisanship that occurred between 1964 and 1974 should be viewed, I think, chiefly from the latter perspective. Whatever the cause(s) of that decline—the mass media, the behavior of govern-

ing elites, Vietnam, Watergate, the civil rights revolution, and on and on
—it seems clear that the parties were more victims than instigators. In ret-
rospect, the late 1960s and early 1970s will probably go down, along with
the Great Depression, as one of the two most turbulent and unsettling periods in twentieth-century American history. The Democratic and Republican parties did play some role in initiating and shaping this upheaval,
but by and large it occurred for reasons and in ways beyond their control.
Perhaps if the parties had been organizationally stronger at that point,
they might have resisted the tide a little better. As it was, they were severely weakened, though they remain a significant electoral force.

But the changes documented in this chapter have also played a major
role in *causing* what is probably the most distinctive phenomenon in
American government during the last third of the twentieth century: divided government. Through most of American history, whichever party
controlled the presidency also had a majority of seats in both houses of
Congress. The years between 1876 and 1896 form a partial exception to
this characterization, though in that period, the division occurred primarily because the two parties were so evenly balanced.[28] In any event, the
realignment that took place in 1896 ushered in an extended period of unified government. Between 1896 and 1954, the United States had divided
partisan control of the national government for only eight years.

To say the least, divided government is no longer such a shocking affair. Indeed, it is now the normal condition of American national government (and of most state governments for that matter). In only six of the
past twenty-eight years has one party controlled the presidency, the
House, and the Senate. A decline in mass partisanship is not, by itself,
sufficient to produce such a situation. But it does seem a *necessary* pre-
condition. In order for divided government to occur, some voters must
split their tickets. And in an era when the number of competitive or
"marginal" congressional districts has actually declined, that number
must be substantial. Whatever else lies behind divided government, it
would quickly disappear if more Americans could be convinced to vote
straight-party tickets.

All of this puts an interesting spin on the state of American political
parties at the close of the twentieth century. In 1950 a special committee
of the American Political Science Association issued a highly publicized
report calling for the creation of a "more responsible" party system in the
United States. Though it has become fashionable of late to impugn the
analysis and recommendations of this committee, the fact of the matter is
that, in a significant number of ways, American politics has moved much
closer to that ideal over the last half-century.

Just as the committee proposed, the national party organizations have become more powerful, more centralized, and more democratic. Party leadership in Congress, especially in the House of Representatives, has become stronger, more programmatically focused, and more capable of disciplining mavericks and recalcitrants. Even the voters have, to a significant measure, cooperated; party identifications, according to several recent accounts, have become more congruent with political ideology. The most striking anomaly in the American party system—the overwhelming identification of conservative white southerners with the Democratic Party—has been substantially whittled away by the forces of realignment and generational succession.[29]

It is largely in subpresidential voting that American politics falls significantly short of the responsible party ideal. Voting for Congress does not seem to be driven very much by policy or national performance issues; and whatever does drive it, the huge increase in split-ticket voting has regularly placed the presidency and Congress under divided party control, thereby thwarting the kind of clear accountability that is so central to the responsible party model. The result is what might be called a "semi-responsible" party system, in which the parties are more ideologically distinct but less clearly accountable for what they actually produce in office.

Notes

1. In particular, it is worth noting that studies of American political parties and electoral behavior written during the 1940s and early 1950s made frequent reference to the existence and importance of partisan "feelings" or "allegiances," though without being very specific about what form these attachments took. See, for example, E.E. Schattschneider, *Party Government* (New York: Holt, Rinehart and Winston, 1942); Samuel J. Eldersveld, "The Independent Vote: Measurement, Characteristics, and Implications for Party Strategy," *American Political Science Review* 46 (September 1952): 732–53; and Bernard R. Berelson, Paul F. Lazarsfeld, and William N. McPhee, *Voting: A Study of Opinion Formation in a Presidential Campaign* (Chicago: University of Chicago Press, 1954).

2. Angus Campbell, Philip E. Converse, Warren E. Miller, and Donald E. Stokes, *The American Voter* (New York: Wiley, 1960), especially chaps. 6 and 7. Earlier, preliminary statements of the Michigan theory of partisanship can be found in George Belknap and Angus Campbell, "Political Party Identification and Attitudes toward Foreign Policy," *Public Opinion Quarterly* 15 (Winter 1951–52): 597–623; and Angus Campbell, Gerald Gurin, and Warren E. Miller, *The Voter Decides* (Westport, Conn.: Greenwood Press), chap. 7.

Important later works that help clarify and extend this framework include

Philip E. Converse, "The Nature of Belief Systems in Mass Publics," in *Ideology and Discontent*, ed. David E. Apter (New York: Free Press, 1964), 206–61; Angus Campbell, Philip E. Converse, Warren E. Miller, and Donald E. Stokes, *Elections and the Political Order* (New York: Wiley, 1966); Philip E. Converse, *Dynamics of Party Support: Cohort-Analyzing Party Identification* (Beverly Hills, Calif.: Sage, 1976); Philip E. Converse and Gregory B. Markus, "Plus ça change ... : The New CPS Election Study Panel," *American Political Science Review* 73 (March 1979): 32–49; and Philip E. Converse and Roy Pierce, "Measuring Partisanship," *Political Methodology* 11 (1985): 143–66.

3. Campbell et al., *American Voter*, 121.

4. See, for example, Warren E. Miller, "The Cross-National Use of Party Identification as a Stimulus to Political Inquiry," in *Party Identification and Beyond*, ed. Ian Budge, Ivor Crewe, and Dennis Fairlie (London: Wiley, 1976), 21–31; Herbert F. Weisberg, "A Multidimensional Conceptualization of Party Identification," *Political Behavior* 2 (1980): 35; Robert C. Luskin, John P. McIver, and Edward G. Carmines, "Issues and the Transmission of Partisanship," *American Journal of Political Science* 33 (May 1989): 441–42; and Warren E. Miller and J. Merrill Shanks, *The New American Voter* (Cambridge, Mass.: Harvard University Press, 1996), 120–26.

My objection to the religious analogy is similar to the revisionist criticism of the Michigan theory of party identification: that an emphasis on emotional attachment and intrafamily socialization significantly understates the rational component of religious belief.

5. The first published exposition of the theory appears in Morris P. Fiorina, "An Outline for a Model of Party Choice," *American Journal of Political Science* 21 (August 1977): 601–25. For a more complete statement, see Fiorina, *Retrospective Voting in American National Elections* (New Haven, Conn.: Yale University Press, 1981), esp. chaps. 4 and 5.

6. See, especially, John E. Jackson, "Issues, Party Choices, and Presidential Votes," *American Journal of Political Science* 19 (May 1975): 161–85; W. Phillips Shively, "The Development of Party Identification among Adults: Exploration of a Functional Model," *American Political Science Review* 73 (December 1979): 1039–54; Charles H. Franklin and John E. Jackson, "The Dynamics of Party Identification," *American Political Science Review* 77 (December 1983): 957–73; Charles H. Franklin, "Issue Preferences, Socialization, and the Evolution of Party Identification," *American Journal of Political Science* 28 (August 1984): 459–78; and Luskin, McIver, and Carmines, "Issues and the Transmission of Partisanship."

7. This insight is usually credited to Anthony Downs, *An Economic Theory of Democracy* (New York: Harper and Row, 1957), chaps. 12 and 13. One of the first to explore its empirical implications was Arthur S. Goldberg, "Social Determinism and Rationality as Bases of Party Identification," *American Political Science Review* 63 (March 1969): 5–25.

8. Fiorina, *Retrospective Voting*, 102.

9. See Campbell et al., *American Voter*, chap. 7.

10. To complicate matters just a bit further, there is also a methodological dispute about whether the variation in party identifications that does exist represents "true change" or "random change" caused by measurement error. See Edward C. Dreyer, "Change and Stability in Party Identifications," *Journal of Politics* 35 (August 1973): 712–22; Douglas Dobson and Douglas St. Angelo, "Party Identification and the Floating Vote: Some Dynamics," *American Political Science Review* 69 (June 1975): 481–90; and Donald Philip Green and Bradley Palmquist, "Of Artifacts and Partisan Instability," *American Journal of Political Science* 34 (August 1990): 872–902.

11. See, especially, Walter Dean Burnham, "The Changing Shape of the American Political Universe," *American Political Science Review* 59 (March 1965): 7–28; Michael E. McGerr, *The Decline of Popular Politics: The American North, 1865–1928* (New York: Oxford University Press, 1986); and Joel H. Silbey, "Beyond Realignment and Realignment Theory: American Political Eras, 1789–1989," in *The End of Realignment? Interpreting American Electoral Eras,* ed. Byron E. Shafer (Madison: University of Wisconsin Press, 1991), 3–23.

12. See Converse, *Dynamics of Party Support,* chaps. 2 and 3.

13. David McCullough, *Truman* (New York: Simon and Schuster, 1992), 523.

14. See, for example, Campbell et al., *American Voter,* chaps. 6 and 7; Gerald M. Pomper, *Voters' Choice: Varieties of American Electoral Behavior* (New York: Harper and Row, 1975), chap. 2; and Norman H. Nie, Sidney Verba, and John R. Petrocik, *The Changing American Voter* (Cambridge, Mass.: Harvard University Press, 1976), chap. 4.

15. Among the best early discussions of the decline in party identifications are Pomper, *Voters' Choice,* chap. 2; Jack Dennis, "Trends in Public Support for the American Party System," *British Journal of Political Science* 5 (April 1975), 187–230; and Nie, Verba, and Petrocik, *Changing American Voter,* chap. 4. For the larger argument about the decline of parties and the consequences this might have for the American political system, see Walter Dean Burnham, *Critical Elections and the Mainsprings of American Politics* (New York: Norton, 1970); and David S. Broder, *The Party's Over: The Failure of Politics in America* (New York: Harper and Row, 1971). For a somewhat later summary, see William J. Crotty and Gary C. Jacobson, *American Parties in Decline* (Boston: Little, Brown, 1980).

16. For an extended discussion of all these points, see Bruce E. Keith, David G. Magleby, Candice J. Nelson, Elizabeth Orr, Mark C. Westlye, and Raymond E. Wolfinger, *The Myth of the Independent Voter* (Berkeley: University of California Press, 1992). The more traditional classification system also has its defenders, however. See, for example, Richard J. Timpone and Francis K. Neely, "Generally Speaking ... The Temporal Dimensions of Party Identification," paper presented at the annual meetings of the American Political Science Association, Washington, D.C., August 1997.

17. An exception is the 1972 survey, in which only three answers were

coded per question.

18. The National Election Studies also ask a parallel series of questions about the presidential candidates. For studies that make extensive use of this database, see, among others, Campbell et al., *American Voter,* chaps. 3, 4, and 10; Nie, Verba, and Petrocik, *Changing American Voter,* chap. 7; Stanley Kelley Jr., *Interpreting Elections* (Princeton: Princeton University Press, 1983); Martin P. Wattenberg, *The Rise of Candidate-Centered Politics: Presidential Elections of the 1980s* (Cambridge, Mass.: Harvard University Press, 1991); and William G. Mayer, *The Divided Democrats: Ideological Unity, Party Reform, and Presidential Elections* (Boulder, Colo: Westview Press, 1996), chap. 6.

19. See Martin P. Wattenberg, *The Decline of American Political Parties, 1952–1994* (Cambridge, Mass.: Harvard University Press, 1996), esp. chap. 4.

20. Ibid., 72.

21. The analysis in this paragraph draws especially on Austin Ranney, *The Doctrine of Responsible Party Government: Its Origins and Present State* (Urbana: University of Illinois Press, 1954); James L. Sundquist, "Needed: A Political Theory for the New Era of Coalition Government in the United States," *Political Science Quarterly* 103 (Winter 1988–89): 613–35; and Paul Allen Beck and Frank J. Sorauf, *Party Politics in America,* 7th ed. (New York: HarperCollins, 1992), chap. 16.

22. For a fuller discussion of this development, see Burnham, "Changing Shape of the American Political Universe."

23. The figures in this table do *not* include, though perhaps they should, respondents who voted in the presidential election but then declined to vote in the congressional race or do not remember which congressional candidate they voted for.

24. See, especially, Angus Campbell and Warren E. Miller, "The Motivational Basis of Straight and Split Ticket Voting," *American Political Science Review* 51 (June 1957): 293–312; and Jerrold G. Rusk, "The Effect of the Australian Ballot Reform on Split Ticket Voting: 1876–1908," *American Political Science Review* 64 (December 1970): 1220–38.

25. There is some ambiguity, it is worth pointing out, as to just what counts as an "uncontested congressional election." The category undoubtedly includes all instances in which either a Democrat or a Republican is the only person listed on the ballot. For the purposes of this chapter, it should also include cases where a major-party candidate was opposed only by an independent or third-party contender. A person seeking to cast a straight Republican ballot in a district without a Republican congressional candidate will find that task no easier if there is a Libertarian on the ballot.

More troubling is the question of how to deal with cases where a single candidate is listed as the nominee of *both* the Republican and Democratic parties. Such a candidate clearly does not have a major-party opponent in the general election, which is why I have chosen to classify these as uncontested seats. But an argument could be made that in such circumstances, both parties' adherents *are* capable of casting a straight-ticket vote: that is to say, they can vote for the official nominee of the same party for every federal office.

More relevant than what the voters thought they were doing, perhaps, is how the ANES survey administrators chose to treat such cases. Unfortunately, the available documentation for the early NES surveys offers not even a hint of an answer. Fortunately, for most of the period being studied here, instances of joint-party endorsement are rare: about 2.3 cases per election from 1956 to 1996. But anyone interested in pushing the analysis a bit further back in time should note that in 1952, there were actually fifteen such cases, fourteen of them in California.

26. The likes/dislikes data are not included in table 5.8 on the ground that, as I have indicated earlier, the results from the 1952 to 1968 surveys are not directly comparable with those from 1972 to 1992.

27. See, especially, Paul Allen Beck, "A Socialization Theory of Partisan Realignment," in *The Politics of Future Citizens*, ed. Richard G. Niemi (San Francisco: Jossey-Bass, 1974), 199–219; Edward G. Carmines, John P. McIver, and James A. Stimson, "Unrealized Partisanship: A Theory of Dealignment," *Journal of Politics* 49 (May 1987): 376–400; and Jerome M. Chubb, William H. Flanigan, and Nancy H. Zingale, *Partisan Realignment: Voters, Parties, and Government in American History* (Boulder, Colo.: Westview Press, 1990).

28. For a good analysis of divided government in the 1876–96 period, see Charles H. Stewart III, "Lessons from the Post–Civil War Era," in *The Politics of Divided Government*, ed. Gary W. Cox and Samuel Kernell (Boulder, Colo: Westview Press, 1991), 203–38.

29. The discussion here draws on Gerald M. Pomper, "From Confusion to Clarity: Issues and American Voters, 1956–1968," *American Political Science Review* 66 (June 1972): 415–28; David W. Rohde, *Parties and Leaders in the Postreform House* (Chicago: University of Chicago Press, 1991); and Gerald M. Pomper, "Alive! The Political Parties After the 1980–1992 Presidential Elections," in *American Presidential Elections: Process, Policy, and Political Change*, ed. Harvey L. Schantz (Albany: SUNY Press, 1996), 135–56.

6

Partisan Rules, 1946–1996

Harold F. Bass Jr.

he post–World War II generation of American political scientists represented a high-water mark in what Leon Epstein calls the "scholarly
commitment" to political parties.[1] This scholarly community placed
parties at the vital center of the study of politics. In doing so, it embraced
enthusiastically the positive portrait of parties developed by the founders
of the discipline of political science in the United States in the late nineteenth century. According to this portrait, parties provided key linkage
mechanisms in the American body politic, perhaps uniquely capable of
connecting masses with elites and of linking the fragmented governing institutions in a system constructed according to the constitutional principles of separation of powers and federalism.[2] In an important new development at midcentury, pioneering students of voting behavior at the
University of Michigan added a focus on party identification as the primary explanatory factor.[3]

Along with these paeans to the role and status of party, highly re-
spected representatives of that generation issued a lament, criticizing
American political parties for their lack of responsibility and enclosing an
agenda for reform. This 1950 report of the Committee on Political Parties
of the American Political Science Association pinpointed, as problematic,
weak party organizations and insufficient discipline among party officeholders.[4] The controversial report elicited a barrage of countercriticism
that reverberated for at least a quarter-century.[5] Critics and defenders

alike, however, acknowledged their mutual understanding of (and commitment to) political parties as key elements of the American democratic political system. Thus, in doing what political scientists do—comprehending, explaining, and predicting—party-centered approaches prevailed in the systematic study of American politics.

A half-century later, an overwhelming scholarly consensus views political parties as in decline, most especially in their electoral connections.[6] Undoubtedly, the contemporary electorate shows a diminished dependence on parties for such traditional provisions as economic employment, social identity, and even information about candidates for public office. This decline has deep roots in reforms of the Progressive era, now a century old, that targeted political party organizations as corrupt and undemocratic institutions. At the same time, however, in a familiar dialectic, other scholars have identified signs of revitalization among party organizations in the past quarter-century.[7] Moreover, party unity scores in Congress have been generally on the rise for well over a decade, reaching record highs in 1995.[8]

Thus, in the years since World War II, a curious inversion has developed with regard to the discipline's understanding of partisanship in American politics. Then, apparently strong and stable party identification in the electorate coexisted with weakening party organizations and poorly disciplined partisans in governmental office. Today, a contrasting climate combines a less party-oriented electorate with invigorated party organizations and heightened party discipline in government. At issue in this work is whether and to what extent changes occurring over the past half-century affect the long-standing assertions of the centrality of parties for understanding American politics.

This chapter assesses transformations of the partisan rules and regulations that not only establish the legal framework within which the American party system operates but also reflect the broader cultural setting. The particular partisan rules and regulations addressed here pertain broadly to the conduct of elections. More specifically, this chapter focuses on issues associated with the ballot. It confronts the topics of ballot form; access to the ballot by parties and, especially, potential voters; and reliance on the ballot for party nominations.

A focus on ballot issues entails a recognition of the significance of the federal principle for American politics. The initial constitutional division of powers placed ballot-related issues clearly in the hands of the several states. Not surprisingly, numerous variations emerged among them. For the past sixty years, the Council of State Governments has published biennially its *Book of the States;* these volumes include authoritative and invaluable data on ballot issues and developments. Meanwhile, one of the central themes to be developed in this chapter is the increasingly assertive role assumed by national political institutions in this regard over the past half-century. This development has substantially reduced autonomy while producing increased uniformity among the states. The South, heretofore the most distinctive of the regions, has coincidentally been the site where the most momentous transformations have taken place. As such, particular attention must be devoted to its changing party politics.

In addition to the *Book of the States,* this chapter relies heavily on three earlier attempts to evaluate partisan rules and regulations pertaining to elections:

• The analytical foundations and framework for this endeavor reside in the model developed in that classic 1960 study of voting behavior, *The American Voter.*[9] In chapter 11, "Election Laws, Political Systems, and the Voter," Angus Campbell, Philip Converse, Warren Miller, and Donald Stokes systematically considered the extent to which electoral laws and regulations facilitate or inhibit partisanship and electoral participation.[10]

• Almost twenty-five years later, David Price addressed the effect of electoral laws on the party role in nominations, elections, and government.[11] Mindful of the indications of party decline mentioned earlier, and endorsing the aforementioned scholarly commitment to parties, he advocated the cause of party resurgence. In doing so, he identified several institutional features that advanced the cause of the parties and the party system.[12] He then proceeded to document the prevailing situation.

• Price's data and analysis ably characterized conditions in the early 1980s. Midway through that decade, the Advisory Committee on Intergovernmental Relations, perceiving the cause of federalism potentially to be enhanced by the revitalization of state and local political parties, issued a report.[13] This report contained a section entitled "State Laws Governing the Role of State and Local Party Organizations in the Electoral Process." Following in Price's footsteps, the report similarly constructed an index of factors facilitating party revitalization.[14]

These three works preface this chapter. Synthesizing their analytical frameworks, it proceeds as follows. First, it surveys key pre–World War II developments in ballot-related issues, to establish the evolving status of partisan electoral rules and procedures prior to the dawn of the post–World War II era. Next, it presents parallel "snapshots" of partisan rules at midcentury and approaching century's end, to offer parallel portraits of the same concerns as this introductory survey. Then, it focuses on central issues in the obvious—and substantial—changes from one portrait to the other, to address the rippling implications of these changes for party competition and for understanding broader changes in postwar American politics. A brief conclusion summarizes and evaluates the findings.

Electoral rules are not neutral. Their political consequences are both manifest and latent.[15] This chapter thus specifies changes in the rules and explores their implications and repercussions for parties, the party system, and the broader political system.

Setting the Stage: Preliminary Developments

The secret ballot became institutionalized in American politics in the late nineteenth century. At the outset of electoral politics in America, oral voting was commonplace. Voters simply informed election officials of their choices. When political parties emerged, they gradually began printing ballots and distributing them. Individual candidates often did so as well. Voters brought their ballots to the designated polling place to be counted.

This arrangement came under attack in the Progressive era as subject to corruption. Reformers proposed the adoption of a ballot procedure developed in Australia, whereby the government prepared uniform ballots and distributed them to voters at authorized polling sites, where they would be marked in secret. The concept of the Australian ballot found widespread support among the states in the 1890s. By the early twentieth century, it had become almost universally accepted.

This ballot reform had important consequences for the political parties. Its manifest intent reduced, though it did not remove, temptations to engage in corrupt behavior. In a latent effect, it also coincided with an increase in split-ticket voting.[16] Where the old-style party-sponsored ballots virtually mandated that votes be cast for the entire party ticket, the secret ballot provided structural opportunities for ticket-splitting. Thus, it undermined a foundation of partisan electoral behavior and promoted a more candidate-centered politics.

Ballot Form and Content

The extent to which the introduction of the Australian ballot affected political parties, however, depended in part on the *form* this ballot took in listing candidates for public office. In the federal system of the United States, individual states still made the key decision regarding how to arrange candidates on the ballot. Two alternative arrangements quickly emerged: office bloc and party column. The office-bloc arrangement, initiated in Massachusetts in 1888, groups all candidates for a particular office. The party-column arrangement, adopted in Indiana in 1889, lists all a political party's candidates for office in a single column, with national offices at the top and local offices at the bottom.

According to Joseph Harris, the initial inclination of states in adopting ballot forms favored the office-bloc style. In the 1890s, however, the tide quickly and decisively turned toward party column, by a two-to-one margin. In the early decades of the twentieth century, the office-bloc alternative began a gradual recovery that still left it the choice of a clear minority of the states.[17] Obviously, the party-column format is more conducive to straight-ticket voting, as is a format that enables the voter to cast a straight-party ballot with a single mark.[18] Within the constraints provided by the Australian ballot, these ballot arrangements can be said to facilitate partisanship, while their counterparts discourage it. In turn, they also advantage the majority party in a given setting.

Jewell and Olson cite scholarly evidence for several additional consequences of differences in ballot form among the states. Forms that encourage straight-party voting result in more votes cast for candidates for minor offices. Such forms produce more straight-ticket voting and thus enhance the likelihood of unified party government, where the same party controls both executive and legislature. In affecting voting behavior by individuals, all these impacts of ballot form are more important for weak partisans than for strong ones. Finally, along with voting machines, ballot forms can discourage write-in voting.[19]

Those are leading questions about the form—the structural configuration—of the ballot. But there are also questions of who, and what, is on it, especially questions of which parties (and their candidates) deserve to be there. Ballot access can thus be addressed from two perspectives. First, and more conventionally, is the issue of access by political parties to the ballot. The long tradition of two-party competition in the United States has featured limitations on ballot access for minor parties. Second, and in a larger sense, ballot access can pertain to the regulation of electoral participation by individuals. As Campbell, Converse, Miller, and Stokes noted, state-imposed restrictions on suffrage have potentially significant partisan implications.

With the advent of the Australian ballot, which mandated government printing, the states had to enact legislation regarding access by office seekers to this printed ballot. Two concerns loomed as paramount. One was a desire to avoid cluttering the ballot with frivolous candidates. The other was to protect a preferred position for the two major parties against emerging challengers. The latter reflected both considerations of self-interest by the established political parties and arguments that a stable two-party system benefited the body politic.

From the outset, ballot-access laws in the states typically granted automatic access to nominees of political parties that had attained a specified threshold of support in a previous election. This feature virtually guaranteed a ballot presence for the (two) major parties. Minor parties, including those below the threshold as well as newly formed entities, usually gained access for their slate of nominees through petitions containing a designated number of signatures of registered voters. This latter procedure normally also applied to independent candidates.

Richard Winger reports that initial ballot-access laws, developed over a century ago, were relatively liberal, affording the numerous minor parties of that electoral era easy access to the ballot.[20] He observes, however, that ballot-access laws began to become significantly more restrictive around 1930. The perceived threat of the Communist Party apparently precipitated the initial wave of restrictions. Six states tightened their requirements in the 1930s, and Georgia followed suit in 1943.[21] Thus, the clear trend in the mid-1940s was toward tighter ballot-access laws.

Suffrage Requirements

The issue of ballot access relates to voters as well as to parties, for states also regulate voter access to (use of) the ballot through suffrage requirements. Throughout the nineteenth century and in the early decades of the twentieth, significant liberalization of suffrage regulations occurred. Traditional property requirements were cast aside in an extended series of state-level reforms, and constitutional amendments prohibited standards based on race or sex. Those remaining by the end of World War II pertained to citizenship, age, residence, and prior registration. The first three can be easily summarized. The latter is more complicated.

The development of a citizenship restriction ran counter to the general trend toward more liberal suffrage requirements. In the nineteenth century, several states had allowed noncitizens to vote. By the mid-1920s, however, all states had prohibited aliens from voting, and they continue to do so. States initially and universally established twenty-one as the age of accountability, at which point one became eligible to vote. In the early 1940s, during World War II, Georgia broke ranks and lowered its voting age to eighteen. Historically, states also made residence in the state, county, and district a standard for voting. They typically established residence requirements in descending fashion: longest for the state and shortest for the voting district. A half-century ago, these requirements were still formidable: a year or more in most states.

Voter registration itself was a Progressive era reform, designed to reduce corruption. Its avowed purpose was to address the possibility of fraudulent voting. The resulting protection, however, which placed the initiative with the prospective voter, contributed to an immediate reduction in participation rates. States actually established two basic forms for voter registration: periodic or permanent. Periodic registration procedures, the norm at the outset of registration requirements in the Progressive era, required voters to reaffirm their eligibility via reregistration at specified intervals.

One alleged virtue of periodic registration rested in the control it afforded the electoral process against the corruption that was the target of the Progressive reformers. On the other hand, this form tended to reduce levels of participation further, by placing a considerable burden of initiative on the voter. The increasingly popular alternative of permanent registration meant that once voters registered, they remained eligible to vote as long as they continued to reside in their particular voting district. Many states nominally embracing this concept also required voters to participate in at least one election within a specified interval to remain registered. This latter test meant that voting became tantamount to reregistration in a periodic system and effectively blurred the analytical distinction.

The voter registration procedures that developed in the South merit special mention, in the light of their systematic efforts to deny suffrage to African Americans. Recall that the Fifteenth Amendment, proposed and ratified in the aftermath of the Civil War, had prohibited states from using "race, color, or previous condition of servitude" as a standard in establishing suffrage requirements. Under federal military rule, the southern states enacted suffrage rules that satisfied this constitutional standard. With the departure of the federal troops in 1877, however, the southern states, with the Democratic Party in firm control, began the process of disenfranchisement of black voters, through such registration-related practices as literacy tests, comprehension clauses, and the poll tax, as well as by economic and physical intimidation.

By the turn of the twentieth century, this process was virtually complete. At the end of World War II, the structure of racial segregation, with its attendant denial of voting rights for blacks, remained firmly ensconced, although it had been dealt a few glancing blows by the Supreme Court. The Court did outlaw the "white primary," which limited participation in the Democratic Party primary, tantamount to election, to white voters.[22] Nevertheless, African Americans remained systematically discouraged, or even simply excluded, from voting, via a variety of legal and administrative standards.

As midcentury approached, then, ballot-access rules purposely discouraged political participation by minor parties. At the same time, suf-

frage requirements created a sizable gap between the voting-age population and the eligible electorate, those that satisfied the requirements.

Party Nominations

Rules and regulations affecting the ballot reach much farther, however,
than just the general election, because the ballot has also become the
main vehicle by which major American political parties make their nominating decisions. Indeed, this development is the factor that most clearly
distinguishes American political parties from their counterparts throughout the rest of the world. In addition, and also distinctively American, is
the extent to which state-level legislation prescribes party nominating procedures.

Nominating procedures have evolved since the appearance of parties
on the American political scene in the 1790s. Initially and informally, legislative caucuses often assumed nominating responsibility. This institution
obviously empowered the party-in-office within the party structure. Later,
nominating *conventions,* representing the official party in a given jurisdiction, became prevalent. This arrangement empowered the party-as-organization instead. Most recently, primary elections, favoring the party-in-
the-electorate, have largely supplanted such nominating conventions. It
was at this stage that state regulation became the norm.

James H. Booser locates the origins of the nominating primary in
1842, in Crawford County, Pennsylvania, from whence it quickly spread
to neighboring counties.[23] The primary became normative in the Progressive era, when advocates attacked control of nominations by the party organization as corrupt and undemocratic. The preferred alternative of the
reformers was the primary election: direct selection of party nominees by
voters through an open and public ballot regulated by the government.[24]

The institution of the primary almost immediately took hold in the
southern states. In the Solid South, Democratic Party domination pre-
cluded meaningful party competition, calling into question the popular
legitimacy of the Democratic nominees who prevailed in the general elections. In a democratic political culture, the appeal of primary elections in
single-party states is probably compelling.[25] For the minority Republicans
in the South, however, party primaries were exceedingly rare. Congressional Quarterly's authoritative *Guide to U.S. Elections,* beginning its survey as late as 1920, still identifies only a handful of Republican gubernatorial and senatorial primaries prior to the end of World War II.

Their low level of popular support usually placed southern Republicans below the thresholds established in state laws instituting primary
elections. As a result, when Republicans did choose to make symbolic,

futile electoral challenges to the regional dominance of Democrats, they typically had to utilize their party organization. This was not, in itself, a cause of distress. Entrenched southern Republican leaders, beneficiaries of federal patronage when the GOP held the White House, predictably preferred not to submit their control to the vagaries of primary elections.

After the turn of the twentieth century, the primary became the accepted norm for nominations among states outside the South as well. Significantly, the states with the strongest party organizations and with two-party competition tended to be most resistant to the tide. Nevertheless, V.O. Key Jr. reports that by 1917, only four states had failed to provide for its exercise, although New York and Indiana subsequently reverted for a time to the nominating convention.[26] The predominance of the primary as a nominating method was thus well established in the early decades of this century.

Political scientists initially categorized party primaries into two further groups: closed and open. The Progressive reformers who advocated primary nominations tended to prefer the open variation. In a closed primary, only party members may participate. In an open primary, by contrast, any voter may participate in the nominating decision of any single party, without officially identifying with it. The ultimate "wide open" primary then features a consolidated ballot, enabling a voter to participate in the primary of more than one party, being limited merely to casting a single vote for any given office.

From the perspective of the party organization, the direct primary places the party's most precious commodity, its nominations, in the hands of the party-in-the-electorate. As such, closed primaries are the least objectionable alternative, and wide-open primaries the most objectionable. Seen from the other side, of course, the wide-open primary affords the individual voter the most discretion, and the closed primary the least. In initially authorizing primary nominations, the states demonstrated a clear preference for closed over open primaries, by a margin of two to one.[27]

Presidential nominations—or more specifically, delegate selection procedures for the national nominating conventions, which have endured despite the triumph of the primary at the state level—remained distinctive. When national nominating conventions came into being, the leaders of state party organizations assumed authority over delegate selection. Candidates seeking a presidential nomination thus had to cultivate the support of these state party "bosses." In response, in the heyday of Progressive reforms, several states enacted legislation establishing presidential primaries, and these addressed delegate selection in various fashions. By 1916, over twenty states had adopted them.[28]

This development opened a new avenue for seeking the presidential nomination, since an aspirant could conceivably demonstrate popular support in this serious minority of primary states and use that support as a lever to attract the support of the still-dominant party organizational leadership. Nevertheless, in the decades following the Progressive era, six states actually abandoned their delegate selection reforms, and reverted to party organizational control of delegate selection. As midcentury approached, the remaining presidential primary states were thus producing well under one-half of the convention delegates.[29] The prevalent trend opposed the expansion of presidential primaries, and their perceived role in presidential selection was slight.

Ballot-Related Practices at Midcentury

That review sets the stage for a capsule description of partisan ballot-related practices at the dawn of the postwar era, circa 1946. At that time, regulations on ballot form itself still clearly favored the organized political parties. Access to the ballot for these parties—which meant, especially, for "third" and "independent" parties—was actually in the midst of a tightening trend. For (potential) voters, residence requirements remained substantial, and the demands of prior registration were also not inconsequential. The primary election had conquered major-party organizations for most offices in most of the nation, although closed primaries remained the norm within them. And the great exception remained presidential selection, where primaries still played an insignificant role.

Ballot Form and Content

With regard to ballot form, states preferred the party-column format by slightly less than two to one (see figure 6.1A, p. 230). Thirty states used the party-column arrangement, while seventeen opted for the office-bloc alternative.[30] (South Carolina managed to remain a lone, long-standing holdout against the Australian ballot into the postwar period.) Moreover, more than half the states facilitated straight-ticket voting by allowing individuals to vote with a single mark[31] (see figure 6.2A, p. 232). Pennsylvania was the lone office-bloc state to facilitate such straight-ticket voting; the others, twenty-six in total, were party-column states.

Existing ballot-access requirements in the states clearly disadvantaged third parties, and a trend toward more restrictive regulations was well into its second decade. The party-as-organization might be—it surely was—in long-term retreat, as the advance of the primary election (see below) powerfully attested. Nevertheless, that retreat *was* long-term, and

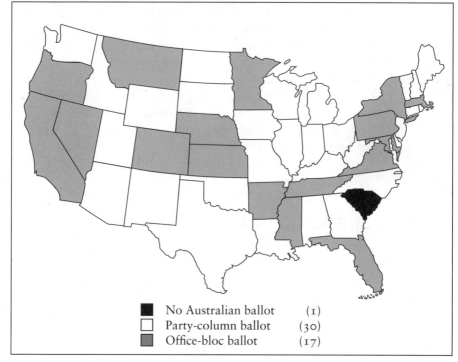

No Australian ballot   (1)
Party-column ballot   (30)
Office-bloc ballot   (17)

FIGURE 6.1A
BALLOT FORMS, 1946

SOURCE: *Book of the States, 1948–1949,* vol. 7 (Chicago: Council of State Governments 1948), 98.

with respect to third and/or independent parties, the two major-party organizations were enjoying a period of advance.

Suffrage Requirements

For prospective voters, suffrage requirements—access to (use of) the ballot by individuals—remained relatively formidable. Major-party organizations had learned to live within these constraints, though not all such
restrictions were equally favored by the parties, nor did all have obvious
and straightforward partisan implications. Nevertheless, at the beginning
of this period, in 1946, suffrage was uniformly limited to citizens among
the forty-eight states, a situation that the subsequent admission of Alaska
and Hawaii would not change. Moreover, it was uniformly limited to

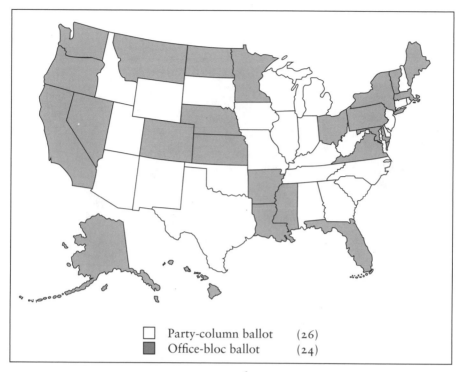

Party-column ballot   (26)
Office-bloc ballot   (24)

FIGURE 6.1B
BALLOT FORMS, 1996

SOURCE: Virginia Graham, "Ballot Format: Trends in Changes by the States," Congressional Research Service, Library of Congress, 1982, 5, 7–8, plus updates.

those age twenty-one or older, with the sole exception of the state of Georgia, which had only recently reduced its voting age to eighteen.

Residence requirements for voting remained hefty. Five states, four of them southern, actually required two years of residence; thirty-two states required one year; and eleven opted for a six-month requirement[32] (see table 6.1, p. 235). Once the residence requirement for voting had been met, thirty-two states then had permanent registration (see table 6.2, p. 235). Of the remainder, seven maintained uniform periodic registration, while another seven combined the forms, having permanent registration in some areas (usually rural) and periodic registration in others (usually urban). The two remaining states did not require registration at all, though one of these exceptions resulted from lack of implementation of a theoretically required scheme.[33]

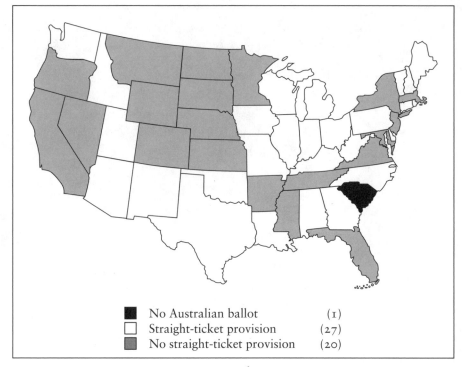

FIGURE 6.2A
STRAIGHT-PARTY VOTING, 1946

SOURCE: *Book of the States, 1948–1949*, vol. 7 (Chicago: Council of State Governments, 1948), 98.

In 1946 seven states, all from the Old Confederacy, imposed poll taxes on voting, effectively discriminating against their (impoverished) black populations, though hardly encouraging low-income whites either. Although a full seventeen states had literacy tests,[34] the six southern states that did so were notorious for their selective administration, intended to discriminate against aspiring black voters. The combined upshot was that black voting was relatively rare and inconsequential in the South.

Party Nominations

The presence of continued resistance and some victories for the party-as-organization—those attractive to partisan theorists, such as party-column formats, as well as those unattractive, including the poll tax—could not gainsay one fact: the major institutional reform of preceding years,

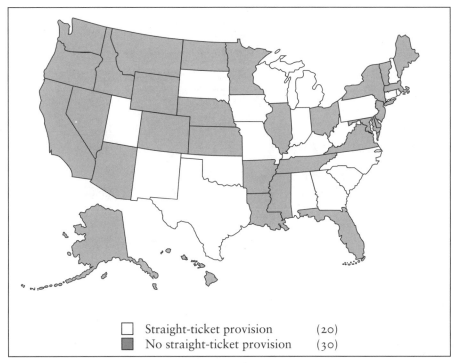

Straight-ticket provision   (20)
No straight-ticket provision   (30)

FIGURE 6.2B
STRAIGHT-PARTY VOTING, 1996

SOURCE: *Book of the States, 1982–1983,* vol. 24 (Lexington, Ky.: Council of State Governments, 1982), 104, plus updates.

nomination by primary elections and not by internal party processes, had largely swept the nation (see figure 6.3A, p. 238). Forty-six states made some provision for primary nominations, with only Connecticut and Rhode Island continuing to resist the tide absolutely.

Contrarily, the widespread acceptance of primary nominations among the states should not obscure the reality that Republican primaries were still exceedingly rare in the Solid South, where the Democratic Party retained its traditional dominance. Democratic Party officials preferred that all the serious political "action" take place within their ranks; Republican Party officials were often content to maintain their (unchallenged) control of minority-party machinery. If the statistics for figure 6.3A were for Republican parties alone, then they would be closer to

TABLE 6.1

STATE RESIDENCE REQUIREMENTS FOR VOTING,
1946 AND 1988

	1946	1988		1946	1988
Alabama	2 years	1 day	Montana	1 year	30 days
Alaska		30 days	Nebraska	6 months	—
Arizona	1 year	30 days	Nevada	6 months	30 days
Arkansas	12 months	—	New	6 months	10 days
California	1 year	29 days	Hampshire		
Colorado	1 year	32 days	New Jersey	1 year	30 days
Connecticut	1 year	—	New Mexico	12 months	—
Delaware	1 year	—	New York	1 year	30 days
Florida	1 year	—	North Carolina	1 year	30 days
Georgia	1 year	30 days	North Dakota	1 year	30 days
Hawaii		—	Ohio	1 year	30 days
Idaho	6 months	30 days	Oklahoma	1 year	—
Illinois	1 year	30 days	Oregon	6 months	20 days
Indiana	6 months	30 days	Pennsylvania	1 year	30 days
Iowa	6 months	—	Rhode Island	2 years	30 days
Kansas	6 months	1 day	South Carolina	2 years	—
Kentucky	1 year	30 days	South Dakota	1 year	15 days
Louisiana	2 years	24 days	Tennessee	12 months	20 days
Maine	6 months	election day	Texas	1 year	30 days
			Utah	1 year	30 days
Maryland	1 year	30 days	Vermont	1 year	—
Massachusetts	1 year	28 days	Virginia	1 year	—
Michigan	6 months	30 days	Washington	1 year	30 days
Minnesota	6 months	election day	West Virginia	1 year	30 days
			Wisconsin	1 year	10 days
Mississippi	2 years	30 days	Wyoming	1 year	—
Missouri	1 year	28 days			

SOURCES: *Book of the States, 1948–1949,* vol. 7 (Chicago: Council of State Governments, 1948), 96; *Book of the States, 1988–1989,* vol. 27 (Lexington, Ky.: Council of State Governments, 1988), 211.

thirty-seven or thirty-eight states making state-level nominations by public primary election.

Of the forty-six states with primary laws, however, a full thirty-six did provide for closed primaries but only ten for open, another measure of the long-running resistance of the party-as-organization to the reform trend represented by the institution of the primary itself.[35] Some note-

TABLE 6.2

VOTER REGISTRATION REQUIREMENTS,
1946 AND 1996

	1946 (Permanent or periodic)	1996 (Cancellation period)
Alabama	Permanent	—
Alaska		6 years
Arizona	Permanent	4 years
Arkansas	—	4 years
California	Permanent	—
Colorado	Permanent	2 general elections
Connecticut	Permanent	—
Delaware	Permanent	4 years
Florida	Permanent	2 general elections
Georgia	Permanent	—
Hawaii		2 election cycles
Idaho	Permanent	4 years
Illinois	Permanent	—
Indiana	Permanent	—
Iowa	Both	2 general elections
Kansas	Both	2 general elections
Kentucky	Both	—
Louisiana	Periodic	—
Maine	Permanent	—
Maryland	Permanent	—
Massachusetts	Permanent	—
Michigan	Permanent	—
Minnesota	Both	4 years
Mississipi	Permanent	4 years
Missouri	Both	2 general elections

Continued ...

worthy additional variations existed, regarding utilization of the primary. An overwhelming majority, thirty-seven, featured uniform and mandatory primaries, above a certain level of support. But four others specified exceptions; New York, for example, required primaries for state legislators, while nominating other state officers by convention. Five more states made primaries fully optional.

Only a distinct minority of these state parties used the institution of the primary in the process of delegate selection to the national nominating conventions. Parties in only fifteen states were relying on the presidential primary—and on only *some form* of the presidential primary, even

TABLE 6.2 — CONTINUED

	1946 (Permanent or periodic)	1996 (Cancellation period)
Montana	Permanent	1 presidential election
Nebraska	Both	—
Nevada	Permanent	4 years
New Hampshire	Permanent	10 years
New Jersey	Both	—
New Mexico	Permanent	2 general elections
New York	Periodic	5 years
North Carolina	Permanent	—
North Dakota	Periodic	—
Ohio	Both	4 years
Oklahoma	Permanent	—
Oregon	Permanent	2 general elections
Pennsylvania	Permanent	—
Rhode Island	Periodic	2 federal elections
South Carolina	Periodic	2 general elections
South Dakota	Periodic	—
Tennessee	Both	—
Texas	—	—
Utah	Permanent	4 years
Vermont	Permanent	—
Virginia	Permanent	4 years
Washington	Permanent	—
West Virginia	Permanent	—
Wisconsin	Both	4 years
Wyoming	Periodic	1 general election

SOURCES: *Book of the States, 1948–1949,* vol. 7 (Chicago: Council of State Governments, 1948), 97; *Book of the States, 1996–1997,* vol. 31 (Lexington, Ky.: Council of State Governments, 1996), 162–63.

then (see figure 6.4A, p. 240). Harry Truman, president in 1946, later referred to these primaries as "eyewash,"[36] and the promise of the early twentieth century, that public primaries would nominate presidents, remained unfulfilled.

The Situation at Century's End

Over the next half-century, substantial changes took place with regard to these partisan rules, and so today the framework governing partisanship differs markedly from that in effect fifty years ago. In general, the party-as-organization has, with one exception, continued to lose more of the battle to make partisan decisions through internal party processes. In some realms, this has been merely an extension of long-term trends; in others, it has been more like a rout. At the same time, suffrage restrictions have been reduced remarkably, though a formally expanded electorate has not always been a practically mobilized one. What has resulted, in these terms, is a less predictable electorate in the aggregate, operating through decreasingly partisan institutional arrangements.

Ballot Form and Content

Changes in ballot form have advanced the long-standing trend away from the party column and toward the office bloc. Postwar movement began in 1949, when Ohio shifted from a party-column to an office-bloc arrangement. This was counterbalanced the following year, when South Carolina finally surrendered its solitary exception to the Australian ballot, coming in under the party-column form. Alaska and Hawaii, new states during the 1950s, at first divided on this arrangement, but Alaska quickly shifted to the office-bloc format. And there was then a continuing trickle in that direction during the 1960s, 1970s, and 1980s. The result, in our time, remains a narrow majority for party column over office bloc, twenty-six to twenty-four[37] (see figure 6.1B, p. 231).

The erosion of partisan institutional incentives continued, more strongly this time, in the fate of the provision for expedited straight-ticket voting, the ability to vote for all of one party's candidates with a single action. In 1946 twenty-seven states had provided a simple straight-ticket option, while twenty-one had not. By 1997 only twenty retained that option, and thirty did not[38] (see figure 6.2B, p. 233). Much of this change was intertwined with changes in ballot format. Alaska and Hawaii, entering with progressive and antipartisan traditions, never introduced this provision, although South Carolina, coming from a pure partisan tradition, did. Moreover, four of the states that switched to the office bloc —Louisiana, Maine, Ohio, and Vermont—also did away with the simple straight-ticket alternative. The aggregate result, in any case, was substantial change.

Given that both of these ballot reforms constitute moves away from the institutional encouragement of partisanship, it should come as no surprise that a major influence for reform in many of these states was a larger national reform movement, itself offering a heavy antiparty emphasis, coming to prominence in the middle 1960s and lasting into the 1980s.[39] This movement was to be much more consequential in the realm of presidential selection, that is, in the final arrival of the primary election

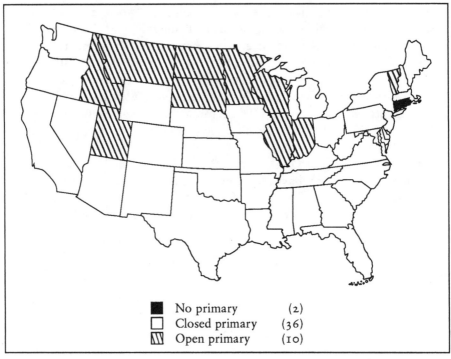

FIGURE 6.3A
TYPES OF PRIMARIES, 1946

SOURCE: *Book of the States, 1948–1949*, vol. 7 (Chicago: Council of State Governments, 1948), 92.

for presidential nominations (see below), but it was also a notable influence on ballot reforms in the individual states.

For a long time, on the other hand, the party-as-organization managed to contain this movement and actually legislate in the opposite direction, in the realm of rules governing access to the ballot by other, minor or independent parties. Initially, the trend was clearly toward continuing to tighten access requirements. Eventually, this trend too reversed, and less restrictive requirements emerged, as public attention increasingly focused on the issue. Yet the resulting changes were largely confined to the presidential race, not to races lower down the ballot, so the formally disadvantaged position of minor parties in ballot access persists, much as it did in the immediate postwar years.[40]

There was some individual state adjustment to the burdens on third

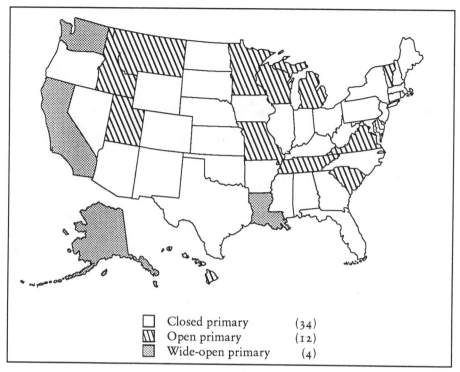

☐ Closed primary	(34)	
▨ Open primary	(12)	
▥ Wide-open primary	(4)	

FIGURE 6.3B
TYPES OF PRIMARIES, 1996

SOURCE: *Book of the States, 1990–1991*, vol. 28 (Lexington, Ky.: Council of State Governments, 1990), 236, plus updates.

parties and independent candidacies, especially in the South and Border States, in response to the independent presidential candidacies of Strom Thurmond of South Carolina in 1948 and George Wallace of Alabama in 1968. All that these candidacies really did, however, was foreshadow a later and more general tendency to *separate* access requirements for presidential candidates from those for lower federal and for state offices, liberalizing the presidential but not necessarily the others. Apart from that, any reforms occurred against a propensity by individual states to tighten their requirements for third-party appearances on the ballot, a trend that continued to run widely through the 1960s and 1970s, when eleven states responded to partisan turmoil by ratcheting up these rules.

Visible and formidable third-party and independent candidacies in presidential elections, on the other hand—recurring with more ultimate

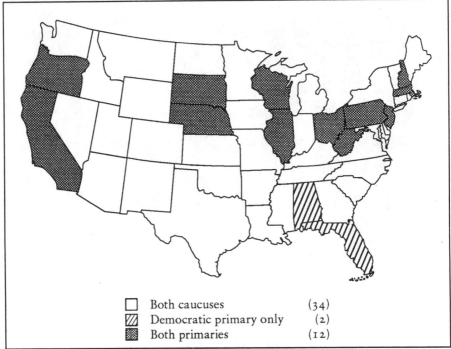

☐	Both caucuses	(34)
▨	Democratic primary only	(2)
▨	Both primaries	(12)

FIGURE 6.4A

PRESIDENTIAL PRIMARY ELECTIONS, 1946

SOURCE: *Presidential Elections since 1789*, 5th ed. (Washington, D.C.: CQ Press, 1991), 31–32.

impact on the rules in 1980, 1992, and 1996—eventually began to reverse this trend, from the 1980s onward. The difficulties that John Anderson in 1980 and Ross Perot in 1992 and 1996 encountered in their dissident efforts did focus public attention and media scrutiny on the restrictive and frequently arcane rules governing access to the ballot. In a chicken-and-egg effect, indications of growing public dissatisfaction with the two major parties both fueled these presidential efforts and encouraged liberalization of ballot-access rules, especially for presidential candidates, in the states.

Suffrage Requirements

By contrast, the last half-century has seen momentous change in suffrage requirements and practices. Throughout this period, all states have con-

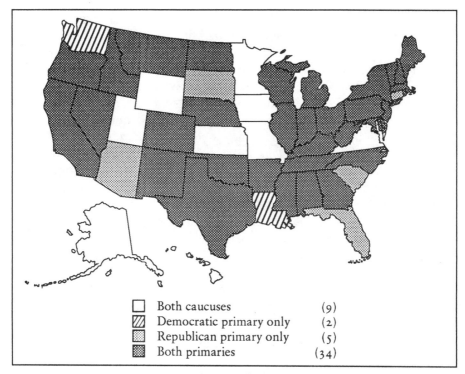

☐ Both caucuses	(9)
▨ Democratic primary only	(2)
▦ Republican primary only	(5)
▦ Both primaries	(34)

FIGURE 6.4B

PRESIDENTIAL PRIMARY ELECTIONS, 1996

SOURCE: *Congressional Quarterly Weekly Report*, 3 August 1996, 63–64; ibid., 17 August 1996, 79–80.

tinued to restrict the suffrage to United States citizens; this was true in 1946, and it was true in 1996. In the other areas, however—age, residence, and prior registration—a transformation has occurred. These changes have nationalized, standardized, and liberalized suffrage requirements, with reverberating partisan consequences for both voter turnout and (even) partisan realignment.

Age requirements underwent piecemeal reduction from the beginning of the postwar years until a dramatic, wholesale move downward in the 1970s. In 1946, forty-seven states retained the long-standing norm of twenty-one as the age of majority (and hence of voting), the sole exception (Georgia) having only recently lowered it to eighteen. During the 1950s, Kentucky followed Georgia's lead, and Alaska and Hawaii entered the Union with lower age requirements (nineteen and twenty, respectively). There matters essentially remained until the Voting Rights Act of 1970, when Congress reduced the voting age nationwide, at a stroke, to eighteen.

This reform was part of a more general effort to expand electoral participation. It was buttressed, more pointedly and specifically, by Vietnam era protests embodied in the slogan, "Old enough to fight, old enough to vote." The Supreme Court, nevertheless, quickly ruled that Congress had authority to make such a change by statute only with regard to federal elections.[41] Because such a division would produce administrative chaos for the states in conducting elections, forcing them to sustain at least two separate age structures simultaneously, Congress responded with a constitutional amendment. This prohibited states from setting the age barrier higher than eighteen; the states quickly ratified, and a new national, lower age limit came into effect in 1971.

Residence requirements have likewise been lowered, even more strikingly. Fifty years ago, the norm was *in excess of* one year. Now the norm is less than one month. Once again, piecemeal liberalizations began in the 1950s and continued into the 1960s, as heightened geographic mobility in society and growing participatory values in mass culture encouraged individual states to adjust.[42] By 1970, under the additional impetus of the civil rights revolution and of antidiscrimination enforcement efforts, the four southern states, which in 1946 had required two years' residence, had all abandoned that category, and several states had pioneered a new minimum of three months.

In the same Voting Rights Act of 1970, then, Congress mandated a thirty-day residence requirement within a state for voting in a presidential election, thereby again creating administrative difficulties for states that did not apply such a standard to all elections within their borders. A year later, the Supreme Court exacerbated those difficulties by striking down a Tennessee statute that retained the twelve-month requirement for state and local elections.[43] The states came rapidly into line thereafter, motivated by a desire to avoid the confusion of having separate standards for different offices, as well as the risk of constant litigation.

Since then, residence requirements have remained stable and minimal. In 1946, five states had required two years, thirty-two one year, and eleven six months. In 1988, according to the most recent volume of the *Book of the States* to bother to report these figures, one state (Colorado) offered a thirty-two-day standard; twenty-three states required a thirty-day standard; thirteen had less than thirty days; and thirteen had none[44] (see table 6.1, p. 234). Residence requirements, in effect, no longer presented meaningful obstacles to voting for otherwise eligible citizens.

The traditional distinction between periodic and permanent registration was already breaking down by 1946. In the intervening years, the acceptance of the hybrid form, in which intermittent voting is sufficient to sustain registered status, has made the old distinction effectively irrelevant. At last count, twenty-six states still specified some interval, but this was almost always at least four years (see table 6.2, p. 235). Twenty-three other states sustain all voters who continue to reside at the same address and participate occasionally in some election or other. North Dakota still requires no voter registration at all.[45]

The move toward more lenient procedures for voter registration has featured another important departure from midcentury practice, whereby the voter appeared personally at city hall or county courthouse to fulfill the requirements of registration. Today, all but four states have procedures for registration by mail, and local election officials customarily cooperate in get-out-the-vote efforts, by registering voters in the evenings and on weekends, and at a variety of locations.[46] In 1993 Congress followed the lead of several states and enacted "motor voter" legislation, requiring all states to allow voter registration to coincide with vehicle registration.

In the wake of such developments over the past five decades, voter registration has become a far less formidable obstacle for prospective voters. The comparatively inhospitable environment of midcentury has given way to an unprecedented array of registration-related incentives and encouragements. Many states are going further by relaxing long-standing restrictions on absentee voting. In a closely related development, several have embraced the concepts of "early voting" and "mail balloting." Under the former procedure, voters can cast ballots at any time within specified parameters prior to election day, without explaining or justifying their absence from the polls. Under the latter device, registered voters can receive and send ballots through the postal service, marking them at their convenience and in advance of specified deadlines.

Party Nominations

At midcentury, the primary had clearly emerged, over the previous five decades, as the preferred alternative for making "party nominations" to public office in the states. Already, by the dawn of the postwar era, the ranks of states without any provision for primary elections had been reduced to two. These soon fell into line: Rhode Island in 1947 and Connecticut in 1955. When Alaska and Hawaii joined the union in 1959, they had already embraced this device for making nominations to all public offices. An evolution begun in the early twentieth century was nearly complete.

There are only lesser variations left within this picture, exceptions not entirely washed away by the primary tide. Thirty-one states specifically establish the primary election as the mechanism for nominating candidates for state office. But twelve others provide *some* alternative nominating procedures, either for certain state offices (typically lower-level ones), for minor parties, or for an especially inconclusive primary outcome. And seven states still provide for a joint formal process, whereby a party organization makes a recommendation before the official primary.[47]

These preprimary endorsements, provided by law in seven states and existing less formally in about that many others, do constitute a mechanism through which political party organizations seek to claw back some control over party nominations. Indeed, this arrangement has become more widespread and formalized in the last half-century. Otherwise, there is just not much significance left in any lesser differences regarding utilization of the primary. In truth, a simple primary versus convention classification arguably oversimplified a complex reality in earlier days, exaggerating the number of true primary states and reducing the apparent differences among them—and thereby masking the degree of change between then and now.[48] Duly noted exceptions notwithstanding, the institution of the primary election has become ever more entrenched in American politics over the last fifty years.

Major-party organizations have largely been reduced to resisting this trend from within, through the provision of closed or open primary rules, rules that require prior registration within the party versus those that do not. This balance actually moved marginally in the closed direction at the beginning of the postwar years because, as Rhode Island and Connecticut surrendered their antiprimary status, they came into the system using closed rules. After that, however, there has been a clear if slow trend in the other direction. In the process, one more counterattack by official parties has been blunted, then eroded.

Alaska and Hawaii, joining in 1959, were both open primary states. In the intervening years, two states did move back from open to closed, but four states moved from closed to open; three more went all the way to the wide-open primary, allowing voters to pick and choose the primary in which they voted, office by office. In 1946, then, there had been two nonprimary states, thirty-six closed primary states, ten open primary states, and no wide-open states. In 1996 there were no nonprimary states, thirty-four closed primary states, twelve open primary states, and four wide-open states[49] (see figure 6.3B, p. 239).

Two very different factors were driving this movement. The first was explicitly partisan. One cluster of states moving toward open primary rules was concentrated in the South and Border States, and the engine of their move appeared to be the rise of an indigenous Republican Party. This took four states—Missouri, South Carolina, Tennessee, and Virginia—from closed to open, and one (Louisiana) all the way to wide open. The other underlying influence was political culture. All the countermoves from open to closed were in the Northeast and industrial Midwest, long the home of organized party politics. The other cluster of reforming states, going in the opposite direction, consisted of West Coast states with a long progressive tradition. Thus Washington reinstated the original wide-open primary, and California, in 1996, took up the device.

In the process, California, given its immense size and media attention, managed to take the wide-open primary from being relatively isolated from mainstream American politics to being a possible wave of the future. Pessimists envision direct consequences for the major parties, and their party organizations in particular; optimists see the reform as manifesting fairness and as liberating increasingly independent voters.[50] Both sides of the debate probably underestimate the degree to which the practical drift beneath the labels of closed, open, or wide open has already gone well down that road.

In fact, only twenty-three states still require a statement of party affiliation *prior to election day* as a condition of voting, and five of these exempt new voters[51] (see figure 6.5, p. 246). In contrast, eleven others —among the thirty-four apparently closed primary states—require the voter to give a statement of party affiliation only on election day, when choosing a primary in which to participate. The difference between this sort of closed system and the open system under which a voter simply chooses one primary ballot to mark is not a large one. Moreover, even among the "true" closed primary states, the date at which a party declaration must be made has crept closer and closer to the primary itself[52] (see table 6.3, p. 247).

Finally, *presidential* primaries represent a different, much more radical shift, inescapable and unmitigated. In this, presidential primaries have risen from relative obscurity and practical insignificance to dominate the process of presidential nomination in every regard. In 1946 presidential primaries were a distant and enfeebled sideshow. In 1996 they are the rule rather than the exception (see figure 6.4B, p. 241). In 1948 the first postwar presidential primaries occurred in only fourteen states, where fewer than 5 million voters participated. In 1996 they occurred in over forty states, whose voters cast almost 25 million ballots—and that in a year when one nomination was uncontested and the other was resolved early[53] (see table 6.4, p. 248).

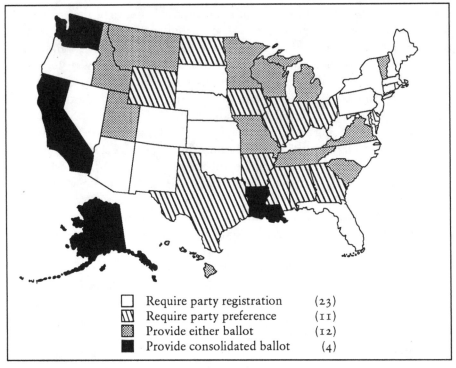

Require party registration (23)
Require party preference (11)
Provide either ballot (12)
Provide consolidated ballot (4)

FIGURE 6.5
TYPES OF PRIMARIES, 1996:
REVISED CATEGORIZATION

SOURCE: *Book of the States, 1990–1991*, vol. 28 (Lexington, Ky.: Council of State Governments, 1990), 236, with updates.

In 1952, the year that President Truman derided the New Hampshire primary as "eyewash," active contests on both sides did produce an increase in real primary voters. The number of primaries remained relatively constant, however, until 1972. In between, John Kennedy demonstrated the incipient power residing in a primary-based nominating strategy, in an era of national press and public attention, though dominance by party organizations remained the characteristic feature of delegate selection. The last hurrah for that system came in 1968, when President Lyndon Johnson's withdrawal and Senator Robert Kennedy's assassination left the nomination to Vice-President Hubert Humphrey—too late to participate in the primaries but still the favorite of the organized party—and fueled an epochal reform agenda afterward.[54]

The 1968 contest featured thirty state primaries, fifteen Democratic and fifteen Republican, with a total of 12 million voters (see table 6.4, p. 248). Four years later, forty-one state primaries, twenty-one Democratic and twenty Republican, drew 22 million voters. By 1980 *seventy* state primaries, thirty-five Democratic and thirty-five Republican, featured 31 million voters. The high-water mark for primary voters, to date, was in 1988, with 35 million; for primary contests, the high points were in 1992 and in 1996, with seventy-seven primaries each.[55] But the central point was that primaries had gone past their irrelevance in 1946, and past the point when they could be used, as John Kennedy did in 1960, to demonstrate *to the organized parties* that their contenders were potential winners. Primaries were now overwhelmingly the story itself of a presidential nomination.

TABLE 6.3
PARTY ENROLLMENT DEADLINES
FOR PRIMARY VOTING, 1996

	Deadline for declaring or changing party affiliation
Arizona	50 days before election
Colorado	25 days before election
Connecticut	6 months before election
Delaware	March 1
Florida	30 days before election
Kansas	20 days before election
Kentucky	30 days before election
Maine	90 days before election
Maryland	84 days before election
Massachusetts	28 days before election
Nebraska	2d Friday before election
Nevada	30 days before election
New Hampshire	10 days before election
New Jersey	50 days before election
New Mexico	January 25
New York	One year before election
North Carolina	21 days before election
Oklahoma	10 days before election
Oregon	20 days before election
Pennsylvania	30 days before election
Rhode Island	90 days before election
South Dakota	15 days before election
West Virginia	30 days before election

SOURCE: *Book of the States, 1990–1991*, vol. 28 (Lexington, Ky.: Council of State Governments, 1990), 236.

TABLE 6.4

VOTER PARTICIPATION IN PRESIDENTIAL PRIMARIES,
1948–96

	Primary states[a]	Party	Total votes	Votes by party
1948	14		4,805,120	
	14	Democratic		2,151,865
	12	Republican		2,653,255
1952	16		12,729,419	
	16	Democratic		4,928,006
	13	Republican		7,801,413
1956	19		11,660,864	
	19	Democratic		5,832,592
	19	Republican		5,828,272
1960	16		11,225,709	
	16	Democratic		5,687,742
	15	Republican		5,537,967
1964	17		12,182,774	
	16	Democratic		6,247,435
	16	Republican		5,935,339
1968	15		12,008,620	
	15	Democratic		7,535,069
	15	Republican		4,473,551
1972	21		22,182,246	
	21	Democratic		15,993,965
	20	Republican		6,188,281

Continued . . .

Elaborations on the Transformation: Why, How, and So What?

A simple comparison of these two period composites begs numerous questions regarding the changes that have taken place in partisan rules over the past half-century. Separated by about five decades, these two snapshots indicate that while specific elements of partisan rules at mid-century can still be understood in the same general terms, many collective features, not to mention their practical impacts, are barely recognizable at century's end. Obviously, numerous and noteworthy changes have occurred. Moreover, they have decisively affected relations both within and between political parties. Their implications and repercussions have contributed to a substantial redrawing of the political landscape.

TABLE 6.4 — CONTINUED

	Primary states[a]	Party	Total votes	Votes by party
1976	27		26,426,777	
	27	Democratic		16,052,652
	26	Republican		10,374,125
1980	37		31,438,276	
	35	Democratic		18,747,825
	35	Republican		12,690,451
1984	31		24,584,868	
	30	Democratic		18,009,217
	25	Republican		6,575,651
1988	37		35,127,051	
	35	Democratic		22,961,936
	36	Republican		12,165,115
1992	39		32,935,932	
	39	Democratic		20,239,385
	38	Republican		12,696,547
1996	42		24,928,183	
	35	Democratic		10,813,135
	42	Republican		14,115,048

a. Includes the District of Columbia (which has been holding presidential primaries since 1952), the territory of Alaska in 1956, and the territory of Puerto Rico since 1980.

SOURCES: Congressional Quarterly, *Guide to U.S. Elections,* 3d ed. (Washington, D.C.: CQ Press, 1994), 508–61; *Congressional Quarterly Weekly Report,* 3 August 1996, 63–64; ibid., 17 August 1996, 79–80.

Ballot Form and Content

Of the three great clusters of partisan institutional rules under consideration here—ballot form and content, suffrage requirements, and party nominations—the first has remained the most recognizable (and changed the least) across the past half-century. The long-running effort to increase the role of the party-in-the-electorate at the expense of the party-as-organization has certainly continued, even before consideration of the spread of the primary election. Thus the office-bloc ballot continues to grow, at the expense of the party-column ballot, just as devices encouraging straight-ticket voting by individual voters continue to recede, more quickly in this case.

At the same time, the tendency to favor the two major parties, at the expense of third parties and independent candidacies, has remained characteristic of rules on ballot access, with only the smallest move away from that tendency. The presidential realm has seen the most liberalization; Emmett Flood and William Mayer have assembled data demonstrating, for example, that the aggregate number of signatures required to get a presidential candidate on the ballot in all fifty states plus the District of Columbia did decline, from over 1.2 million in 1967 to slightly over 700,000 in 1994.[56] Even then, disaggregating the data by state indicates that only fifteen states plus the District actually reduced their requirements, and significant moves by California and Ohio account for virtually all the difference. Twenty-nine states actually imposed more stringent requirements, while six have remained stable. Liberalization for lower offices, in any case, has been less.

Exploring how much this contributes to the great partisan change and diagnostic partisan characteristic of our time, split partisan control of national government, must wait until the concluding section of this chapter—except to say that it is hard to make a case that having office-bloc, rather than party-column, ballots, and then explicitly doing away with a provision for simple straight-ticket voting, is a recipe for encouraging unified (rather than divided) party government. This seems only more true, given the characteristics of the reformed electorate following from changes in suffrage requirements, explored in the next section.

In contrast, minor-party proponents lament that restrictive ballot-access laws effectively fortify this two-party system, "split" as it may be, against erstwhile challengers.[57] And indeed, over the past fifty years, minor parties have made no significant inroads on the virtual monopoly of the major parties on the offices of government. Especially at the subpresidential level, formidable restrictions persist. What remains are only several clear lines of skirmishing over them. In one such line, about half the state parties have introduced and then defended a "sore loser" stipulation.[58] This prevents losing candidates in primary contests from appearing on the general election ballot, either as independents or as nominees of another party. As such, it protects the integrity of the party's nomination, even if achieved through a primary election, and promotes the power of the party to unite behind its primary nominee.

From the other side, provision for "cross-filing" allows a candidate to compete in the primary of more than one party, potentially even producing "fusion" slates, whereby victorious candidates appear on ballots as the nominees of several parties. Fusion obviously benefits minor parties, by allowing them to form coalitions with the major parties or with other minor parties. The overwhelming majority of the states have opposed this practice; ten states currently permit fusion tickets; but only New York regularly features them. Moreover, a 1997 Supreme Court decision upheld the constitutionality of Minnesota's prohibition, challenged on First Amendment (freedom of association) grounds.[59] The decision suggests that minor parties will continue to face political restrictions on ballot access.

The other attempted route to reform in matters of ballot access, then, for third and/or independent parties, has been (as the Minnesota case suggests) the courts. But while there have been successes on both sides in court, although such cases are usually brought by the liberalizers, there has been no consistent trend, and certainly no uniform national impact. The Supreme Court has denied jurisdiction, accepted jurisdiction, and denied it again. It has thrown out access limits, sustained access limits, and sent the issue elsewhere.[60]

Suffrage Requirements

Changes in suffrage requirements, and hence in both the potential size and the composition of the electorate, have been much larger in the past half-century than those affecting ballot form and content. Moreover, most of these changes have featured a clearly expected partisan impact, and most have proved in operation to have at least partisan implications. In operation, however, what their expanded electorates have largely introduced into electoral politics is a greater degree of unpredictability, of partisan volatility. And where their impact has had a clear partisan thrust, it has often been opposite to the one expected by *both* major parties.

In their original look at the partisan implications of changing suffrage requirements, Campbell, Converse, Miller, and Stokes noted that the effect of easing those requirements depends on two factors: the likelihood that the newly enfranchised electorate will in fact vote, and its likely partisan preference.[61] The ratification of the Twenty-Sixth Amendment (1971), lowering the voting age to eighteen, raised the hopes of Democrats, heartened by survey data indicating that among newly enfranchised young voters, their party outnumbered Republicans by more than two to one. Even initially, however, this optimism had to be weighed against enduring evidence that younger voters were the least likely to vote.

The outcome of the 1972 presidential election disappointed those who saw the youth vote as providing an edge that would carry the Democrats to victory. New voters, aged eighteen to twenty-four, narrowly favored the Republican nominee, incumbent President Richard Nixon. Still, survey data from presidential elections from 1952 to 1980 indicate that, until 1984, the percentage of support given to Democratic nominees by younger voters consistently exceeded those nominees' overall vote percentage. From 1984 through 1992, by contrast, Republican presidential nominees exceeded *their* overall national averages in drawing support from younger voters. In 1996, the tide turned, again favoring the Democrats.[62] A clearer partisan trend may well emerge in future elections. For now, this evidence suggests a heightened volatility and unpredictability for this low-turnout population.

More liberal residence requirements have been a striking change in the past half-century, and more liberal residence requirements, by definition, benefit newcomers to a voting area at the expense of their entrenched counterparts. What this implies for parties and partisan competition, however, is less clear. In an environment of heightened mobility, easing residence requirements surely increases the aggregate voter turnout, just as it surely decreases the overall turnout rate.[63] Otherwise, it probably just exaggerates any ongoing transformations of traditional patterns of party competition, by allowing newcomers to participate electorally without having undergone socialization to established local norms.

All these elements have come together in the case of the substantial relaxation of prior registration requirements in recent years: a major and multifaceted suffrage reform; clear partisan expectations before the fact; an increased raw potential for the electorate but a decreased rate of actual turnout; and partisan results that did *not* accord with expectations. Students of political participation have traditionally identified socioeconomic status as the key factor associated with both registration and voting. Generally, both forms of electoral participation rise with increasing socioeconomic status. Less restrictive suffrage requirements should thus affect mainly those at lower socioeconomic levels, both expanding the eligible electorate and reducing the turnout rate of that electorate—and this particular expectation has indeed been borne out.[64]

On the other hand, persistent social-class differences between the two major parties have also characterized party competition in the United States. In the New Deal party system, clearly in effect at the outset of the post–World War II era, the Democratic Party had its dominant electoral base in the support of working-class voters; the minority Republicans drew disproportionate support from middle- and upper-middle-class voters instead. Fifty years later, the social-class foundations of party identification are more blurred, but these outlines remain intact.[65]

This view of socioeconomic status, as central both to whether one votes and for which party, strongly suggests that liberalized suffrage requirements over the past half-century should have advantaged the Democratic Party. Indeed, the responses of the two major parties to proposals for easing suffrage requirements reflected this expectation; such initiatives found greater support at the national level among Democrats generally than among Republicans. Ironically, however, this expansion of the suffrage has coincided with the deterioration of the New Deal coalition, and with a corresponding rise in Republican Party fortunes from their New Deal depths. Thus, in broad outline at least, the repercussions of more liberal suffrage requirements have been counterintuitive. Or at least, any expansion of the Democratic (New Deal) base that followed from these reforms has been more than compensated by Republican demographic or issue trends.

Clearly, the most sweeping changes in voter registration procedures and practices have occurred in the southern states, where all these other reforms have been added to an explicit assault on discriminatory practices aimed specifically at African Americans but with some larger fallout.[66] Voting by African Americans was a relatively rare phenomenon right after World War II, effectively restricted by a variety of legal and extralegal mechanisms. In the 1950s these traditional mechanisms came under increasing attack, as black Americans and their political allies lobbied, litigated, and demonstrated for reform. Reformers looked to the national government, far more than the states, for remedies.

Landmark civil rights legislation, including the Civil Rights Act of 1957, the Civil Rights Act of 1964, and the Voting Rights Act of 1965, caused black voter registration in the South to increase exponentially. Significantly, so did the registration of white southerners. Conventional explanations of this phenomenon depicted it as racial countermobilization. But Harold Stanley convincingly contends that other factors were more compelling. They include "enhanced political competition; shifts in attitudes toward the parties; easier registration requirements; greater use of the media, particularly television, to follow campaigns; and socioeconomic development, especially advances in educational attainment."[67] Although black registration still lags slightly behind white registration, the gap has narrowed dramatically.

In any event, these newly enfranchised black voters typically exercised their suffrage on behalf of the Democratic Party, which at the national level had been advocating increased civil rights for blacks since 1948. This development coincided with a substantial shift of white southerners to the ranks of the heretofore discredited Republican Party. On balance, this shift of whites to the Republican camp, including both traditional Democratic voters and, especially, previous nonvoters, has outweighed the infusion of blacks into the Democratic camp. At a minimum, the effective elimination of discrimination in voter registration in the region has transformed the demographics of electoral participation. But it has also changed the structure and character of party competition.

One benefit of these changes is that the Republicans have steadily eroded the long-standing regional dominance of the Democrats. At this writing, in presidential voting, they have actually supplanted the Democrats as the majority party in the region. A trickle-down effect has then extended Republican voting preferences increasingly farther down the ticket. In the process, the emergence of meaningful two-party competition has heightened participation in heretofore meaningless general elections. As a result, voter participation in party primaries in the South, once abnormally high, has come more into line with the lower levels found in the rest of the states. Along the way, southern voters have become less distinctive in these expressions of their electoral behavior.[68]

There are still other suffrage changes on the political landscape that have not yet had a chance to demonstrate their effect. For example, the significance of motor-voter legislation is not yet clear. The conventional wisdom, reflected in debate over the legislation, was that its enactment would advantage the Democratic Party, for the aforementioned socioeconomic reasons. Some tentative findings in a handful of southern states suggest that, to date, "motor voter" may be bringing more likely Republican voters into the fold instead, in that region of growing Republican strength.[69]

The expansive reforms of absentee voting and the adoption of early voting procedures are also proving undeniably popular. As yet, however, partisan ramifications are uncertain. These reforms do provide party organizations with significant new opportunities to get out the vote and thus shape electoral outcomes. Indeed, some contemporary critics, fearful of corruption, echo the concerns of Progressive era reformers; they raise the specter of a return to the conditions that inspired the adoption of the Australian ballot. Increasing potential for vote fraud notwithstanding, substantial early voting certainly alters traditional campaign dynamics, along with the conception of an election as a singular event.[70]

This remarkable record of changes in suffrage requirements has swept away many of the traditional obstacles associated with nonvoting. Ironically but predictably, voter turnout has declined, diminishing the potential effects arising from lowered barriers. With a larger potential electorate and declining turnout, the possibilities for partisan volatility have also increased.

Party Nominations

The great institutional initiative on behalf of the party-in-the-electorate, as specifically contrasted with the party-as-organization, has been, of course, nomination by primary election. This is also the great institutional embodiment of the notion of the political party as a public utility, formally in private hands but publicly regulated in great detail, so that the voters, not party officials, get to make key decisions.

The largest part of the success of this initiative, nomination by primary for most public offices in almost all states, had been completed by the beginning of the postwar period. In the interim, the primary has collected the few missing states. It has mopped up the few missing state and local offices elsewhere. It has reached out and engulfed the last major institutional hold-out, the nomination of major-party candidates for president. And it has spread to the last great partisan "oversight," in the form of Republican primaries for state and local office in the South.

At the dawn of the postwar era, the primary was already firmly institutionalized as the means by which state parties nominated candidates for public office. The now-unanimous provision for it among the states does not appear to have disadvantaged the party organization further. In effect, that damage had already largely been done. Indeed, in legal and procedural terms over the past half-century, the party organization has probably managed to hold its own, in an ongoing intraparty struggle over nominations with the party-in-the-electorate. Nevertheless, in popular culture, the expansion of participatory norms has doubtless heightened the legitimacy of the primary, and hence of decisions made by the party-in-the-electorate, at the expense of the party organization.

The main, new, and further twist on all this comes with current reforms in the state of California. Steve Finkel and Howard Scarrow have demonstrated that "party enrollment systems affect the way some voters perceive the nature of partisanship."[71] This specific finding reinforces the broader thesis of Campbell, Converse, Miller, and Stokes regarding the influence of institutional structure on political behavior.[72] In that light, California's decision to abandon not just the closed primary but party registration as well could, over time, contribute to a loosening of partisan attachments in the nation's most populous state, with increased possibilities for emulation elsewhere. Whether that would still permit parties to adapt and cope, much less to prosper, remains to be seen.

The largest advance for the primary in aggregate terms in the postwar years has been, of course, in making presidential nominations. Every aggregate here tells the same story: total primaries to select delegates, up from fourteen to forty over the past half-century; total primary electorate, up from 5 million to 35 million; total primaries with an explicit presidential preference attached, up from *eight* to forty, and so on.[73] Such totals speak for themselves, so only several final points need to be made regarding the party reforms that produced this new dominance of presidential primaries.

First, this proliferation of primaries decisively altered the locus of decision making in presidential nominating politics. The nominating convention now essentially ratifies the choice of the participants in these primary elections. As such, the reforms reflected an assertion of participatory and egalitarian values within the party, empowering the party-in-the-electorate at the expense of the party-as-organization. They also effectively imposed the need for personal candidate organizations, rather than campaigns based on a party organization, along the way to a nomination. James Ceaser locates this development within a much longer-running and more general conflict between values of representative decision making and direct democracy in presidential selection.[74]

Second, this proliferation of presidential primaries was accompanied by an unprecedented assertion of national party authority by the Democrats, to which the state parties and the state legislatures acquiesced. Heretofore, states unilaterally controlled their delegate selection processes. After 1968 the national party effectively restricted the state parties, mandating specified procedures, lest the state delegation be denied seats at the national party convention. This power shift received Supreme Court endorsement in 1981.[75] Through an altogether different process of providing needed services, the Republican Party has likewise become far more centralized, though its nominating practices were also shaped in many cases by state legislation enacted at the behest of majority Democrats.

Nelson Polsby has identified further consequences of these presidential party reforms for the broader political environment. Writing over a decade after their enactment, he judged the faction-ridden Democrats to be relatively disadvantaged by the reform process, when compared with the more homogeneous Republicans. Accordingly, the process itself worked against the Democrats in contesting presidential elections.[76] On the other hand, in the 1990s, as the GOP's factions became both more visible and more intense, Republicans appeared to be suffering from some of the same reformulated problems that bedeviled the Democrats in the 1970s and 1980s.

Finally, the greatest comprehensive growth for the primary—local, state, and national together—has come among Republican parties in the South. Though here, it must be noted at the outset that institutional changes in ballot form and in suffrage requirements have interacted with the rise of the primary election to shift the character of partisan politics. The largest of these other changes, the shift in suffrage limitations and the huge increase in black (and secondarily in white) voter participation, has been central to this shift. But variables such as the office-bloc (or party-column) ballot, the provision (or lack) of a straight-ticket mechanism, and the provision of open (or closed) arrangements within the primary have all interacted with it, too.

Recall that during the Progressive era, the southern states quickly and enthusiastically embraced primary nominations as a means of legitimizing Democratic Party candidates who were otherwise virtually assured of election, absent meaningful party competition. The minority Republicans, in contrast, were not part of this development and rarely relied on primary nominations. Moreover, in the early postwar years, when the primary was mopping up missing states and missing offices nationwide, the incidence of Republican primaries in the South increased only slightly, and the number of participants remained low. A state such as Tennessee, with an established "mountain Republican" tradition, could draw a turnout in excess of 100,000 to its 1948 gubernatorial and senatorial primaries. That same year, a state such as Florida, without that tradition, could attract only 16,000. And most southern states had no such (Republican) primaries on offer.

In more recent years, this situation too has changed dramatically. Primaries became more commonplace and participation rose sharply. In fact, the rise of southern Republican primaries for state and local office eliminated the two great anomalies of the spread of the primary as a device for party nominations. Southern states were no longer an exception to the totals on the rise of the primary as an institution. Moreover, turnouts in excess of Tennessee's early postwar standard of 100,000 voters were gradually achieved, for example, in gubernatorial primaries in Texas in 1962, in Florida in 1964, in North Carolina in 1968, in Georgia in 1970, in Virginia in 1989, and in Alabama in 1990. In the 1979 nonpartisan primary in Louisiana, a Republican candidate also comfortably exceeded that standard, leaving only Arkansas, Mississippi, and South Carolina as yet beneath it. Indeed, more populous states such as Texas and Florida can now attract over 750,000 voters to nominate Republican candidates for governor and senator.[77]

It should be noted that these totals still generally pale in comparison with voter participation in the parallel Democratic primaries in the region, though the gap continues to narrow. So far, the regional Republican realignment remains distinctly top-heavy, and public offices at the local and county levels remain overwhelmingly in the control of Democrats. This reality effectively encourages many Republican "converts" to continue to participate in Democratic primaries. Oddly, the coming of the office-bloc ballot and the disappearance of a straight-ticket provision probably encouraged this pattern. When there was no serious Republican Party in the South, party-column ballots and straight-ticket provisions were a barrier to its creation. When there was a serious Republican Party, office-bloc ballots and the disappearance of the straight-ticket provision hampered its ability to translate victories at the top of the ticket into victories at the grassroots.

The rising incidence of Republican primaries in the South was probably an inevitable by-product of the above-mentioned regional electoral realignment. Growing electoral support for Republican candidates for high-level federal and state offices in general elections usually triggered existing state laws requiring primary nominations. Moreover, the erstwhile Democrats joining Republican ranks were culturally conditioned to view electoral participation in party nominating decisions as an entitlement. From the other side, then, existing party organizations were generally unwilling to risk offending the large influx of party shifters by seeking to maintain their traditionally restrictive nominating practices.[78]

As a result, for the Republican Party in the South, a curious departure from conventional wisdom regarding the effect of the primary on party organization has occurred. Recall that Progressive era reformers initially promoted the primary as a device for weakening the control of strong but allegedly corrupt party organizations. In the case of southern Republicans, whose party organizations were notoriously weak, the primary ironically has become instead a party-building institution. It affords the state parties an attractive opportunity to generate public attention and support; most emergent Republican parties actually *want* to achieve the status of deserving a primary election.

Reinforcing this latter trend have been several judicial decisions over the past decade that have affirmed the right of a political party to control the rules within its nominating process, state law to the contrary notwithstanding. The most important of these, though still ambiguous in its full implications, came in Connecticut. One of the last states to adopt a primary form of nomination, Connecticut had a closed primary. State Republicans, however, preferred an open contest and enacted party rules to that effect. The resulting dispute went all the way to the Supreme Court, and the Court sided with the party.[79] On the other hand, the facts of the case make it difficult to label this as a clearly proparty decision, since, traditionally, party organizations have preferred closed to open primaries. Regardless, the decision does place the Connecticut Democratic Party organization in the position of not welcoming independents to its (closed) primary, whereas Connecticut Republicans do welcome them to an open counterpart.

The same kind of counterintuitive impact, where a reform device can facilitate party *building* in certain specific situations, involves other rules governing implementation of the primary. For example, the southern states traditionally fell into the closed primary category, though they typically did not require party registration. (Florida and North Carolina were the traditional exceptions.) This rule arguably facilitated regional party realignment. It eased the move toward Republicanism, by minimizing institutional barriers in the way of potential party switchers who desired to participate in the increasingly frequent Republican primary contests. More recent moves by Tennessee and South Carolina from the "loose closed" to the "open" category, along with Louisiana to "nonpartisan," even further ease time-honored regional obstacles associated with voting Republican.

The other great advance for the primary in the postwar years has been in the making of presidential nominations. Here, closer examination of voter participation provides further convincing evidence of the rise of the Republican Party in the South, a development that roughly corresponds to the expansion of presidential primaries. In 1948 there were no Republican primaries in this region. Florida introduced a Republican presidential primary in 1956, though for a decade it operated largely in isolation, joined only by Texas in 1964. The Florida primary, even then, typically attracted about 50,000 voters, less than 1 percent of the total Republican primary votes in a given year (see table 6.5, p. 260).

With the advent of the reform era in 1972, the number of southern primaries rose to three, and participation increased to almost 700,000, about 11 percent of the Republican total. By 1980 nine states had Republican presidential primaries, and more than 2 million voters participated, over 17 percent of the party total. The high-water mark to date occurred in 1988, when all eleven former Confederate states held Republican primaries; these drew almost 4 million voters, over 30 percent of the party total. Since then, virtually all the states continue to hold Republican primaries, and the number of voters has consistently been in excess of 3 million, over a quarter of that Republican total.[80]

The framework of partisan rules in effect at midcentury has thus given way to a very different one at century's end. Contemporary understandings of issues relating to ballot form and content, suffrage requirements, and party nominations in general attribute far more significance to participatory values, while attaching less importance to the needs and interests of party organizations.

TABLE 6.5

PARTICIPATION IN REPUBLICAN PRESIDENTIAL PRIMARIES
IN THE SOUTH, 1948–96

	Primaries	Voters	Percent of national GOP primary vote
1948	0	0	0.0
1952	0	0	0.0
1956	1	43,147	0.7
1960	1	51,036	0.9
1964	2	240,033	4.0
1968	1	51,509	0.1
1972	3	696,595	11.0
1976	3	884,895	8.5
1980	9	2,242,824	17.7
1984	6	814,390	12.0
1988	11	3,859,766	31.7
1992	10	3,329,742	26.2
1996	10	3,741,595	26.5

SOURCES: Congressional Quarterly, *Guide to U.S. Elections,* 3d ed. (Washington, D.C.: CQ Press, 1994), 508–61; *Congressional Quarterly Weekly Report,* 3 August 1996, 63–64; ibid., 17 August 1996, 79–80.

Conclusions

This chapter has sought to identify noteworthy changes in electoral rules over the past half-century, to consider the foundations of these changes, and to probe their partisan implications. The changes in ballot form have been relatively slight and in themselves relatively insignificant. Office-bloc formats are marginally more popular, and fewer states simplify straight-ticket voting. Both developments hinder the expression of partisanship. Moreover, the impact of ballot forms that discourage partisanship has likely been increased, owing to weakening partisan attachments in the electorate. As Campbell, Converse, Miller, and Stokes noted, now nearly forty years ago, "formal political institutions have their greatest impact on behavior when the attitudes relevant to that behavior are least intense."[81] With party identification in general decline in the electorate, making for both relatively fewer partisans and fewer strong partisans, it follows that any structures discouraging partisanship have become more significant.[82]

In the area of ballot access for parties, the changes have been slightly more extensive, but their impact as yet has not. Contemporary minor parties do have generally easier access to the ballot than did their predecessors in recent decades, but the change is not great, and they have yet to make noteworthy inroads on public voting loyalties to the two major parties. Indeed, independent candidacies appear to have been relatively better able to take advantage of these changes than have minor parties. Regardless, the Democrats and Republicans retain a virtual monopoly over state and national public office. Independent candidates have not succeeded; minor parties even less so. If the two major parties are increasingly "public utilities," they retain the oligopolistic character associated with that status.

It has been in the areas of suffrage requirements and the use of primary ballots in presidential nominating politics that changes have been both extensive and meaningful. Expansion of suffrage has perhaps inevitably been accompanied by declining *rates* of electoral participation as more marginal voters have been added to the rolls. Outside the South, as a result, the predicted benefits of an expanded electorate, predictably accruing to the Democrats on socioeconomic grounds, have not been readily apparent. Indeed, this era of suffrage expansion has, paradoxically, coincided with a general upsurge of Republican electoral fortunes.

The South is a notable exception to some of this. There, the enfranchisement of African Americans helped stimulate a parallel mobilization of white voters, heightening voter turnout and transforming party politics. More competitive general elections are a major factor in explaining higher voter turnout. Regional repercussions reverberate throughout the country. The movement of the South toward the Republican camp, for example, has broadened the party's electoral coalition, decidedly benefiting the GOP in presidential contests, and increasingly in congressional ones as well.

The rise of presidential primaries has tremendously expanded the raw base of popular participation in the presidential nominating process. Primaries have, quite simply, supplanted the traditional nominating role of the national party convention. Reliance on them has also arguably heightened the disengagement between campaigning and governing, a disengagement that characterizes the contemporary political scene. Presidential nominations were long the great holdout against that distinctively American institution, the primary election. In the last generation-plus, that has ceased to be the case.

Two other changes associated with these reforms, one clearly partisan and one whose partisan implications are less clear, deserve mention in any conclusion. The first of these involves "divided government," split partisan control of national government. Whatever its sources, this situation, heretofore rare, has become the norm during the postwar era. Indeed, over the past fifty years, the president and majorities of both houses of Congress have belonged to different political party fully 60 percent of the time. In contrast, divided government occurred during only eight years of the previous half-century (see table 6.6). Divided government by definition undermines the prospects for party responsibility.

The postwar era has also experienced an unprecedented rise in split-ticket *voting,* and ticket-splitting is an essential element of sustained split-party control of government.[83] This development should not be attributed exclusively to shifts in ballot form, to suffrage expansion, or to the spread of the primary. Other factors, such as an increasingly literate electorate, a more candidate-centered politics, and declining party loyalties are evidently important. Yet these changes in ballot-related practices have, at a minimum, coincided with declining partisanship in voting behavior and with the rising incidence of divided party government. At the least, they

TABLE 6.6
DIVIDED PARTY GOVERNMENT, 1895–1997

	Party affiliation		
	President	*House majority*	*Senate majority*
1895–97	Democratic	Republican	Republican
1911–13	Republican	Democratic	Republican
1919–21	Democratic	Republican	Republican
1931–33	Republican	Democratic	Republican
1947–49	Democratic	Republican	Republican
1955–57	Republican	Democratic	Democratic
1957–59	Republican	Democratic	Democratic
1959–61	Republican	Democratic	Democratic
1969–71	Republican	Democratic	Democratic
1971–73	Republican	Democratic	Democratic
1973–75	Republican	Democratic	Democratic
1975–77	Republican	Democratic	Democratic
1981–83	Republican	Democratic	Republican
1983–85	Republican	Democratic	Republican
1985–87	Republican	Democratic	Republican
1987–89	Republican	Democratic	Democratic
1989–91	Republican	Democratic	Democratic
1991–93	Republican	Democratic	Democratic
1995–97	Democratic	Republican	Republican

do not interfere with these developments. In fact, they surely facilitate them—which is not to deny that the situation may already have reached the point where the causal link runs in the other direction; as voters appear more inclined to split their tickets, changes in ballot form, for example, will increasingly accommodate them.

The second change deserving some final notice concerns the locus of decision making in American politics. In the constitutional system of the United States, the principle of federalism long dictated that electoral laws were largely the province of the separate states. In the period under consideration, by contrast, the institutions of national government and politics have asserted unprecedented authority. In ballot access for parties, the Supreme Court has exercised some initiative in liberalizing access requirements, thus benefiting minor parties. In suffrage requirements, all three branches of national government have acted to minimize restrictions. In presidential nominating politics, the national Democratic Party has virtually mandated that state parties use primaries in the process of delegate selection to the national convention, and the Republican Party has largely followed suit.

The states have generally acquiesced in these assertions of national authority, for a variety of reasons. In some cases, they felt that they had no choice but to bend to the sovereignty of the national government. In others, their objective was to avoid administrative confusion; when the national government imposed new suffrage standards for federal elections, for example, states extended them to state and local elections to spare election officials the responsibility of maintaining separate standards. In still others, the national government acted in the wake of reforms already initiated and intact in most *states,* promoting uniformity by imposing those standards on the laggards. Finally, when the reforms reflected participatory values that were popular in the electorate, state officials, admittedly with varying degrees of enthusiasm, again perceived no choice but to endorse them.

A half-century has passed since the dawn of the postwar era. As American political science approaches its centennial, the scholarly commitment to political parties endures, even though the triumph of the behavioral movement in the discipline has removed some traditional normative underpinnings. On the other hand, as the objects of this disciplinary affection, contemporary political parties find their support among the electorate in decline, even as the party-in-the-electorate has gained strength within the party structure. The rise of split-ticket voting nationally has established an unprecedented contemporary norm of divided party government.

Party organizations, undeniably weakened by the persistent assault that began over a century ago in the Progressive era, nevertheless endure. Although the old-style urban party machines have atrophied, party organization is correspondingly stronger at the national level. Further, state parties generally exhibit enhanced elements of institutionalization. Meanwhile, the party-in-office, less beholden to the party organization, is on the one hand more clearly connected with (and potentially constrained by) the party-in-the-electorate, via nominations. On the other, the potency of name recognition and other benefits of incumbency in contemporary electoral politics leave officeholders arguably more autonomous and less accountable than ever within this party structure.

Nevertheless, parties in government have been demonstrating noteworthy party responsibility. Much of this is due to increasing ideological polarization between the two major parties, a polarization that contributes to this heightened responsibility as it simultaneously diminishes the prospects for bipartisan cooperation, which the modern era of divided party government apparently demands. Partisan electoral arrangements and institutions thus continue to occupy a central role in the changing landscape of American politics. Indeed, they remain the institutional underpinnings of the party system. A heightened cultural emphasis on participatory values has added salience to their status in the postwar era.

Notes

1. Leon Epstein, *Political Parties in the American Mold* (Madison: University of Wisconsin Press, 1986), chap. 2.

2. See Avery Leiserson, "The Place of Parties in the Study of Politics," *American Political Science Review* 51 (December 1957):943–54.

3. See Angus Campbell and Robert Kahn, *The People Elect a President* (Ann Arbor: Survey Research Center, University of Michigan, 1952); and Angus Campbell, Gerald Gurin, and Warren Miller, *The Voter Decides* (Evanston, Ill.: Row, Peterson, 1954).

4. Committee on Political Parties of the American Political Science Association, "Toward a More Responsible Two-Party System," *American Political Science Review* 44 (September 1950): supplement.

5. See, for an example of an immediate response, Julius Turner, "Responsible Parties: A Dissent from the Floor," *American Political Science Review* 45 (March 1951):143–52. For a retrospective, see Evron Kirkpatrick, "Toward a More Responsible Two-Party System: Political Science, Policy Science, or Pseudo Science," *American Political Science Review* 65 (September 1971): 965–90.

6. See Norman H. Nie, Sidney Verba, and John R. Petrocik, *The Changing American Voter,* enlarged ed. (Cambridge, Mass.: Harvard University Press, 1979); William J. Crotty and Gary C. Jacobson, *American Parties in Decline*

(Boston: Little, Brown, 1980); and Martin P. Wattenberg, *The Decline of American Political Parties, 1952–1992* (Cambridge, Mass.: Harvard University Press, 1994).

7. See Cornelius P. Cotter and John F. Bibby, "Institutional Development and the Thesis of Party Decline," *Political Science Quarterly* 95 (Spring 1980): 1–27; and Cornelius P. Cotter, James L. Gibson, John F. Bibby, and Robert J. Huckshorn, *Party Organizations in American Politics* (New York: Praeger, 1984).

8. See "Party Line Vote Rate Soars," *Congressional Quarterly Almanac, 1995* (Washington, D.C.: CQ Press, 1996), C8–10. In 1996, party unity support scores declined very slightly but still remained above previous levels. *Congressional Quarterly Weekly Report*, 21 December 1996, 3461. In 1996, however, party unity votes that split the parties, with a majority of Democrats opposing a majority of Republicans, declined precipitously from their 1995 highs. "GOP's Election Year Worries Cooled Partisan Rancor," ibid., 3432–36.

9. Angus Campbell, Philip E. Converse, Warren E. Miller, and Donald M. Stokes, *The American Voter* (New York: Wiley, 1960).

10. They looked first at formal facilitation of partisanship. Here, they considered type of primary election, arrangement of the primary ballot, party tests for voting in the primary, existence of a nonpartisan primary, form of the general election ballot, and provision for a presidential primary. Then they turned to formal restrictions on voting. Their conclusions were twofold. First, "formal political institutions have their greatest impact on behavior when the attitudes relevant to that behavior are least intense." Ibid., 283. Second, "informal environmental factors have the greatest direct relevance for political behavior when political motivations pertaining to that behavior are reinforced by formal institutional arrangements." Ibid., 287.

11. David E. Price, *Bringing Back the Parties* (Washington, D.C.: CQ Press, 1984), chap. 5, "Parties and the Law."

12. (1) Does the party partially or potentially make its nominations through conventions? (2) Does the party regularly make preprimary endorsements? (3) Does the state use a caucus convention system rather than a primary for choosing and allocating its delegates to the national convention? (4) Do the laws governing voter participation in primaries adequately protect the integrity of the parties? (5) Do the laws governing access to the general election ballot adequately protect the integrity of party nominations? (6) Does the state provide public funding of campaigns, and do the monies go partially or entirely to the parties? (7) Does the ballot facilitate straight-ticket voting? (8) Are elections timed to facilitate party voting and reduce the likelihood of divided government? (9) Do electoral arrangements foster unified party leadership within the executive branch? Ibid., 125–36.

13. Advisory Committee on Intergovernmental Relations, *The Transformation of American Politics: Implications for Federalism* (Washington, D.C.: Advisory Committee on Intergovernmental Relations, 1986).

14. "(1) Does the state allow or require party nominating conventions?

(2) Does the state require or specifically allow preprimary endorsements of the candidates? (3) Does the state have a closed primary? (4) Does the state prevent candidates who contest but lose a party's primary from running in the general election under another party label? (5) Does the state provide in its ballot a means to vote a straight-party ticket?" Ibid., 144–57.

15. See Douglas Rae, *The Political Consequences of Electoral Law* (New Haven: Yale University Press, 1967).

16. Jerrold G. Rusk, "The Effect of the Australian Ballot Reform on Split Ticket Voting: 1876–1908," *American Political Science Review* 64 (December 1970): 1220–38.

17. Joseph P. Harris, *Election Administration in the United States* (Washington, D.C.: Brookings Institution, 1934), 155; Price, *Bringing Back the Parties,* 134–35.

18. See Rusk, "The Effect of the Australian Ballot Reform on Split Ticket Voting"; Jack L. Walker, "Ballot Forms and Voter Fatigue: An Analysis of the Office Bloc and Party Column Ballots," *Midwest Journal of Political Science* 10 (August 1966):448–63; Angus Campbell and Warren E. Miller, "The Motivational Basis of Straight and Split Ticket Voting," *American Political Science Review* 51 (June 1957):293–312; and Ronald E. Weber, "Gubernatorial Coattails: A Vanishing Phenomenon," *State Government* 53 (Summer 1980):153–56.

19. Malcolm E. Jewell and David M. Olson, *American State Parties and Elections,* rev. ed. (Homewood, Ill.: Dorsey Press, 1982), 157–58.

20. Richard Winger, "How Ballot Access Laws Affect the U.S. Party System," *American Review of Politics* 16 (Winter 1995):321–50. This essay relies heavily on the information presented in Winger's comprehensive survey. In addition, for over a decade, Winger has provided extensive coverage of ballot-related developments in *Ballot Access News.*

21. Ibid., 326–27.

22. *Smith* v. *Allwright,* 321 U.S. 649 (1944).

23. James H. Booser, "Origins of the Direct Primary," *National Municipal Review* 24 (1935):222–23, cited in V.O. Key Jr., *Politics, Parties, and Pressure Groups* (New York: Crowell, 1946), 371.

24. The authoritative account of the rise of the primary is Charles E. Merriam and Louise Overacker, *Primary Elections* (Chicago: University of Chicago Press, 1928).

25. V.O. Key Jr., *Southern Politics in State and Nation* (New York: Vintage Books, 1949), 417; also see Harold F. Bass Jr., "Change and Democratization in One-Party Systems," in *Building Democracy in One-Party Systems: Theoretical Problems and Cross-Nation Experiences,* ed. Gary D. Wekkin, Donald E. Whistler, Michael A. Kelley, and Michael A. Maggiotto (Westport, Conn.: Praeger, 1993), 74–80.

26. Key, *Politics, Parties, and Pressure Groups,* 373.

27. *Book of the States, 1943–1944,* vol. 5 (Chicago: Council of State Governments, 1943), 120.

28. Paul T. David, Ralph M. Goldman, and Richard C. Bain, *The Politics*

of National Party Conventions (Washington, D.C.: Brookings Institution, 1960), 528–42. There were four different levels of connection to the presidential contest in existence at that time: (1) the ballot must not show the delegate's preferences among candidates; (2) the ballot may show the delegate's preference if the candidate consents; (3) the ballot may show the delegate's preference whether or not the candidate consents; (4) the ballot must show the delegate's preference for a candidate who has given consent.

29. Ibid., 218–49, 528.

30. *Book of the States, 1948–1949*, vol. 7 (Chicago: Council of State Governments, 1948), 98.

31. Ibid.

32. Ibid., 96.

33. Ibid., 96–97.

34. Ibid., 96.

35. Ibid., 92.

36. W.H. Lawrence, "Truman Bars Test in New Hampshire," *New York Times*, 1 February 1952, 1, 10.

37. Virginia S. Graham, "Ballot Format: Trends in Changes by the States," Library of Congress, Congressional Research Service, January 1982, cited in Daniel R. Grant and Lloyd B. Omdahl, *State and Local Government in America*, 5th ed. (Boston: Allyn and Bacon, 1987), 134–35. These authors note that after the report was prepared, North Dakota also adopted the office-bloc format. Their sixth edition (Madison, Wis.: Brown and Benchmark, 1993), 132, shows no change in these figures.

38. *Book of the States, 1982–1983*, vol. 24 (Lexington, Ky.: Council on State Governments, 1982), 104; *Ballot Access News*, 10 February 1997, 4.

39. For the authoritative account, see Byron E. Shafer, *Quiet Revolution: The Struggle for the Democratic Party and the Shaping of Post-Reform Politics* (New York: Russell Sage Foundation, 1983).

40. *Ballot Access News*, 12 December 1996, 6–8, reports that for nonpresidential races, petition requirements have actually risen since 1994.

41. *Oregon v. Mitchell*, 400 U.S. 112 (1970).

42. Paul Allen Beck, *Party Politics in America*, 8th ed. (New York: Longman, 1997), 173–74.

43. *Dunn v. Blumstein*, 405 U.S. 330 (1972).

44. *Book of the States, 1988–1989*, vol. 27 (Lexington, Ky: Council on State Governments, 1988), 211.

45. *Book of the States, 1996–1997*, vol. 31 (Lexington, Ky: Council of State Governments, 1996), 162–63.

46. Ibid., 162.

47. Ibid., 157–58.

48. For example, in the 1970s New York began to use primaries to nominate gubernatorial (and not just legislative) candidates. Arguably, New York merits classification as a primary state more now than it did before. Jewell and Olson, *American State Parties and Elections*, 112.

49. *Book of the States, 1948–1949*, 92; *Book of the States, 1990–1991*, vol. 28 (Lexington, Ky: Council of State Governments, 1990), 236; various intervening volumes; see also note 50.

50. See Michael Ross, "California Voters Adopt an Anti-Party 'Open' Primary," *Party Developments* 2 (June 1996), 5–6; Eugene C. Lee, "The Open Primary Will Revitalize California Politics," *Public Affairs Report* 37 (May 1996), 6; J. Morgan Kousser, "The Open Primary Will Ruin California Politics," ibid., 7.

51. *Book of the States, 1990–1991*, 236.

52. Ibid.; see also Craig L. Carr and Gary L. Scott, "The Logic of State Primary Classification Schemes," *American Politics Quarterly* 12 (October 1984):465–76.

53. Congressional Quarterly, *Guide to U.S. Elections*, 3d ed. (Washington, D.C.: CQ Press, 1984), 508–9; *Congressional Quarterly Weekly Report*, 3 August 1996, 63–64; ibid., 17 August 1996, 79–80.

54. Shafer, *Quiet Revolution*.

55. *Guide to U.S. Elections*, 3d ed., 522–61; *Congressional Quarterly Weekly Report*, 3 August 1996, 63–64; ibid., 17 August 1996, 79–80; Charles D. Hadley and Harold Stanley, "Surviving the 1992 Presidential Nomination Process," in *America's Choice: The Election of 1992*, ed. William Crotty (Guilford, Conn.: Dushkin Publishing, 1993), 37.

56. Emmett T. Flood and William G. Mayer, "Third-Party and Independent Candidates: How They Get on the Ballot, How They Get Nominated," in *In Pursuit of the White House: How We Choose Our Presidential Nominees*, ed. William G. Mayer (Chatham, N.J.: Chatham House, 1996), 295–302.

57. For example, Winger, "How Ballot Access Laws Affect the U.S. Party System," 338–44.

58. Price, *Bringing Back the Parties*, 132–34.

59. *McKenna* v. *Twin Cities Area New Party*; see Linda Greenhouse, "Court Says States Don't Have to Allow Fusion Tickets," *New York Times*, 29 April 1997.

60. In 1948 *McDougall* v. *Green* (335 U.S. 281) saw the Supreme Court deny that the Constitution even addressed the issue of ballot access. Twenty years later, *Williams* v. *Rhodes* (393 U.S. 23) saw a changed Court invalidate Ohio laws on ballot access that denied a place to George Wallace's American Independent Party, holding that First Amendment freedoms of association and Fourteenth Amendment guarantees of equal protection did apply. But three years later, in *Jenness* v. *Fortson* (403 U.S. 431), the Court upheld relatively restrictive laws in Georgia, while three years after that, in *Storer* v. *Brown* (415 U.S. 724), it showed a disinclination to go into existing petition requirements. Again in 1983, however, in *Anderson* v. *Celebreeze*, the Court revisited Ohio to throw out another ballot access law.

61. Campbell, Converse, Miller, and Stokes, *The American Voter*, chap. 17.

62. "Vote By Groups: Presidential Elections Since 1952," *Gallup Poll*

Monthly, November 1996, 17–20.

63. In previous instances of suffrage expansion, turnout similarly declined. William H. Flanigan and Nancy Zingale, *Political Behavior of the American Electorate,* 6th ed. (Boston: Allyn and Bacon, 1987), 8–13.

64. See Raymond E. Wolfinger and Steven J. Rosenstone, *Who Votes?* (New Haven: Yale University Press, 1980), chap. 2.

65. James L. Sundquist, *Dynamics of the Party System: Alignment and Realignment of the Political Parties,* rev. ed. (Washington, D.C.: Brookings Institution, 1983), chaps. 10–18.

66. Beck, *Party Politics in America,* 178, summarizes the relevant data from U.S. Bureau of the Census, *Statistical Abstract of the United States* (Washington, D.C.: Government Printing Office, 1980), 514, and U.S. Bureau of the Census, *Current Population Report P20-466,* (Washington, D.C.: Government Printing Office, 1980), table 4. Also see Harold W. Stanley, *Voter Mobilization and the Politics of Race: The South and Universal Suffrage, 1952–1984* (New York: Praeger, 1987).

67. Stanley, *Voter Mobilization and the Politics of Race,* 145.

68. Jewell and Olson, *American State Political Parties and Elections,* 131–32; also Stanley, *Voter Mobilization and the Politics of Race,* esp. chap. 5.

69. John Harwood, "In a Surprise for Everyone, Motor-Voter Law Is Providing Boost for GOP, not Democrats," *Wall Street Journal,* 11 June 1996, A16.

70. Richard Smolka, "Election Legislation," *Book of the States, 1990–1991,* 228–29.

71. Steve E. Finkel and Howard A. Scarrow, "Party Identification and Party Enrollment: The Difference and the Consequence," *Journal of Politics* 47 (May 1985): 638–39.

72. See notes 9 and 10.

73. See note 55.

74. James Ceaser, *Reforming the Reforms: A Critical Analysis of the Presidential Selection Process* (Cambridge, Mass.: Ballinger, 1982).

75. *Democratic Party of the United States* v. *Wisconsin ex rel La Follette,* 450 U.S. 107 (1981).

76. Nelson W. Polsby, *Consequences of Party Reform* (New York: Oxford University Press, 1983).

77. Congressional Quarterly, *Guide to U.S. Elections,* 3d ed., 717–73, 849–911.

78. Virginia remains the conspicuous exception to this generalization. State law authorizes party organization officials to substitute party conventions for primary nominations, and both parties have repeatedly demonstrated their willingness to do so.

79. *Tashjian* v. *Connecticut,* 479 U.S. 208 (1986).

80. Congressional Quarterly, *Guide to U.S. Elections,* 3d ed., 508–61; *Congressional Quarterly Weekly Report,* 3 August 1996, 63–64; ibid., 17 August 1996, 79–80.

81. Campbell, Converse, Miller, and Stokes, *The American Voter,* 283.

82. See Bruce E. Keith and others, *The Myth of the Independent Voter* (Berkeley: University of California Press, 1992), 14, for a presentation of data on party identification, 1952–92, indicating a drop in the number of self-identified strong partisans. They themselves go on to contend that rising numbers of self-described independents notwithstanding, most voters continue to behave as partisans.

83. Beck, *Party Politics in America,* 8th ed., 158, cites data from the Center for Political Studies, University of Michigan, on straight-ticket voting among party identifiers, 1952–84. Over that interval, the percentage of ticket-splitters in the various categories increased by about 30 percentage points. Also see Walter DeVries and V. Lance Tarrance, *The Ticket-Splitter: A New Force in American Politics* (Grand Rapids, Mich.: Wm. B. Eerdmans, 1972).

Index

About the Authors

Byron E. Shafer is Andrew W. Mellon Professor of American Government at Oxford University. He is editor and coauthor of *Present Discontents: American Politics in the Very Late Twentieth Century; Postwar Politics in the G-7: Orders and Eras in Comparative Perspective; The End of Realignment? Interpreting American Electoral Eras;* and *Is America Different? A New Look at American Exceptionalism.*

Harold F. Bass Jr. is Moody Professor of Pre-Law Studies at Ouachita Baptist University. He received his Ph.D. from Vanderbilt University in 1978. He is the author of several journal articles, including "Comparing Presidential Party Leadership Transfers: Two Cases," in *Presidential Studies Quarterly,* Winter 1993, as well as several chapters in edited collections, such as "The President and the National Party Organization," in *Presidents and Their Parties: Leadership or Neglect?* edited by Robert Harmel.

John F. Bibby is Professor of Political Science at the University of Wisconsin–Milwaukee and a specialist in American political parties. He is the author of *Politics, Parties, and Elections in America* and a coauthor of *Party Organizations in American Politics* and *Two Parties—Or More? The American Party System.* In addition to his scholarly activities, Professor Bibby has held political party leadership positions at the national, state, and local levels.

William G. Mayer is Associate Professor of Political Science at Northeastern University. Since receiving his Ph.D. from Harvard University in 1989, he as done research primarily in the areas of public opinion, elections, political parties, and presidential nominations. His publications include *In Pursuit of the White House: How We Choose Our Presidential Nominees* and *The Divided Democrats: Ideological Unity, Party Reform, and Presidential Elections.*

Nicol C. Rae is Associate Professor of Political Science at Florida International University. His publications include *The Decline and Fall of the Liberal Republicans; Southern Democrats; Conservative Reformers:*

The Republican Freshmen and the Lessons of the 104th Congress; and *Governing America* (with Tim Hames).

Randall W. Strahan is Associate Professor of Political Science at Emory University. He has been a Guest Scholar at the Brookings Institution and has held the Fulbright Distinguished Chair in American Studies at Odense University in Denmark. His publications include *New Ways and Means: Reform and Change in a Congressional Committee,* and he is currently working on a book on leaders who have influenced the development of the U.S. House of Representatives from the early nineteenth century to the present.